The Long Shadow of the Civil War

The Lon

SOUTHERN DISSENT AND ITS LEGACIES

ıadow of the Civil War

Victoria E. Bynum

THE UNIVERSITY OF NORTH CAROLINA PRESS *Chapel Hill*

© 2010
THE UNIVERSITY OF NORTH CAROLINA PRESS
ALL RIGHTS RESERVED
MANUFACTURED IN THE UNITED STATES OF AMERICA

Designed by Courtney Leigh Baker and set in Bembo by Rebecca Evans. The paper in this book meets the guidelines for permanence and durability of the Committee on Production Guidelines for Book Longevity of the Council on Library Resources. The University of North Carolina Press has been a member of the Green Press Initiative since 2003.

Frontispiece and chapter opening illustration: Photograph courtesy of Library of Congress; shadows © iStockphoto.com/Sven Klaschik.

Library of Congress Cataloging-in-Publication Data
Bynum, Victoria E.
The long shadow of the Civil War : southern dissent and its legacies / Victoria E. Bynum.
p. cm. Includes bibliographical references and index.
ISBN 978-0-8078-3381-0 (cloth : alk. paper)
1. Southern States—Social conditions—1865–1945. 2. Confederate States of America—Social conditions. 3. United States—History—Civil War, 1861-1865—Social aspects. 4. Unionists (United States Civil War)—Confederate States of America. 5. Reconstruction (U.S. history, 1865–1877)—Social aspects. 6. Southern States—Politics and government—1865–1950 7. United States—History—Civil War, 1861-1865—Influence. I. Title.
F215.B 956 2010
973.7′1—dc22   2009039272

14 13 12 11 10   5 4 3 2 1

Contents

Illustrations

Preface

The Long Shadow of the Civil War takes us inside the worlds of men and women whose deepest commitments were to family, community, and the principles of government that they believed best served both. In this book, you'll meet Southerners like Newt Knight, Warren Collins, and Anna Knight, who were at once profoundly traditional in their beliefs and unorthodox in their actions. Whether they opposed the Confederacy in the Civil War, rejected conventional politics and religion after the war, or refused to accept race-based rights of citizenship, these Southerners fiercely defended their choices. For their efforts, they were frequently branded as renegades, outlaws, or even deviants.

There are few more vivid images in popular culture than those purporting to portray "typical" Southerners. Television, movies, novels, and even mainstream newscasts have long presented us with white Southerners who take unusual pride in ancestry, revere military traditions, and glory in the causes of both the American Revolution and the Civil War. Popular images of African American Southerners commonly center on slavery, segregation, and the civil rights movement. Less common are images of white Southerners who rejected the "Lost Cause" of the Confederacy or of the deep ties of kinship that linked whites, blacks, and Native Americans in a world bounded by unequal relations of power.

Regardless of whether one views the South sympathetically or critically, white Southerners are almost invariably assumed to have supported the Confederate cause in the Civil War. In popular memory, the war became a chief symbol of white Southern cultural identity. The "proof" for such assumptions is often found in old obituaries, reports of family reunions, or local histories that note the illustrious Confederate service of individual family members. As every courtroom lawyer knows, however, there are the "facts" and there are the "true facts." The mere publication of family facts does not make them true, nor did enlistment in the Confederate Army prove that one supported the Confederate cause.

The Civil War home front schisms presented in this book demonstrate the extraordinary power of kinship, family, and community in people's lives. In protecting what was closest to them—loved ones, land, and the daily rituals of neighborhood—men and women struggled to meet the concrete and immediate needs of life. Abstract notions of honor or political valor often had no place in this struggle.

Yet political ideology did have its place. For Southern Unionists, ideology was grounded in the struggles of the American Revolution of their ancestors, the nationalizing War of 1812, and the settling of frontier communities that marked their family's participation in building a republican nation. For enslaved Southerners, the war brought an exhilarating struggle for freedom while simultaneously threatening their safety and their very lives. For all, the American Civil War was at once a local and a national crisis.

As the Civil War ripped at the fabric of society, it created a home front of uncertainty, deprivation, and grief, forcing people to draw on their deepest psychological and material resources to sustain themselves and each other. When we look back, it is comforting to think of people "pulling together" in a time of such intense stress and to imagine that their suffering led to a deeper appreciation of fellow human beings. The Civil War home front was far too complicated, however, for glib characterizations. True, there were many touching instances of kindnesses shared between strangers, as well as some unexpected alliances between groups separated by barriers of class, race, and gender. Yet home front conditions also remind us of how rigid those barriers were.

For the past twenty-five years, I have researched Civil War dissenters and their descendants in North Carolina, Mississippi, and Texas. As a result of my research in North Carolina records, I encountered the Free State of Jones, a Civil War uprising in which my own Bynum ancestors participated. The Free State of Jones in turn led me to the Big Thicket jayhawkers. Here I expand upon that research in a series of discrete, yet interrelated, chapters. The North Carolina Piedmont, the Mississippi Piney Woods, and the Big Thicket region of Hardin County, Texas, form the geographic bases for six chapters, as well as an introduction and epilogue. The Southern stories they tell offer compelling narratives of bold actions and expressions of outrage by white people who did not honor the cause of secession, who in fact hated the Confederacy with a passion, so much so that their backyards ran with blood. People of mixed-race ancestry tell yet another story. Their participation in inner civil wars, Reconstruction politics, and household governance offers new perspectives on gender and race relations in the Civil War–era South.

The chapters that follow, then, are stories of human struggle. In some chapters, two or all three of these regions are combined for comparative purposes or to explore a connecting theme or story. Whether about North Carolina Quaker Belt women who protested against Confederate soldiers or Newt Knight's efforts to gain compensation from the U.S. government for having supported the Union, each chapter features ordinary people who were plunged into extraordinary times that transformed their lives and the lives of future generations. The legacies of the American Civil War include Southern Unionists who evolved into New South populists and socialists and multiracial communities, such as the one in Mississippi, which emerged from anti-Confederate collaboration between blacks and whites. Truly, these are living histories that connect past and present.

The Long Shadow of the Civil War

Kinship, Community, and Place
in the Old and the New South

An unlikely defender of the rights of common people in the Civil War was North Carolina physician Samuel L. Holt, first cousin to textile entrepreneur Edwin M. Holt. Moved by his conversation with a poor man of Randolph County whose only plow horse had been seized by a Confederate "press gang," Holt fired off a letter to Governor Vance on 24 May 1863, charging that "this county has sent many & true men to this piratical war," while the "coxcombs, cowards, & puppies," of the planter class manage "to screen their own carcasses from yankee bullets."[1]

The ordinary people defended by Samuel Holt are the subject of this book. So also are their multiracial neighbors and kinfolk—some were slaves and others were free before the war. Three central questions run throughout: 1) How prevalent was support for the Union among ordinary Southerners in the war, and how was it expressed? 2) How did Southern Unionists and freedpeople experience the Union's victory and the emancipation of slaves during the era of Reconstruction and beyond? 3) What were the legacies of the Civil War, Reconstruction, and the South's white supremacist counterrevolution in regard to race, class, and gender relations and New South politics?

To answer these questions, this book spotlights three Civil War home fronts seared by violent wars within the larger war. These community wars continued into the bloody era of Reconstruction. To further understand their legacies for twentieth-century Southerners—indeed, for present generations—I have included a section that examines the long shadow cast by the Civil War and Reconstruction upon descendants of both Unionists and multiracial families. Their stories remind us that, truly, the past is prologue.

The very phrase "home front" evokes images of women, children, and old folks struggling to perform the daily routines of life amid the disruptions of war. As the opposite of battle fronts, home fronts are commonly imagined as places where people react to, rather than participate in, war. In reality, the boundaries between Civil War battlefields and home fronts were quite fluid. Communities, in fact, were complex arenas of interactions among civilians, soldiers, and governments that directly shaped the course of war. For the Confederacy, those interactions directly influenced the outcome of the war.

The Southern Civil War home front was not simply the domain of women, children, and old folks; it included young men, many of whom were slaves. Others were disabled soldiers or men who had obtained exemptions or furloughs from military service or had paid substitutes to serve in their places. In addition, units of soldiers frequently camped nearby. The home guard, too, stationed men nearby who fulfilled their military duty by offering protection to their own communities. Thus, home fronts were not simply places where families waited out the war but were focal points of ongoing political debates and conflicts, many of which derived from the presence of so many men of soldiering age, in and out of uniform.[2]

Hence the angry words of Samuel Holt. Samuel's own cousin, Edwin Holt, became a favorite target of suffering families. As wealthy speculators in scarce goods became the scourge of society to small farmers, nothing better exemplified the ill-gotten profits of war than Edwin M. Holt's Alamance County factory. Although Confederate laws established price controls during the war and although the Holts occasionally donated goods to hospitals and Ladies Aid Societies, the family profited handsomely by charging high prices to customers, who often paid in wheat, corn, or meat. The Holts profited further by denying credit to poor people who sought cloth, thread, and yarn from the Alamance factory at a time of dire shortages. Edwin also took advantage of conscript laws that favored manufacturers and planters by obtaining exemptions for at least eleven men who worked for him. Although three of his sons served as Confederate soldiers, two others received exemptions on account of the family business.

The sight of privileged young men from the planter class strolling about the community during wartime irked plain farming families. Like Edwin Holt, Samuel Andrew Agnew, of Lee County, Mississippi, was frequently derided for sitting out the war. Agnew, the son of a slaveholding physician, avidly supported the Confederate cause but was exempted from military duty due to his status as a Presbyterian minister. A diarist and scrupulous chronicler of local and national events during the war, he spent much of his time preparing and delivering sermons, as well as reading newspapers, novels, and books on Roman history. By his own account, he frequently spent days "lolling" or "lying" about the home he shared with his parents. For many farmers by 1863, men such as Agnew personified the Civil War as a "rich man's war and poor man's fight."[3]

Thus, white men's wartime experiences were most directly affected by their conscript status, which itself was affected by age and economic status. But it was not only about who had to fight. Wealthier civilians such as Agnew might suffer for want of daily comforts, but many poor people struggled simply to eat and stay warm. For African Americans, geographic proximity to Yankee soldiers or the ability to form alliances with disaffected whites greatly influenced their experiences of the Civil War. Since slaves might have greater access to food than poor whites, cross-racial communication accordingly increased during the war.

Women's wartime experiences varied every bit as much as did men's, and many white farm women were anything but secessionist in their sympathies. The 1865 narrative of Yankee sergeant Richard W. Surby illustrates this point. Two years after participating in a raid on Mississippi under the command of Yankee colonel Benjamin H. Grierson, Surby published a memoir that revealed strong Unionist sentiments among the plain people of Mississippi's "timberland" (Piney Woods). On the ninth day of Grierson's mission, in late April 1863, the cavalry approached Smith County, gateway to the state's southeastern Piney Woods, where they encountered a "modest double-log house" wholly occupied by women. The women, mistaking Grierson's men for Confederate conscript officers, reported their menfolk to be with the Confederate Army in Vicksburg. They remained aloof, offering the soldiers nothing more than a drink of water.[4]

Real conversation began only after an "old lady" asked Surby when he thought "this cruel war" would end. When he replied with a few pro-Union comments, her true feelings tumbled out. "I always did like that old flag and think this ere war [is] all wrong." She spoke not a word about God or morality, emphasizing instead that politicians had trampled on the rights of law-abiding citizens. "If it hadn't been for these big larned folk, we'd all be living in peace," she declared, and then began to cry. What sort of government, she wondered aloud, would force her husband of thirty-six years into the army, even though he owned no slaves, "minded his own business," and had no "law suits in court." And what government would leave wives and mothers without the protection of their husbands and fathers. Confederate officers might as well conscript the women, she lectured Surby, since "we have no one left to care for us."[5]

The women's attitude toward Surby and his fellow soldiers shifted dramatically once he convinced them that they were Yankees. Then, he wrote, "we were called into the house," where "pies, bread, butter, and milk in abundance were placed upon the table." Amid this womanly presentation of food, the older woman now pulled a chest out from under a bed, from which she retrieved a U.S. flag, which she displayed before the Yankees with pride. Another woman wished aloud that their menfolk, hiding in the woods, might join them in their feast.[6]

Unfair conscript laws, increasingly desperate economic conditions, and reverence for the "old flag" generated social upheaval among ordinary farm folks, particularly in regions outside the cotton belt. The women encountered by Colonel Grierson's army lived just above the "Free State of Jones" County, where violence rippled across the Confederate home front by mid-1863. Such women found themselves at the forefront of social unrest as they urged men to return home, protested high prices, and deplored the hoarding of food and rampant speculation in commodities by unscrupulous merchants.

The famous 1863 food riot of Richmond, Virginia, epitomized women's public outcries against the war. One wife of a Confederate Army colonel, identified only as "Agnes," had a chance encounter with a young woman on her way to that very riot. When Agnes asked her to explain the ruckus, the emaciated woman declared: "We celebrate our right to live. We are starving." Soon after, Agnes expressed shame for her own complaints about missing the "petty comforts" of "hats, bonnets, gowns, stationery, books, magazines, [and] dainty foods" to her equally well-placed friend, Sara Rice Pryor. "This is a frightful state of things," she wrote Sara. "Your General has been magnificent. He has fed Lee's army all winter—I wish he could feed our starving women and children."[7]

A year and a half after the Richmond bread riots, Agnes was still haunted by "the pale, thin woman with the wan smile" who chose to riot rather than beg. Politicians' rants, she told Sara, were responsible for the starvation that now drove women to riot. "Ah! These are the people who suffer the consequence of all that talk about slavery in the territories you and I used to hear in the House and Senate Chamber. . . . I am so shocked and disturbed I am hysterical. It is all so awful."[8]

Rising desertion rates and bread riots convinced many Confederate politicians, too, that something "awful" was happening: their government was losing legitimacy among plain people. Beginning in early 1864, the Confederate Congress responded by tightening standards for class-based exemptions such as the Twenty-Negro law, which provided military exemptions for owners of twenty or more slaves. The hiring of substitutes was also ended, and price controls were established.[9]

Confederate efforts to distribute the burdens of war more equitably had their greatest effect in regions where the Union Army wreaked its greatest havoc on men and women. By no means, however, did such reforms win over all disaffected Southerners. In nonplantation regions such as the North Carolina Piedmont, the Mississippi Piney Woods, and the East Texas Big Thicket, where desertion and disaffection were common (and Yankees rare), Confederate tax-in-kind collectors, home guard soldiers, and special militia forces remained the enemy for many plain folk. These were the men who seized precious food and animals, forced sons and husbands into the Confederate Army, occasionally tortured women who hid their men in the woods, and summarily executed deserters.

Chapter 1 compares and contrasts leaders of the guerrilla community wars that erupted in the above three regions of the Confederacy. During the final years of war, bands of deserters roamed these areas, raiding pro-Confederate homes to obtain provisions. The fiercest was led by Bill Owens, whose men terrorized the North Carolina Piedmont, robbing slaveholders and punishing Confederate militia. Likewise, Confederate home guard and pro-Confederate vigilantes raided the homes of deserters' families and scoured the woods in search of disloyal men, frequently abusing civilians in the process.

Civil unrest and unconventional behavior by nonslaveholding farmers, slaves, and free people of color during the war reminds us that the "Solid South" never existed. By 1864, communities of dissent existed throughout the Confederacy, made up of evaders or deserters of the Confederate Army and civilian populations willing to harbor and defend them. Inadequate food and shelter would make unlikely associates, even allies, of some black

Sites of Three Inner Civil Wars in the Confederate South:
North Carolina, Mississippi, and Texas

WEST VIRGINIA

MISSISSIPPI   NORTH
               CAROLINA   VIRGINIA

                                       Raleigh

               TENNESSEE

ARKANSAS

                              SOUTH
                              CAROLINA

        Jackson
                          GEORGIA
• Dallas   Vicksburg •
                    ALABAMA
TEXAS

Austin   LOUISIANA
                                       FLORIDA
  Houston

Angelina   Smith
                                          Jasper

Polk   • Laurel
        Tyler   • Ellisville
                         Covington
                                       Jones
        Hardin

Liberty   Marion   Perry
        • Beaumont
      Jefferson

Big Thicket, Texas

                         Free State of Jones,
                         Piney Woods, Mississippi

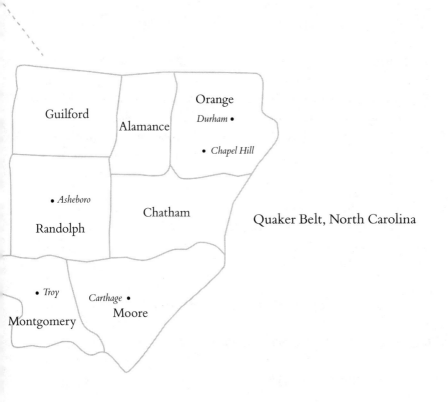

Guilford

Alamance

Orange

Durham •

• Chapel Hill

• Asheboro

Randolph

Chatham

Quaker Belt, North Carolina

• Troy

Carthage •

Moore

Montgomery

and white Southerners, who organized underground networks for pillaging and mutual defense. In such regions, the Confederacy came under siege without the presence of a single Yankee.

The most notorious hotbed of dissent was the "Free State of Jones," so-called because Jones County, Mississippi, allegedly seceded from the Confederacy. According to legends, some 55 to 125 men organized themselves, took over the county, and fought against the Confederacy. Their leader was Newt Knight, the nonslaveholding grandson of a Jones County slaveholder. The "Knight Company" was so powerful and well known by late 1863 that Confederate officials dispatched numerous troops to the area and launched two major raids in efforts to subdue them.[10]

So deep were the ideological roots of the Jones County uprising that several brothers of the leading lights of the Knight Company—Simeon, Jasper, and Riley Collins—led a separate band of deserters in East Texas. In 1852, about half of the Collins family headed to Texas. Among them was Warren, commonly described as the leader of the Big Thicket "jayhawkers." When all the fighting was over, seven of eight Collins brothers had stood against the Confederacy: Vinson, Simeon, Jasper, and Riley in Mississippi and Warren, Stacy, and Newton in Texas. Only the youngest Texas brother, Edwin, remained a loyal Confederate soldier at the time of his death, in 1862.[11]

The wives, sisters, and daughters of these kin-related uprisings provided shelter and food. So, too, did neighboring and enslaved women. The Knight Company's most famous accomplice was Rachel Knight, a slave of Newt Knight's grandfather. Rachel was credited with using red pepper and ground glass to confound and kill militia hounds on the trail of deserters. After the war, she gave birth to several light-skinned children reputed to have been fathered by Newt. Rachel and Newt's alliance bound them together for the rest of their lives, creating a multiracial community that endures to this day.[12]

Local religious traditions varied greatly among these communities. North Carolina's Quaker Belt, so named because of heavy Quaker settlement in the eighteenth century, was a stronghold of Unionism during the Civil War. Stretching from Surry County in the west to Orange County in the east, this region has received renewed attention during the past twenty years from historians of Southern Unionism and the Southern home front. The heart of the Quaker Belt, labeled the "Randolph County area" because it encompassed parts of Randolph, Montgomery, and Moore Counties, exhibited immediate and fierce opposition to the Confederacy, compelling military occupation by late 1862.[13]

A legacy of religious dissent was reawakened in the Randolph County area by the rise of Wesleyan Methodism, which intellectually and morally challenged Baptist and Presbyterian conventions. The Wesleyan-Episcopal split in the Methodist Church, carried into the North Carolina Piedmont via ministers and New York newspapers, emerged within the growing national debate over slavery and its expansion west. As a result, the free soil ideals espoused by President Lincoln and the Republican Party, and even abolitionism, resonated with this region's yeoman farmers.[14]

Especially in the heart of the Quaker Belt, moral outrage, as well as fear and suffering, motivated women and men to openly defy the Confederacy.[15] Chapter 2 places women front and center in the inner civil wars that erupted among neighbors and between Confederate forces and dissident civilians. By late 1863, Piedmont women were writing plaintive letters to officials that detailed abuse of civilians by militia and home guard soldiers sent to their neighborhoods to "protect" citizens, arrest deserters, and force slackers into uniform.

To highlight the militancy of Quaker Belt Unionists, chapter 2 contrasts the Randolph County area with its northeastern neighbor, Orange County, a microcosm of Old South diversity. In Orange County, yeoman farmers were interspersed with planters, business entrepreneurs, professors and lawyers, slaves, poor whites, and free blacks. The county's antebellum court records reveal a lively interracial subculture in which participants exchanged goods and engaged in gambling, drinking, and sexual and social intercourse. During the war, these networks proved vital to poor folks' survival, as illicit commerce in stolen goods flourished between them and deserters of the Confederate Army.[16]

Chapter 3 follows Orange County's subculture into Reconstruction. In Orange and surrounding counties, interracial family groups were frequently targeted by the white supremacist revolt against Republican rule. With help from the Ku Klux Klan, North Carolina's Conservative Union Party (a coalition of anti-Republican Whigs and Democrats) attacked not only former Unionists and politically active African Americans but also poor whites and blacks and their mixed-race descendants.[17]

In Mississippi's Free State of Jones, Union victory and emancipation of slaves also created hope and generated excitement among white and black opponents of the Confederacy. Class pride permeated the political activism of former Unionists, many of whom were radicalized by the "rich man's war and poor man's fight." Thomas G. Crawford, a former Unionist and Jones County's delegate to Mississippi's 1865 Constitutional Convention, taunted embittered former Confederate delegates who disdained Jones County Unionists as ignorant "mossy backs." Proudly accepting the label, Crawford minced no words: "Yes, sir, we did secede from the Confederacy, and, sir, we fought them like dogs, we killed them like devils, we buried them like asses—yes, like asses, sir."[18]

Crawford's words, likely directed at pro-Confederate forces inside as well as outside his own county, revealed Jones County's deep divisions and fierce struggle for power. In October 1865, less than two months after his speech, ninety-nine Jones County citizens lamented their county's "mortifying" reputation in a petition to the state legislature. In order to dissociate themselves from the "dark deeds" of the men that Crawford defended, they asked that the county's name be changed from Jones to Davis, in honor of Jefferson Davis. In December of that year, the legislature complied. In 1870, however, Davis County once again became Jones County under terms set by the Republican-dominated "radical" legislature of 1868.[19]

Unionist victories during Reconstruction were short-lived. After less than a decade of Republican rule, former Confederate Democrats made political comebacks amid campaigns promising white supremacy and fiscal responsibility. Their election victories were often achieved through violent intimidation and fraud. Aided by the Ku Klux Klan, Mississippi Democrats overthrew Reconstruction, curtailing the power of Unionists in Mississippi and throughout most of the South.[20]

With the overthrow of political Reconstruction came a growing commitment to racial segregation as the appropriate and only safe social arrangement for blacks and whites, now that blacks might freely roam the land. But segregationists ignored America's long history of race mixing, which belied campaigns of racial purity. They also ignored white dependence on black services, which necessitated interracial contact. Clearly, segregation was not so much about separating the races as it was about asserting political, economic, and social control over multiracial people, whether their skin was black, brown, or white.

A stunning example of the absurd and twisted logic of race-based legal judgments in the immediate aftermath of Reconstruction was exhibited in an 1877 divorce case, for which North Carolina Supreme Court justice William B. Rodman wrote the final decision. In granting a husband's divorce from a wife accused of having an interracial affair, Judge Rodman stated as fact that if a white woman gave birth to a black man's child, all her future children, even those fathered by white men, would forever carry the "taint" of African blood. Here was the ultimate indictment of interracial sexual intercourse: the permanent pollution of a white woman's bloodstream, to the point where she could no longer produce a pure white child for her white husband.[21]

Judge Rodman's pseudoscientific logic marked the beginning stages of the sweeping racial segregation being mandated by law in piecemeal fashion throughout the South. Little more than a decade later, an Orange County property dispute, detailed in chapter 3, demonstrated the degree to which interracial socializing conferred grave legal as well as social disabilities in the emerging New South. In 1888, five siblings of the Granville County Hopkins family challenged the right of Ann Bowers Boothe to inherit sixty-eight acres of land that had belonged to her late husband, Nash Boothe, the Hopkinses' uncle. The litigants claimed rights to their uncle's land on grounds that his marriage to Ann Bowers was invalid. Ann, they charged, was rumored to have African ancestry and therefore could not legally have married Nash Boothe, a white man.[22]

This environment of white supremacy and segregation coincided with the blossoming between 1880 and 1900 of the multiracial Knight community in Jasper County, Mississippi. More shocking than Newt's own crossing of the color line were the interracial weddings that followed between two of his and two of Rachel's children. In 1878, Matt and Mollie Knight, Newt's children by his white wife, Serena, married Fannie and Jeffrey, respectively, Rachel's children by a white man. From that point forward, the interracial Knight community, which grew larger every year, was an open secret in the Jones County area.

Chapter 4 moves beyond Newt's interracial community to focus on his decades-long effort to win financial compensation from the U.S. government for himself and the other members of the Knight Company. Perhaps in part because he could no longer run for office and hope to win, in 1889 Newt resumed efforts begun in 1870. The files generated by these efforts provide a rich source of first-person testimony and speak to several controversial issues regarding the Jones County uprising. First, they refute arguments that the uprising was politically insignificant or merely a cloak for banditry. Second, they directly address the popular controversy over whether Jones County seceded from the Confederacy during the war. While no "secession within secession" appears to have occurred, several former Knight Company men vigorously asserted that they had proclaimed their loyalty to the U.S. government in a mutually agreed-upon oath of allegiance during the war.[23]

Unfortunately for Newt and his Knight Company associates, as the last vestiges of Republican rule were defeated throughout most of the South, the era of Reconstruction gave way to the age of the "New South." In this toxic political environment, Newt would struggle until 1900 without success to win federal compensation for surviving members of the Knight Company.

The Populist movement briefly gave new hope to Newt and other Unionists. Populism's potential for radically restructuring the political and economic structure of the postwar nation was expressed in the Omaha Platform of 1892, in which leaders denounced the concentration of wealth enjoyed by capitalists and the greed and political corruption that facilitated it. Attendees demanded currency reform, government ownership of railroads, a graduated income tax, and various reforms of the workplace consistent with demands by organized labor.[24]

Chapter 5 links key Unionists to new forms of political radicalism they assumed in New South Mississippi and Texas. In both states, Populism and Socialism attracted hardcore Unionists (and their offspring) with connections to the Free State of Jones. In Texas, Populism arrived earlier and stayed later; the Socialist Party also took hold there with greater force than in Mississippi. In both states, the Collinses and their kinfolk were active in these and other alternative political movements. In Mississippi, Jasper Collins also switched his religious allegiance from Baptist to Universalist.[25]

Jasper's religious conversion may in part have reflected his disgust for the close ties between the Baptist Church and the Democratic Party in Mississippi. Democratic leaders presented the institutions as twin halves of the only "true faith." With their "redemption" of state politics, former Unionists such as Jasper were expected to accept a Baptist God who favored the wealthy and well placed, having decreed them once again the "true" leaders of society. But if that were so, the "rich man's war and poor man's fight" was paralleled by a "rich man's heaven and poor man's hell." Jasper and a small cohort of friends and kin would have none of it. They joined the People's Party as well as the Universalist Church.[26]

The national and state Democratic Party weakened its third-party challenger by appropriating several agrarian reforms, most particularly that of "free silver," which had great appeal in western mining states. The 1896 national presidential "fusion" ticket of Democrat William Jennings Bryan and Populist Tom Watson epitomized the party's success in co-opting Populism by embracing free coinage of silver while abandoning meaningful reforms of financial policies responsible for the South's devastating crop lien system.[27]

In Mississippi, Progressive Democrats such as James K. Vardaman and Theodore Bilbo now spoke for plain whites, capitalizing on the racial fears previously whipped up by conservative Democrats to build a white base across class lines. In Texas, politicians such as James T. Hogg, Martin M. Crane, and Thomas M. Campbell did the same. Thus, the Democratic Party's successful appropriation of agrarian rhetoric and watered-down Populist goals effectively squelched third-party challenges. From 1902 until 1964, Mississippi was, in effect, a one-party state. In Texas, militant Populists refused to compromise with Democrats, and many more than in Mississippi became Socialists rather than return to that party. Nevertheless, Democrats eventually prevailed in Texas, too.[28]

Conservative politics and racial discrimination enforced by violence thus characterized much of the first half of the twentieth century. The Myth of the Lost Cause flourished, while multiracial people were socially and legally lumped together as "black" and expected to stay in their "place." This, however, many descendants of Rachel Knight refused to do.

Chapter 6 returns to the multiracial community begun by Newt and Rachel Knight. Often called "white Negroes" or "Knight's Negroes" by their white neighbors, many of these Knights refused to consider themselves black. Before we judge them as "passing," it is well to remember that they grew up in a racially mixed community overseen by white grandparents. Reflective of their European, Indian, and African heritage, other twentieth-century Knight descendants self-identified as people of color but did not mix with people defined as "Negroes." Still others considered themselves African American despite their mixed ancestry.

Marriage patterns best indicated a person's sense of identity. Some of the Knights married only whites; others married cousins or acquaintances who were as light-skinned as they were. Still others affirmed African American identities by marrying partners whose skin shades were darker than their own. Davis Knight, for example, considered himself white. During World War II, he enrolled in the U.S. Army as a white man. In 1946, he married Junie Lee Spradley, a white woman. Two years later, he found himself convicted of the crime of miscegenation.

The absence of published material about the Knight community before Davis Knight's 1948 trial is particularly striking given that the legend of the Free State of Jones has long been a vital part of Mississippi folklore and history. Before Davis's trial, historians and folklorists ignored Rachel's role in the Civil War uprising, covering only those aspects of Newt's wartime behavior that pertained directly to his resistance to the Confederacy. In

1951, however, Ethel Knight broke that silence with *Echo of the Black Horn*. Unlike previous authors, Ethel extended the history of the Free State of Jones well beyond the war, providing readers with fanciful accounts of the descendants of Newt and Rachel, whom she repeatedly labeled as "strange" people. As a result, for more than half a century, multiracial Knights have lived with images that sometimes seem carved in stone.[29]

White descendants of the Knight Company, too, have lived with legends and stories that seemed to assume a life of their own. Although few scholarly books have been written about the Free State of Jones and the Big Thicket jayhawkers, both uprisings have received ample literary attention, much of it from descendants of their three best-known Unionist guerrillas: Newt Knight, Jasper Collins, and Warren Collins.

Although folklorists and historians have provided cultural and political profiles of these men, the published and unpublished histories produced by their kinfolk express ongoing family arguments over ancestors' dissident behavior and, by extension, the meaning of the Civil War and Reconstruction. Tom Knight, Loren Collins, and Vinson Collins, the sons of Newt, Jasper, and Warren, respectively, each wrestled with telling the story of his own father's life. An epilogue, "Fathers and Sons," thus concludes this book to illuminate the burdens of memories passed on from legendary fathers to twentieth-century sons. Each son, it shows, approached that burden differently, inadvertently reflecting the legacies of place, kinship, and community that so profoundly shaped their lives.

PART I   Home Front

LATE IN THE CIVIL WAR, John Beaman of Montgomery County, North Carolina, fired off an angry letter to Governor Zebulon Vance blasting Confederate war policies. Complaining that planters and manufacturers received exemptions from the army while he and other "farmers and mechanics" produced vast quantities of corn and beef, Beaman demanded that the governor explain why he should be forced to "fight for such men as thes[e]?" Around that same time, Romulus Sanders, the sheriff's son, was charged with stealing a mare from John's wife, Malinda. These were perilous times for the Beamans, who found their daily lives turned upside down by war.[1]

John and Malinda Beaman were among the small farmers in the South who vigorously opposed the Confederacy. The couple lived on the Montgomery-Randolph county line where they raised corn, wheat, and hogs alongside neighbors and kinfolk. The upheaval caused by war, however, prompted John Beaman to warn Governor Vance that farmers would be forced to "revolutionize unles this roten conscript exemption law is put down, for they air laws we don't intend to obey."[2]

And revolutionize they did. By late 1863, the Randolph County area in which the Beamans lived was a hotbed of Unionism, desertion, and guerrilla warfare. No isolated example, such pockets of resistance emerged in nonplantation regions throughout the Confederate South.

Chapter 1 of part I tells the stories of three such regions of resistance: the Piedmont Quaker Belt of North Carolina, the Piney Woods of Mississippi, and the Big Thicket of East Texas. Within their respective states,

Unionist communities spilled over the borders of several counties, making the phrases "Jones County area," "Hardin County area," and "Randolph County area" the most useful ways to designate them. All three communities had solid nonslaveholding majorities, with slaves making up only 10 to 14 percent of their populations. Those who owned slaves were generally the wealthiest citizens in each community, but they did not culturally dominate their neighbors to the extent, or in the manner, commonly associated with plantation regions. Nor did nonslaveholders always defer to or share the worldview of slaveholders, even though some interacted and even intermarried with them.

Using a comparative context, chapter 1 reveals common and unique cultural features that shaped yeoman farmers' responses to secession and war. The profiles of these three communities' most notorious guerrilla leaders—Bill Owens, Newt Knight, and Warren Collins—provide further evidence that although similar class issues linked the uprisings across state lines, each setting was distinct, giving each its own particular characteristics.

The most dramatic difference was displayed in the Randolph County area of North Carolina's Quaker Belt, where dissent among plain folk such as the Beamans was motivated by religious principles as well as class. Not only did these farmers live outside the plantation belt, but they also lived among large populations of Quakers, Moravians, and Wesleyan Methodists.

So important was religion to the Randolph County area uprising and so visible was women's participation that chapter 2 focuses exclusively on the Quaker Belt to provide a detailed examination of the role of both. Women did far more than wonder and wait while husbands marched off to war or hid in the woods. Take the Beamans' cousin, Martha Sheets, for example, who was arrested in early 1865 for threatening the sheriff of Montgomery County. Although Sheets's behavior was hardly typical of Unionist women, it spoke directly to the issues of class and religion, as well as women's personal desperation, which motivated protest in the Quaker Belt.

In chapters 1 and 2, retaliation by Confederate forces against Union militants and their families is highlighted. Men who hid in the woods rather than serve the Confederacy relied on female kin to feed and shelter them. As a result, women were in danger of harassment and torture and the men were in danger of execution.

The most thoroughly documented example of retaliation against deserters' wives is the torture of "Mrs. Owens," wife of guerrilla leader Bill Owens. Deputy Sheriff Albert Pike, of Randolph County, unapologetically recounted his men's abuse of Owens's wife to Judge Thomas Settle, who investigated the matter. To Pike and his men, Mrs. Owens was simply an outlaw's wife, and a mouthy one at that. Over and over, officers and soldiers repeated the dirge that no respectable woman would engage in disloyal behavior and that no disloyal woman therefore deserved the respect of a Confederate soldier. As for himself, Sheriff Pike declared he would not remain "in a country in which I cannot treat *such people* in this manner."[3]

Whereas chapter 1 compares and contrasts guerrilla uprisings in three different states, chapter 2 contrasts women's wartime experiences in the Randolph County area with that of women in nearby Orange County. Unlike the women of the militant Randolph County area, who boldly and publicly confronted Confederate forces, Orange County's women rarely challenged Confederate authority, although they frequently complained about food prices and shortages and committed greater numbers of thefts to feed themselves and their families.

These differences reflected counties where economic, political, and ethnic development had diverged over time. Although Orange County was included in the Quaker Belt, by 1860 Quaker cultural influences had been diminished by migrating Virginian, Scots-Irish, and German settlers. Slavery grew more rapidly than in the Randolph County area, creating larger gaps in wealth among citizens and enabling Orange County's Confederate leaders to suppress Unionist sentiment more easily.

The contrasting behavior of women in two geographically close counties reveals the effects of race, class, and culture on female unruliness. In the heart of the Quaker Belt, Confederate abuse of Unionist women (and sometimes children) outraged both pro- and anti-Confederate citizens, encouraging militant Unionism and mistrust, even hatred, of Confederate soldiers.

CHAPTER ONE

Guerrilla Wars

Plain Folk Resistance to the Confederacy

From their states of Mississippi, Texas, and North Carolina, Newt Knight, Warren Collins, and Bill Owens led guerrilla bands that waged war on the Confederacy. By early 1864, the most infamous of the bands, headed by "Captain" Newt Knight, had crippled the government of Jones County, Mississippi. Thanks to historians, novelists, moviemakers, and a long-standing family feud, his "Free State of Jones" is the best known of the uprisings. All three of these Unionist uprisings, however, generated regional inner civil wars. Each challenged the Confederacy on its own turf and struggled to restore the power of the U.S. government.

As for the leaders themselves, they possessed forceful, even charismatic, personalities. Newt Knight, a tall, eagle-eyed, and remarkably self-possessed man with extensive family ties in the community, quickly rose to prominence among deserters after escaping his Confederate captors, who, early in 1863, tried to force him back into the Confederate Army. Later that same year, deserters from the Jones County area formally organized themselves, unanimously electing him as "captain" and naming their "company" after him.

Newt Knight, captain of the Knight Company, the guerrilla band that held sway over Jones County, Mississippi, during the Civil War. Photograph courtesy of Earle Knight.

Befitting the leader of a guerrilla band, Newt could be ruthless as well as charismatic. The cold-blooded murder of Major Amos McLemore, Jones County's most powerful Confederate officer, is universally attributed to Newt, although he was never charged in court. That murder, committed on 5 October 1863, triggered formation of the Knight Company.[1]

In contrast to Newt Knight, Warren Collins, of Hardin County, Texas, appeared more adept at eluding capture than at murdering Confederate leaders. Not that Collins was necessarily less capable of murder—his reputation as a backwoods, bare-knuckled fighter suggests otherwise. But an entire body of folklore surrounds the life of this so-called Daniel Boone of East Texas, in which he appears more as trickster than as guerrilla leader. His home, the Big Thicket of East Texas, encompassed all or parts of five counties. Distant and isolated from major theaters of the Civil War, the Big Thicket offered an almost impenetrable fortress for the men it sheltered.[2]

By all accounts, Bill Owens, of North Carolina, appears to be the most ruthless and least charismatic of the leaders. Owens's Civil War exploits inspired no romantic tales of heroism, and one searches the internet in vain for even one genealogy site that claims him. In fact, it seems Owens has been disowned. Perhaps because the North Carolina Piedmont boasted such an array of articulate Unionists among its political, intellectual, and religious leaders, Owens is known in popular memory (if remembered at all) only as one of the war's many terrifying outlaws.[3]

More positively remembered leaders from the Randolph County area include militant Unionist Bryan Tyson, who was descended from Quakers, and Daniel Wilson and Daniel Worth, both of whom were Wesleyan Methodist abolitionists. Hinton Rowan Helper, author of the free soil/abolitionist tract *The Impending Crisis of the South*, was from nearby Davie County, and John Lewis Johnson, founder of the underground Unionist organization the Heroes of America, was from Forsyth County, another Quaker Belt county.[4]

Particularly in the Piedmont's Randolph County area, where Bill Owens was born and raised, religious principles as well as class interests motivated loyalty to the Union. The same cannot be said of the uprisings in Jones County, Mississippi, and Hardin County, Texas, where religious irreverence rather than piety may have diluted the effects of pro-Confederate sermons. Neither Newt Knight nor Warren Collins appeared to be particularly devout. Nor is there evidence of organized abolitionist activity among families who rallied in support of either the Mississippi or the Texas uprisings.[5]

Despite a less ideological reputation than his Quaker and Wesleyan Meth-

Family of Warren Jacob Collins, leader of the jayhawker guerrillas who hid out in the Big Thicket of East Texas during the Civil War. Seated on the left is his wife, Tolitha Eboline Valentine. On their laps are daughters Cora and Lillie. Photograph courtesy of Mary Allen Valentine Murphy.

odist peers, Bill Owens was solidly rooted by kinship and neighborhood in North Carolina's Unionist networks. Nearby kin included Murphy Owens, age forty-two, of Montgomery County, a self-proclaimed Union man, and Joseph Owens of Moore County, a cousin or perhaps even a brother, who refused to join the Confederate Army and protested the forced conscription of his sixteen-year-old son, Daniel, in 1864.[6]

Historians continue to struggle to understand the guerrilla bands that roamed the South during the Civil War. The communities of dissent that produced Newt Knight, Warren Collins, and Bill Owens were located in widely separated states and provide an opportunity to study Southern Unionism in a comparative context. Each man's community differed in expression and level of dissent, demonstrating the importance of physical, economic, and political environments, as well as community traditions and cultural beliefs, in generating sustained resistance to Confederate authority.[7] Despite wide distances between the communities, they are linked to one another by migration patterns from the settled East to the Southwest and onward to the West. In the wake of the American Revolution, families migrated from the backcountry of North Carolina to that of South Carolina and then on toward Georgia, Alabama, and Mississippi. The quest for fresh forests and grazing lands amid expanding plantation agriculture continued into Texas, particularly after its annexation to the United States in 1845.

But the connections among these communities are about more than migration patterns. North Carolina was the ancestral seedbed for migrants to Jones County, Mississippi. In turn, many citizens of Jones County moved on to East Texas before the Civil War. Somewhere between North Carolina and Mississippi, Newt Knight's Quaker heritage was replaced by Baptist allegiances. And, in Texas, Warren Collins of Mississippi entered a state where prosecession rhetoric would be tied to Texas's 1836 revolution and its annexation a decade later to the United States.

Still, similarities among the communities are striking: most obvious are their locations outside the cotton belt, which extended across the South. In all three, men who deserted the Confederacy received strong civilian support, not only for rejection of Confederate military service but also for waging war on the Confederate government. Men hid in the woods to avoid conscription but also organized and armed themselves for battle much like any regular soldier. Extensive ties of kinship and neighborhood were essential, and women, children, and slaves aided their missions.[8]

Genealogical research on participants in the Free State of Jones confirms both their kinship and their migration patterns. Twenty-six of the fifty-five men who made up the core of the Knight Company carried the surnames of Collins, Knight, Valentine, Welch, Welborn, and Whitehead. The ancestors of these men were chief among the region's founding families, many having intermarried with one another for several generations—in some cases long before entering Mississippi Territory. As a result, all were related either to Captain Newton Knight or to his first and second lieutenants, James Morgan ("Morgan") Valentine and Simeon Collins. More accurately, this was the Knight-Valentine-Collins band.[9]

The ancestry of Texas's Warren Collins epitomized the frontier trail that linked the three Southern regions. His father, Stacy Collins, left the South Carolina backcountry as a young man, settling in Georgia, then Mississippi, then Texas. Along the way, around 1808, he met and married Sarah Anderson Gibson, of Georgia. The Collinses arrived in Mississippi Territory around 1812. By 1826, the year that Jones County was formed in the state of Mississippi, they and their allied families were settled farmers and herders who chose not to own slaves despite its increasing popularity throughout the South.[10]

By 1850, ten of Stacy and Sarah's fourteen children were married with families of their own and were among the most prosperous and civic minded of Jones County's nonslaveholding farmers. For some, the frontier once again beckoned. Shortly before 1850, the Collinses' oldest child, Nancy Riley, moved to Texas with her husband; in 1852, sons Stacy Jr., Newton, and Warren followed suit. Though getting on in years, Stacy Sr. and Sarah decided to accompany them. They and their youngest child, Edwin, age twelve, packed their belongings and joined the caravan west. Remaining in Mississippi were brothers Vinson, Simeon, Riley, and Jasper and two sisters, Sarah Parker and Margaret Bynum.[11]

In the dense forests of the Big Thicket of East Texas, the Collins brothers farmed less land and raised more hogs. They built homes from seemingly endless pine trees, planted corn, built smokehouses, and purchased a few cows for milk. Wild game and hogs from the surrounding woods supplied their meat. Warren Collins so preferred East Texas to Mississippi that he returned to Jones County in 1854, married Eboline Valentine, and brought her back with him. For this couple, settling in Texas continued their ancestors' precedent of leaving societies in which slavery was on the rise. During the Civil War, the Big Thicket of East Texas provided refuge for nearly 100 deserters. From Hardin County, Warren, Newton, and Stacy Collins Jr. played a central role in organizing resistance to Confederate authority. Relative newcomers to the state, the brothers had participated in neither

Texas's revolution nor its annexation but simply sought a more unsettled, unspoiled Piney Woods.

The Collinses did indeed find that pristine setting, but they now lived in a state where secession would soon enjoy widespread support among slaveholding and nonslaveholding citizens alike. In 1861, with Texas's history inextricably tied to the 1850s' sectional crisis, leaders successfully trumpeted secession as the only means for saving Texans' cherished freedoms and independence from ruin. Anyone who disagreed faced harassment, even murder, in the Lone Star state.[12]

There were plenty of Unionists in Texas, including Governor Sam Houston, as well as the Collinses, but few that dared voice—or, in some cases, even vote—their objections. Given that German Texans of the Hill Country and North Texas farmers were harassed and even murdered for publicly supporting the U.S. government, the extent of silent support for the Union can never be known. In any case, and in distinct contrast to voters in Randolph County, North Carolina, and Jones County, Mississippi, 73 percent of Hardin County's voters supported Texas's prosecession referendum of 23 February 1861.[13]

Hardin County's prosecessionist vote illuminates important differences among the three communities. Created in 1858 from parts of Liberty and Jefferson Counties, Hardin County lacked the intricate, extensive bonds of kinship and long histories that characterized the communities of North Carolina and Mississippi. Although Hardin County's citizens shared the ancestral roots and class backgrounds of their distant cohorts, the context and environment in which they experienced the sectional crisis made all the difference. These differences in turn hampered the emergence of local leaders (such as Warren Collins) who might have galvanized a wider antisecession movement among nonslaveholding citizens.

Take the case of Angelina County, the only East Texas County where voters rejected secession (by 57 percent). During the war, that county's Confederate enrolling officer was reported in late 1863 to be in "deadly fear of his life from a large force of deserters" harbored there. Local citizens refused to aid the officer, forcing him into hiding.[14]

Unlike Hardin County, Angelina County was part of East Texas's cotton-growing plantation region. Yet, like Hardin County, its nonslaveholding majority was not dominated by slaveholders. At the same time, cross-class alliances strengthened Angelina County's support for the Union. Slaveholding attorney James W. Guinn, for example, endangered his own life by aggressively campaigning against secession. Plain folk uprisings benefited enormously from such cross-class support; Unionist uprisings in both the Randolph and Jones County areas of North Carolina and Mississippi included a distinct minority of slaveholders who adamantly and publicly opposed secession.[15]

In contrast, Hardin County's guerrilla band emerged despite lacking a well-organized Unionist movement. Instead, Unionists like Warren Collins looked to Governor Sam Houston, rather than any local leader of status, as their model of reasoned opposition to secession. Like most Unionists, the Collins brothers enlisted in the Confederate Army rather than face arrest but soon deserted and retreated to the woods. From then on, they were labeled "jayhawkers," after the radical abolitionist and free soil jayhawkers of Kansas.

Big Thicket jayhawkers were joined by many other ex-Confederate soldiers previously "rarin' for a fight" with the Yankees. Labeled "bush-whackers," these soldiers revealed that Lone Star loyalty did not so easily translate into allegiance for the new Southern republic. Poor pay and rations, disease, and suffering families back home soon convinced them that the cause they had enlisted to fight for was not worth risking their lives after all.[16] The Collinses' migration into Texas forged the most remarkable link of all between the future guerrilla bands. Newt Knight and Warren Collins, it turns out, led bands that shared more than socioeconomic similarities. Warren Collins and his wife, Eboline, were kin to at least fifteen members of the Mississippi Knight Company. Eboline's brother, James Morgan Valentine, was Newt's 1st lieutenant; three of Warren's brothers, Simeon, Jasper, and Riley, also joined the Knight Company guerrilla band.[17]

Simeon Collins, who joined the Knight band along with several of his sons, was Newt's 2nd lieutenant, and Jasper was his 1st sergeant. In essence, there were two branches of the same band in separate states. Collins men formed the core of Newt Knight's Knight Company in Mississippi while leading a remnant band of guerrillas in East Texas.[18] It is testimony to Newt's charismatic personality that he was elected captain of Mississippi's Knight Company. His flagrant disregard for the color line further ensured that he would become the band's most famous member. Yet, when we expand our focus beyond race and class to include kinship and gender, a fascinating portrait of Unionism across state lines emerges, one that places the Collins family center stage.

An important aspect of Warren Collins's band of guerrillas, then, is its connection to Mississippi's more famous Free State of Jones. The failure of this avowedly Unionist family to participate in an organized movement

James Morgan Valentine, 1st lieutenant to Newt Knight of the Free State of Jones and brother-in-law of Warren J. Collins, leader of the Big Thicket jayhawkers of East Texas. Photograph courtesy of Dwayne Coats.

against secession in Texas, as they did in Mississippi, until two years into the Civil War underscores the importance of the political and social environment, as well as economic interests, to organized resistance against the Confederacy.[19]

Returning to North Carolina, the ancestral home of Free State of Jones and Big Thicket guerrillas, we find the most explosive mixture of political, social, and economic forces of all. Violent, widespread, and protracted inner civil wars raged throughout the state's Piedmont region. More North Carolina soldiers deserted the Confederacy than in any other state, and numerous outlaw bands roamed the countryside almost from the very beginning of the war.[20] Because of fierce resistance to secession in the Piedmont, local home guard units were organized as early as May 1861 but soon proved inadequate to the task of enforcing loyalty. Confederate militia who were sent to the area essentially occupied a region in which many people never accepted the Confederate government as legitimate.[21]

As a result, confrontations between anti- and pro-Confederate forces were ongoing in the North Carolina Piedmont, whereas in Jones County they were sporadic and in Hardin County they were few and far between. Acts of resistance and revenge were also more amply documented. Numerous letters, official reports, and court cases reveal wartime breakdowns in class relations. References abound to deserter bands such as that led by Bill Owens, who hailed from a neighborhood made up primarily of plain farmers and craftsmen.[22]

Located in the heart of the Quaker Belt, the Randolph County area became North Carolina's center of militant Unionism during the war. Violence erupted among pro- and anti-Confederate citizens of the North Carolina Piedmont almost immediately after war was declared. Large numbers of men evaded or deserted Confederate Army service from the outset; others waited until after the first year of war to desert, returning to supportive families and communities mobilized in opposition to the Confederacy.

Like "Captain" Newt Knight, "Colonel" Bill Owens headed a disciplined band of men that emulated official military organization and practices. Both bands took oaths of allegiance to the United States and engaged in standard military practices, such as "paroling" captured militia officers.[23] After chasing militia officers throughout the fall of 1862, the Owens band captured Captain Peter Shamburger, a militia officer, and forced him to march through rain with them as they robbed, pillaged, and abused families of the area.[24]

By mid-1863, Governor Vance had been informed of the Owens guerrilla band. In a detailed letter to the governor, three Montgomery County men gave explicit details of the band's behavior. Describing the "Owens crowd" as residing in the "extreme eastern edge" of Montgomery County and on the edge of Moore County, they accused the men of robbing a "Mr. Allen" of $1,000 in gold and silver and several "poor women of all their wheat and bacon."[25]

The men attributed their own reluctance to join the army to fear of leaving their community unprotected. They asked the governor to send guns and ammunition so that they might "subdue these vandals." Others in the neighborhood, however, especially those from Unionist families, claimed that such men sought home guard duty merely to harass pro-Union neighbors. Court records indicate an inner civil war in which both sides plundered, pillaged, and occasionally murdered one another.[26]

A prime example of the Owens band's mode of operation occurred early in 1863, when it invaded the workshop of Pleasant Simmons, a slaveholder and silversmith, seeking to repair guns the band members had obtained by theft and trade. The men's bold actions turned Simmons's world upside down. He had once employed the labor of men such as Riley Cagle, a member of the Owens band, and the same men now assumed control over his property. It was enough to make a man fear for his life, and, just two months after the men's "visit," sixty-three-year-old Pleasant Simmons wrote out a new will and filed it in court.[27]

Before the war ended, that will was executed. In February 1864, less than one year after the Owens band took over Simmons's workshop, a deadly shoot-out between him and the same band ended his life. According to newspaper accounts, the gun battle erupted when Simmons and Jacob Sanders, a neighbor who was visiting his home, rushed from the house to challenge the Owens band's latest forced entry, this time into Simmons's smokehouse. Sanders fired on the intruders, wounding two of them, including Bill Owens, but the gang members fired back, killing both Simmons and Sanders. "Damned secessionists," they cried out as they fled the scene. "The yard was strewn with human gore," reported one witness, that "stood in some places in puddles where the men lay." The Civil War had converted neighbors into cold-blooded killers of one another.[28]

Pleasant Simmons belonged to a social network of slaveholding artisans, planters, and lawyers who actively supported the Confederacy. Militia officer Peter Shamburger was his son-in-law; nephew Alexander P. Leach was captain of the Montgomery County Home Guard. Too often, it appeared to plain folk that wealthier folks escaped the worst effects of war. Unwilling to risk their lives any longer, they not only deserted the army but also regularly harassed their pro-Confederate neighbors. With religious antislavery ideals providing moral fervor for some, protests against the "rich man's war and poor man's fight" gathered steam, pitting family against family and slaveholder against nonslaveholder.[29]

As the Owens band's takeover of Pleasant Simmons's property revealed, divisions of class and kinship quickly eroded reciprocal economic relations between planter and yeoman, employer and employee. Still, wartime divisions were not always drawn cleanly along lines of slaveholding status. The murdered Jacob Sanders, a carpenter who owned no slaves, may also have worked for Simmons. Yet Sanders remained a fierce supporter of the Confederacy and was said to favor the "extermination" of all deserters.[30]

In all three communities, especially in the Randolph County area, Confederate militia were reported to have tortured civilians in the hope of finding deserters. Army officials correctly surmised that many farmwives encouraged desertion in the first place, thus helping to motivate the formation of deserter bands. These same women, they also knew, sheltered, fed, and spied for outlying husbands, brothers, and sons.[31] Confederate abuse of Bill Owens's wife (whose first name was not given) is particularly well documented. Mrs. Owens was washing clothes outdoors while tending her year-old baby when deputy sheriff Alfred Pike and his men rode up in search of her husband. Demanding that she reveal her husband's whereabouts, the men became impatient when she refused to cooperate. Insisting that Bill was "dead & buried," she snapped and cursed the men, especially after Pike demanded that she take him to her husband's grave. She proceeded to "abuse us for everything that was bad," reported Pike.[32]

"Bad," from Mrs. Owens's perspective, was a protracted war that left her alone to run a farm and care for a child while her husband led a guerrilla band of deserters. To make matters worse, the last time she had seen Bill, he had been suffering from wounds sustained from the shoot-out at the Simmons place. Nor was this her first visit from Confederate militia. After cursing the men, she grabbed her baby and refused to cooperate. Deputy Pike then slapped her across the face and forced her to relinquish her baby and submit to his authority.[33]

Pike and his men tied Mrs. Owens's thumbs together behind her back. They then took a cord and tied her to a tree limb, suspending her body so that her toes could barely touch the ground. She soon admitted her husband was alive and promised to tell all if they released her. Once freed, she began lying again, according to Pike, who applied more torture.[34] Only after Pike's men jerked Mrs. Owens to the ground and pressed her thumbs under the corner of a fence did she behave "respectfully" by providing information about the whereabouts of her husband. Downplaying their actions, Pike described the fence rails as flat and not very sharp. "I don't think she was hurt bad," he told Judge Thomas Settle. More to the point, Pike added, Confederate soldiers must have the "right" to treat Bill Owens and his wife in such a manner.[35]

Although not continually under occupation, Mississippi's Free State of Jones was also frequently visited by Confederate militia. The Knight Company fought some fourteen battles against the Confederacy, the most famous against Colonel Robert Lowry, who was sent to the region to restore a disintegrating Confederate order. The anguishing scene faced by families in the Jones County area in mid-April 1864 as a result of Colonel Lowry's incursion demonstrates why Civil War guerrilla wars were simultaneously community wars.[36]

In the space of two days, Confederate Colonel Robert Lowry and his forces killed ten of Newt Knight's men, shooting some and hanging others. Morgan Valentine narrowly escaped death. Wounded on 16 April at the battle of Knight's Mills, he was captured and imprisoned at Shubuta, Mississippi, for two months. In searching out the deserters, Lowry's forces allegedly seized aged fathers and children and held them captive, while lifeless bodies of deserters were allegedly flung on wives' doorsteps. Following a rout on 25 April, at least sixteen men of the Knight Company were captured and forced back into the Confederate Army. Others escaped and fled to Union forces in New Orleans. That left about twenty of a core group of fifty-five band members, including Newt Knight and Jasper Collins, hiding in the swamps and woods after Colonel Lowry's departure.[37]

Jasper Collins by chance escaped Lowry's raid because he had traveled to Memphis and Vicksburg between March and July 1864 to seek Union aid for the Knight Company. Several of his relatives, however, suffered the consequences of that raid. His brother, Riley Collins, and his nephew, Prentice Bynum, were among those who fled to the Union Army's 1st Regiment of New Orleans Infantry. Exactly four months later, on 30 August 1864, Riley died from the effects of chronic rheumatism and diarrhea. Prentice Bynum survived the war but was dangerously ill throughout his Union Army service. Almost continuously hospitalized, he was mustered out of service on 20 May 1965, from McDougall General Hospital in New York harbor.[38]

Jasper Collins's older brother, Simeon, was wounded by Lowry's forces and eventually surrendered, along with three of his sons. On 3 May 1864, an anonymous officer reported to the *Mobile Daily Advertiser and Register* that "terror was struck" among the Jones County deserters, causing many to come "flocking in asking for mercy." He specifically noted that "Sim and his sons" had "reported." Disdaining the notion that there had ever existed "any organization of men in Jones," the same officer characterized the area's Unionists in a manner typical throughout the South. The entire population of Jones County, he wrote, was "very poor and very ignorant." He blamed "older citizens" for inducing men of the Knight Company to believe they were the "strong party," who might therefore "defy the government and stay home."[39]

In a letter to Governor Charles Clark, Colonel William N. Brown, another of Lowry's men, similarly attributed the "Union ideas" of the Knight Company men to "old and influential citizens, perhaps their fathers or relatives." Yet Brown indicated, probably unintentionally, that these were not "ignorant" degraded poor whites after all; rather, they were sturdy yeoman farmers who, he wrote, embraced Unionist "principles" associated with the "agrarian class."[40]

Stacy Collins, Allen Valentine, Benagah Mathews, and Mark Bynum were no doubt among the "older citizens" or "fathers" referred to by the officers. All four men were nonslaveholders who had migrated to Mississippi Territory from South Carolina early in the nineteenth century. Stacy Collins, we already know, was the father of six sons who armed themselves against the Confederacy in Mississippi and Texas. Although he did not live long enough to witness their rebellions, his Unionist ideals were well established before his death. Valentine, Mathews, and Bynum actively assisted their sons in resisting Confederate service by obtaining arms and other supplies for them during the war.[41]

The adult children of these patriarchs intermarried with one another, a fact that reinforced their Unionist beliefs. Mark Bynum's daughter Lydia married Simeon Collins; Benagah Mathews's daughter Caroline married Simeon and Lydia's son Matt. Wives did not simply assume their husband's views of the Union; many brought those same views to the marriage. Truly, the Free State of Jones was a family affair, characterized by intricate, tangled lines of kinship.[42]

Not surprisingly, then, women played direct roles in these inner civil wars. Simeon Collins's wife, Lydia, fearing that her husband and three sons might at any moment be seized and executed and perhaps worried that her wounded husband would die in the woods if left untreated, reportedly begged Colonel Lowry to allow the men to surrender without penalty of death.[43] Colonel Lowry offered a deal. The lives of those men who came in from the woods would be spared on condition they return to the Confederate Army. Among the men who complied were Simeon and three of his sons. They and twelve other men from Mississippi's best-known band of deserters were soon fighting the Yankees near Kennesaw Mountain, Georgia. Captured by General William Sherman's forces on 3 July 1864, the men were sent to prison, most to Camp Morton, Indiana.[44]

All of the men were incarcerated for the final year of the war; several died in prison. Indicative of the tendency of Northern whites to view all Southern white men as slaveholders, one Yankee sergeant stationed at the Camp Morton prison reportedly beat Confederate prisoners about the head and body with a heavy stick while crying out, "This is the way you whip your Negroes." Such treatment was cruel irony for men who had never owned slaves and who had supported neither secession nor the Confederacy.[45] At the time of their arrival, Camp Morton housed nearly 5,000 prisoners, over half of whom had entered during the previous three months. The following winter was a cold one, with temperatures dropping to 20 degrees below zero on New Year's Day, 1865. Under these conditions, forty-five-year-old Simeon Collins struggled to survive the wound he had sustained while battling Colonel Lowry's forces. Simeon did survive his incarceration, only to die within months of being exchanged at war's end.[46]

In Texas, the remaining three Collins brothers, Warren, Stacy Jr., and Newton, maintained a hideout with fifteen to twenty other deserters near Honey Island at the northwestern end of Hardin County. Collins and his men were well armed and well supplied living in these woods and creeks, which offered wild oats, game, and fish. They knew the woods, which were thicketed with vines and creepers, like no one else and even dug and camouflaged three wells (later appropriately called "Union Wells") near the Polk County line to ensure a fresh supply of water.[47]

In this remote corner of the state, neither conscripts nor the civilians who aided them could be easily captured, executed, or tortured by Confederate militia and home guard soldiers. Historians of Civil War Texas argue that exceptional frontier skills made Texans particularly effective Confederate soldiers; clearly, such skills served jayhawkers and bushwhackers as well.[48]

An "informant" to the *Houston Tri-Weekly Telegraph* reported in late November 1864 that on the western edge of the Big Thicket some twenty-eight deserters had "built comfortable shanties, cleared land, planted corn [and] erected a tan yard for making leather of the hides of stolen cattle." The informant proudly reported that twenty-four of the men had been captured by some forty "reserve corps" who tracked down the deserters "with a pack of negro dogs." In what may have been a reference to the band headed by Warren Jacob Collins, he admitted that some twenty more deserters remained at large in "another place in the Thicket."[49]

Like deserters throughout the Civil War South, Big Thicket jayhawkers relied on civilians, especially wives, to provide them with staples such as coffee, corn, tobacco, and salt. Surrounded by beehives, the Collins band cut down the trees, gathered honey from the hives, and set up a thriving system of barter. According to local memories, the men took a large plank and placed it between two pear trees to fashion a table. There they laid out honey, venison, and whatever else the woods had to offer. Wives and friends then retrieved the goods and sold them in Beaumont, where they bought tobacco and coffee to return to the deserters' makeshift table. Other Hardin County women confronted the supervisor of a government corn crib, demanding that he, as a "gentleman," allow them free access to his corn that they might feed their hungry families.[50]

But the Collins band would eventually have its showdown, too, with Confederate forces. The story comes mainly from folklorists. Lacking military reports and letters from the *Official Records* of the Confederate Army, historians have relied on tales told by old-timers, such as pipe-smoking, seventy-five-year-old Cornelia Sutton, affectionately called "Aunt Deal." News feature writer Dean Tevis interviewed Sutton in 1930 in her "picturesquely lonely back-country house in the depths of the Hardin County thicket," wearing a "patterned calico dress." Folksy in content rather than scholarly, such interviews are forerunners of today's genre of oral history and provide intriguing narratives of the past, which are often the first steps toward historical verification.[51]

The most enduring and popular Civil War folktale about Warren Collins is that of the "Kaiser Burnout." According to legend, Captain Charles Bullock of the 24th Texas Cavalry was determined to capture the jayhawkers of the Big Thicket. At one point he is said to have done so, only to have them escape under his nose. Ever the trickster, Warren Collins reportedly played the fiddle and danced a jig for guards in the front part of the jail while his men slipped out the back. Somehow Warren was able to slip away too.[52]

In spring 1865, a frustrated Bullock ordered Captain James Kaiser into the Big Thicket with orders to capture the jayhawkers. Legend has it that Captain Kaiser, unable to penetrate their hideout, decided, literally, to burn the men out. At his command, Kaiser's forces set the woods on fire, eventually burning two to three thousand acres of land in the Thicket. In the end, the tactic did not work. Although two outliers reportedly died in the flames, none were captured, and Warren Collins and his brothers remained outlaws in a Confederate nation that was taking its last breaths.[53]

Historians have verified the actions of Captain Charles W. Bullock, and environmental experts agree that someone burned between two and three thousand acres of the Big Thicket, but a Captain James Kaiser in Texas military records is not to be found. Historians have, however, located a Captain H. W. Kyser (the only officer in Texas with that surname) who belonged to Co. G of the 12th Texas Cavalry. This Kyser, records show, was a member of a battalion commanded to hunt jayhawkers and deserters in Hardin County, and thus it appears that the folk legend of Kaiser's Burnout is based on solid historical evidence.[54]

In the aftermath of these guerrilla wars, questions inevitably center on what became of the leaders. The Union, after all, was victorious. Unfortunately for Bill Owens, who languished in a jail cell as Confederate forces surrendered, that victory spelled his doom. Reportedly using information extorted from Owens's wife, deputy sheriff Alfred Pike and his men captured the outlaw leader on 28 April 1864 and imprisoned him at the Asheboro jail in Randolph County.[55]

Owens's trial was moved to eastern Chatham County sometime in 1865 and was set to begin just as General Sherman's troops approached the Piedmont. Perhaps fearing the consequences of convicting a staunch, well-known Unionist in the wake of Confederate surrender, the presiding judge "declined to try the case," inflaming the pro-Confederate community. According to newspapers, on 22 March 1865 Bill Owens was forced from his cell by "unknown" persons and shot to death.[56]

Newt Knight and Warren Collins would remain in their communities for the rest of their lives, achieving legendary status in the process. They and their wives survived the war and lived to ripe old ages. The men did not fade into oblivion after the war, and both continued to defy conventional social and political mores.[57] Warren Collins never apologized for refusing to serve the Confederacy and defended his Civil War actions for the rest of his life. He considered his support for the Union "the greatest patriotic act of his long eventful life." Newt Knight was equally unrepentant. Newt lived openly among his mixed-race kin, and he clearly wished that the plain folk had resisted more, not less. Shortly before his death, in 1922, he signed off with the remark, "I guess we'll all die guerrillas."[58]

The Civil War brought a violent end to Bill Owens's life. Had he lived to see the Union restored and the nation at peace, would he have returned to farming and lawful behavior? The postwar behavior of Newt Knight and Warren Collins suggests that he would have. Yet, although Newt and Warren never again led outlaw bands, the choices forced upon them by secession and the stands that they took profoundly and forever reshaped their view of the world and themselves. In matters of religion, race, and politics, they and several of their followers became lifelong dissenters against the status quo.

CHAPTER TWO

Occupied at Home

Women Confront Confederate Forces in
North Carolina's Quaker Belt

Early in 1864, near the county seat of Carthage, in Moore County, North Carolina, Franny Jordan followed a "squad of soldiers" who had seized her teenaged son with the intention of forcing him into the Confederate Army. Fearful of what lay ahead, she stopped at the home of a neighbor and enlisted the aid of two young women in retrieving her son. As the women approached the Confederate soldiers, the soldiers cursed them for daring to challenge their authority. When one of the women retorted that they intended to do "no such thing," the soldiers surrounded her. Crying out "god dam her," one man urged the others to "take her along too."[1]

At first, the young woman stood her ground, warning the men not to touch her. But when they drew their bayonets and one pretended to drive his through her, she bolted and ran. As she scrambled over a fence, another soldier grabbed her dress, ripping it before she could escape his grip. "Shoot her," a man's voice rang out, prompting another to cock his gun and take aim. In the end, although the same man continued to holler, "Shoot her," none of the soldiers had the stomach to kill an ordinary white farm girl. They held their fire as the three women ran away.[2]

During the Civil War, such home front skirmishes occurred regularly in North Carolina's Quaker Belt. Although historians now recognize women as active participants in the war, forced as wives, mothers, or slaves to protect home and family from intruding soldiers and deserters alike, the very nature of women's wartime struggles makes it difficult to view them outside their biologically and socially constructed roles, as anything other than victims. Because white women such as Franny, emotionally and economically devastated by the loss of husbands and sons, appear in past records mostly as wives and mothers, they are rarely viewed as individuals—that is, citizens—who publicly asserted opinions or influenced the course of wartime policy.[3]

We should not discount, however, the possibility that Franny acted as both a mother and a citizen when she and her female companions contested the right of the Confederate state to impress her child into military service. A strong sense of cultural solidarity, nurtured by nonconventional religious traditions, characterized the Randolph County area.[4]

Quaker Belt women developed a public voice in response to the Civil War's violation of their cultural values and traditions and particularly to Confederate military occupation. Yet, because occupying forces are typically understood to be enemy soldiers who have seized control over a rival government's lands, it is easy to overlook the Confederacy's occupation of disloyal regions and its punishment of pro-Union citizens. As a result, Civil War tales about occupation of the South regularly recount harassment of citizens by Yankees and deserters but rarely include women like Franny Jordan who were abused by their new government's forces.

Race and class, as well as culture and religion, influenced many people throughout the South to view the Confederacy as an illegitimate, occupying government. Certainly, few enslaved, free black, or landless poor white Southerners expressed much affection for the Confederacy. Free African Americans, a visible reminder of the possibility that all blacks might soon be free, were more stringently policed, sometimes harassed, by methods resembling those of an occupying force.[5]

The case of Elizabeth Burnett, of Goldsboro, Wayne County, demonstrated the dangers of open resistance to Confederate authority by women of color. During the war, Burnett's home was a popular meeting place for blacks. Goldsboro's mayor, worried that she might be involved in a theft ring, ordered Officer Blount King to investigate. During King's investigation, a fight broke out between him and Elizabeth Burnett. After the war, the reconstructed court charged King with assault and battery. In October

1867, however, in what presaged coming race relations, about 120 white citizens protested the indictment of Officer King. Rather, they praised the officer for keeping free blacks in their "proper place" during the war. Citing Burnett's "rude and insulting" behavior toward the officer and her well-known "high temper," these white members of the community argued that a beating was just what Burnett deserved. They accordingly petitioned Governor Jonathan Worth to drop all charges against Officer King.[6]

White people's fears of black women like Elizabeth Burnett symbolized the Confederacy's difficulty in mobilizing support for the war, especially among certain segments of the South's population. Like free black women, poor white women—especially those who lacked husbands or whose husbands lacked property—were not particularly loyal to the cause of war. Unlike yeoman farmwives such as Franny Jordan, however, such women rarely dared to openly defy the new government. As conditions worsened, thefts, rather than political protests, became increasingly common. Such striking differences among women of the same general region reveal much about the intertwined, but varied, effects of gender, class, and culture on people's reactions to the war.

In Orange County, for example, prosecession politicians had asserted control over the local population by mid-1861. A striking example was the swift reprisal that Henry Harrison Blalock, a forty-five-year-old mechanic of the Patterson community, received after he denounced the Confederacy. On 25 March 1861, Blalock declared that "I wish I had a rifle that would carry a two-ounce ball; I would try to kill the head man of the South." Quickly arrested, he was further accused of predicting that slaves would soon be freed and with uttering "insurrectional, conspiratorial words against the Confederacy."[7] The arrest of Blalock demonstrated the power of coercion in silencing opposition to the war. By April 1861, prosecession politicians had assumed control over the levers of local government in Orange County. Charles Long, a shoemaker, was threatened with death by a "rebel" for refusing to provide shoes to a Confederate supporter. If not for "sickness in my family," Long commented, "I should have gone across the lines. I always hoped the Yankees would get here and put down the rebellion."[8]

Wealthy Unionists, though less easily intimidated than ordinary farmers, were also harassed. Chapel Hill slaveholder Sheffey Lindsey was cursed, abused, and called a "traitor" on account of being a Unionist. Similarly, James Pleasant Mason declared that he would have rather given up every slave he owned "than to have a war. . . . Nothing was worth breaking the Union up." As a Baptist preacher, however, Mason dared not speak his true feelings for fear of losing his ministry license. Not surprisingly, as Mager Green of Durham Township later commented, Orange County Unionists "were not very plenty there in those times."[9]

Local authorities had less success in curbing the effects of hunger on people's loyalty to the new order. Orange County's laboring people faced great hunger and need during the war, despite public officials' efforts to supply grain to the destitute. Significantly, the county had an unusually large number of female-headed households whose average household wealth was lower than that of single women in surrounding counties. This fact, combined with the wartime deaths of so many men, sapped the vitality of neighborhoods in which most farmers were self-sufficient at best before the war.[10]

Crime dockets swelled with the names of poor white women in Durham Township, noted for its unruly population even before the war, as hunger threatened to unhinge Confederate authority. In spring 1864, Rebecca Davis, Nancy Bowers, and Nancy Carroll were charged with forcible trespass after helping themselves to government flour stored at William Mc-Cown's mill. Similarly, in winter of early 1865, William McCauley charged two poor white women, Elizabeth Gilbert and Hawkins Browning, with stealing bedclothes and blankets from his home.[11]

These women, linked by kinship, class status, and neighborhood, had lived precarious lives even before the war. All were from families of small farmers and laborers whose ability to support themselves was severely strained or broken by the war. Unlike women of the Randolph County area, they did not dare assert their rights as independent citizens who happened also to be wives or mothers; dependency defined their existence.[12]

Being female brought a greater likelihood of poverty to women such as these from economically marginal families. Dependent upon marriage for economic support, yet sexually vulnerable, all except Gilbert had diminished their chances for marriage by giving birth to illegitimate children. Nancy Carroll lived much of her adult life with her parents. The mother of a mentally deficient illegitimate child, she was unable to support herself or her child, forcing her to request aid from the county wardens of the poor in 1845. Nancy Bowers, like Carroll, was granted a cash payment of ten dollars per year by poorhouse officials for support of her illegitimate child.[13]

Hawkins Browning (whose legal name was Hawkins Hicks) had lived with Jefferson Browning, her neighbor since childhood, until his death during the Civil War. Because the couple had three children together, the courts regularly charged Hawkins with bastardy and illegal fornication. The poorhouse was also familiar to this couple. From 1846 to 1857, Jefferson's mother, Nelly Carroll Browning, received aid from the wardens of the poor for support of another son, David, who was blind.[14]

Elizabeth Gilbert was also from a network of poor families. Most of the male Gilberts who lived in Orange County during the 1850s were laborers; a few were small farmers. None owned slaves. Like Carroll, Bowers, and Browning, Elizabeth was familiar with the wardens of the poor, at least indirectly. A decade before the war, in 1852, two Gilbert women, Tabitha and Eady, had died in the poorhouse. Another Gilbert relative, Penny Gilbert, struggled to make a living during the war by operating an illegal tavern. Arrested in 1862 for operating a "disorderly house," Penny may also have engaged in prostitution. The Civil War drove such women ever more deeply into the precarious underworld of petty crime and illicit sexual affairs merely to survive.[15]

Women's reactions to Confederate authority in the Randolph County area, where some broke laws in broad daylight, provide a vivid contrast. In early 1865, for example, a white farm woman openly threatened the life of the Montgomery County sheriff if he did not supply her family with wheat and corn. In a letter that revealed both gender and class consciousness, Martha Cranford Sheets raged at Sheriff Aaron H. Sanders, a wealthy slaveholder, for having done nothing for the "pore wiming" of the neighborhood and for telling lies to keep his sons home, while "my husband is gon, and he has dun work for you." Calling Sanders a "nasty old whelp" who cared nothing for the county's suffering families, Sheets issued a final warning: "If you don't bring that grain to my dore you will sufer, and that bad." She then signed the letter with her full name.[16]

The ease with which Sheets threatened to "send" deserters to punish the sheriff attested to neighborhoods where deserters, civilians, and Confederate forces met one another on the "battlefields" of their own farms and nearby woods. Whether or not Sheriff Sanders obtained military exemptions for his sons, as Sheets implied, is not clear. What is clear is that his twenty-year-old son, Romulus, was at home in the fall of 1864, assisting the sheriff in identifying and harassing deserters. Both father and son served as state's witnesses against several men arrested for desertion.[17] Sheets's subsequent threats against the sheriff would not have surprised distinguished educator Braxton Craven, who warned Governor Henry Clark from Randolph County in early 1862 that "it was a great mistake to leave [punishment of the disloyal] to the County authorities. Deep, inveterate hate to this government abounds and the authorities of the county will never crush it." By

March 1865, Randolph County harbored an estimated 600 deserters, many of them members of armed bands.[18]

The Quaker Belt's potential for class conflict was grounded in the non-slaveholding landed majority to which Martha Sheets belonged. Throughout this region, reciprocal economic relations, kinship, and relatively isolated, cohesive neighborhoods diminished the potential for class conflict among slaveholders and nonslaveholders before the war. Class differences were soon laid bare, however, by Confederate conscript policies that favored slaveholders, tax-in-kind laws, and military impressment of vital farm goods that drove nonslaveholding families to the brink of starvation. Any semblance of class reciprocity was soon destroyed, as Sheets intimated when she commented to the sheriff that her husband had "dun work" for him, yet there he was, claiming privileges for his own sons that were unavailable to her family.[19]

The persistence of Quaker and Moravian traditions added moral force to this resentment of the Randolph County area's small but powerful slaveholding class. Although Quaker antislavery convictions had faded over time, the emergence of Wesleyan Methodism around 1848 planted outright abolitionism in this portion of the Quaker Belt. Martha Sheets's evident sense of moral authority over the sheriff was no doubt reinforced by her own religious connections. Many of her Cranford kin had intermarried with the founding members of the Wesleyan Methodist Lovejoy Church, where, in 1851, the Reverend Adam Crooks was mobbed for denouncing slavery from the pulpit. As part of this Wesleyan Methodist circle, Martha was likely familiar with the views of pro-Union leaders who seamlessly blended religious antislavery views with republican free soil ideologies.[20]

Piedmont Unionists such as Bryan Tyson, Daniel Wilson, Daniel Worth, and the nationally known Hinton Rowan Helper all had Quaker or Wesleyan Methodist backgrounds. Unlike in the North, where women like Lydia Maria Child and Harriet Beecher Stowe carved out public careers as abolitionists long before the war, these antislavery Southern male leaders may appear distant from the world of women. Indeed, Hinton Helper belittled the abolitionism of "yankee housewives" like Stowe in favor of his own sturdier (that is, masculine) economic analysis of the horrors of slavery. Yet Martha Sheets's confrontation with Sheriff Sanders revealed a sense of moral and economic outrage equal to that expressed by Child, Stowe, or Helper.[21]

So determined was Helper to distance himself from Northern abolitionism and, by extension, feminized abolitionism (since his primary audience was nonslaveholding Southern men), that critics often dismiss him as a Southern racist who objected to slavery only because he wished to rid the South of blacks or because of the white class divisions it perpetuated. In fact, Helper objected to slavery on the same grounds as did most Northerners: because it was morally wrong to enslave human beings and because it privileged one class over another, creating an economically backward society in the process.[22]

Helper's racism, as well as his effort to distance himself from Stowe's "feminine" critique of slavery, was also typical of Northern abolitionist men. Throughout this patriarchal society, politics was the province of men, and male efforts to prove masculine fitness was an ongoing work-in-progress. Nevertheless, religious training, considered the special province of women, had an enormous impact on their behavior, adding special urgency in the Randolph County area to perceptions of the Confederacy as an alien, intrusive force.[23] Buoyed by local political leaders who refused to be silenced and by a powerful secret organization, the Heroes of America, nonslaveholding families in the Randolph County area only grudgingly supported the rebel government, if at all. By 1863, many of the area's men refused altogether to serve in the Confederate Army. North Carolina had the highest desertion rate among Confederate states; Randolph County had the highest desertion rate in the state.[24]

The enforcement and the abuse of Confederate policies further deepened people's disaffection. The military seizure of Franny Jordan's son, for example, was a direct result of Governor Zebulon Vance's proclamation of 11 September 1862, in which he condemned Confederate disloyalty and desertion. Soon after, Vance authorized the use of military campaigns to suppress Unionist activities. Major Peter Mallett, head of North Carolina's Confederate Conscript Bureau, ordered militia officers to take charge of such efforts in the Randolph County region. On 1 February 1863, Captain Nathan A. Ramsey requested that Governor Vance authorize him to lead North Carolina's 61st Regiment into Chatham, Randolph, and Moore Counties to aid in "exterminating all enemies to our great and glorious cause." Ramsey would head the forces that captured Franny Jordan's son in Carthage the following year.[25]

Confederate arrests of resistant conscripts and those who harbored them, forced enlistments, and executions of deserters occurred over and over again in the Randolph County area, as local and state Confederate forces worked together to suppress dissent and desertion. Captain Ramsey's forces were accompanied by fifty-four-year-old Adams Brewer, a self-appointed vigilante who roamed the woods in search of men disloyal to the Confederacy. It was Brewer who commanded Ramsey's soldiers to shoot the young woman who confronted them after they captured Franny Jordan's son. A slaveholder, he lived just across the Moore County border in the Brower's Mills neighborhood of Randolph County. Brewer was part of a distinct minority in a community noted for pro-Union, even abolitionist, families. Militant Unionist Bryan Tyson, who lived in Moore County, was born in the Brower's Mills neighborhood and maintained contact with friends and kinfolk there. Tyson's and Brewer's neighbors considered Brewer a "hot head secesh [secessionist]" and kept close track of his movements.[26]

In a letter to Governor Vance, Thomas W. Ritter, a prosperous non-slaveholding farmer who served in North Carolina's House of Commons, reported Franny Jordan's confrontation with Adams Brewer and the 61st Regiment. Aware that the reputation of any woman assaulted in public was immediately suspect (hence the euphemism "public woman" for prostitute), Ritter assured the governor that Franny's assaulted companion was from as "respectable a family as any in the country." Adams Brewer, he explained, was a menace to civil society, a pro-Confederate zealot dedicated to hunting down and killing his less-than-zealous neighbors even though he was not enlisted in military service. Brewer was instead "piloting" Captain Ramsey and his men through the woods, directing their depredations on local citizens. A few days before the soldiers seized Franny's son, claimed Ritter, the same group shot to death a seventeen-year-old boy accused of having evaded conscription. Ritter reminded the governor that Brewer had also murdered another Moore County man, George Moore.[27]

Assaults and murders in the name of Confederate loyalty were common enough that women like Franny had every reason to panic when their menfolk were seized. Franny certainly would have known about the murder of Neill McDonald, a young man who, shortly before the war, worked on a farm just two households away from her own. In separate letters to Bryan Tyson, two of Adams Brewer's neighbors claimed that Adams and his son, Stephen, were "behind" the murder of McDonald, who had deserted the Confederate Army and was accused of robbing and pillaging his neighbors (common activity among deserters). According to H. K. Trogden, Stephen Brewer pulled the trigger, shooting McDonald after he refused to reveal the whereabouts of other deserters. "They shot him through the Boddy," wrote Trogden to Tyson. "Hiz foalks heard the gun. They went out in the woods wher they [had] taken him and found him Shot." Soon, Adams Brewer himself became a hunted man. Another of his neighbors told Tyson in late 1864, perhaps more wishfully than accurately, that Brewer had been murdered by deserters.[28]

Vigilante murders and military executions of men accused of desertion intimately involved women, who surely were among the "foalks" who heard the shot that killed Neill McDonald and retrieved his body in the nearby woods. Less murderous efforts by overzealous militia and the home guard to police pro-Union men and women in this section of the Quaker Belt sometimes even spilled over into abuse of women of the slaveholding class. Henry W. Ayer, state agent on contracts, wrote a lengthy letter to Governor Vance after a visit to Randolph County, during which he learned of numerous abuses committed in the Asheboro region under the command of 1st Lieutenant William A. Pugh. A crisis ensued after Pugh's cavalry burned the distilleries of several men accused of providing whiskey to conscripts and deserters. In the process, Pugh's soldiers appropriated hogs, tobacco, and various goods from the citizens of Asheboro.[29]

Although this confrontation began as a clash between male soldiers, deserters, and moonshiners, women were soon drawn into the fray. One of the accused men, nonslaveholder Loton Williams, countered the Confederate charge of illegal bootlegging with an image of innocent women's work. Williams insisted that he had not produced any liquor since January 1862 but that his wife was "in the habit of washing her clothes in the still house, and using the kettle to boil them, which accounts for the fire under the kettle." Although Williams's explanation sounded plausible to Agent Ayer, Lieutenant Pugh scoffed at it, commenting that Mrs. Williams must wash clothes in "hot swill." Pugh and his cavalry proceeded to burn Williams's still, and several others, to the ground.[30]

In need of food and rest after the day's activities, the troops next entered the home of "Esquire Foust" over the objections of his daughter, even though there was not "another white male person on the place at the time." Foust's daughter watched helplessly as the soldiers cooked a hog they had taken from yet another citizen. Ayer seemed particularly disturbed by the cavalry's dishonoring of a wealthy patriarch's daughter, and equally so by the disrespect shown to Nancy Hoover, a slaveholder and the proprietor of a hotel located in Asheboro.[31]

Hoover fell victim to what Confederate sympathizers today would term "collateral damage." Their stomachs full, the soldiers prepared for an evening's rest by appropriating a quilt and four blankets from Hoover's hotel. As a result of their behavior, reported Ayer, the people of Randolph County "say the deserters and conscripts do them less injury than those sent to take them do." Lieutenant Pugh defended himself and his men against these accusations, proclaiming the guilt of every man whose still or mill they had burned and denying that Foust's daughter had been treated with disrespect. In regard to Nancy Hoover's complaints, Pugh insisted that after a diligent search of his troops' supplies, her goods were not found.[32]

Governor Vance was infuriated by Pugh's "plundering" of Randolph County citizens but stopped short of dismissing him from his post. In fairness to the Confederate troops, rounding up deserters and those who sheltered them was a thankless task. They were sent to restore order in a region they were told was under siege by lawless bandits. What they found were neighborhoods of families and extended kin who resisted with arms the authority of what *they* considered to be a lawless government created in defiance of the will of the people. Never truly understanding the perspective of these Unionists, Confederate officials routinely dismissed them as merely ignorant. Commander Pugh's most revealing statement came near the end of his letter of defense. After carefully addressing each charge against his unit, he denigrated Randolph County as a region where few "respectable people" lived and where people displayed "little or no refinement."[33]

Pugh's use of the word "refinement," with its feminine connotations, justified his men's harsh treatment of Randolph County citizens by conflating class and gender. His cavalry was assigned the task of punishing disloyal lawless men, not that of defiling or robbing helpless women. By presenting the people of Asheboro as neither loyal nor culturally refined, Pugh suggested that neither its men nor women deserved his soldiers' respect. Lieutenant Pugh was hardly alone in caricaturing rural plain folk as degraded, ignorant, or unrefined when it served his purposes. Even Confederate congressman Andrew C. Cowles, a "peace man," referred to leaders of the Heroes of America as "still house orators" because of their popularity among common people. Thomas Morris, described as "extremely poor" on his petition for a military exemption, was dismissed by enrolling officer D. C. Pearson as belonging to a "class of individuals in Montgomery County noted for their thriftlessness and want of energy." Captain Pearson cavalierly proclaimed the benefits of Confederate service for such a poor man, ignoring the probable effects of Morris's lengthy absence, or death, on his dependent wife and children.[34]

Politically and socially, military occupation encouraged people in the Randolph County area to accept desertion and evasion of Confederate service as appropriate behavior. Shortly after Captain Ramsey and his men cut a swath through Moore County, Congressman Thomas Ritter joined other leading members of the county to sponsor a peace meeting in Carthage, on 10 February 1864. Less than six months later, Moore County enrolling officer P. H. Williamson described Ritter's voting precinct as "one of the worst holes in the Confederacy." Deserters, he reported, were "stealing a good deal. . . . Still, the citizens don't care about arresting them." It was not that men and women did not care; many lived in neighborhoods that openly approved of desertion. One citizen commented in a personal letter that "deserters and conscripts" in Moore County were "doing a bout the same" and could be seen "at the Sunday School every Sunday."[35]

John Milton Worth, relief commissioner of Randolph County and brother of state senator Jonathan Worth, refused to accept that church-going and otherwise law-abiding people supported disloyalty to the Confederacy. In August 1864, Worth complained to Governor Vance that "more than half of this county, Moore, and Montgomery are now in the hands of *desperadoes*." How otherwise to explain why Randolph County's voters would elect as sheriff Zebedee F. Rush, a member of the Heroes of America and the candidate recommended by Bill Owens, the most notorious leader of deserters in the region? On Christmas Eve of the same year, Moore County slaveholder Iver D. Patterson likewise expressed his disgust with Lincoln-loving "tories" and recommended to Vance that the state legislature strip deserters of their right to vote and confiscate the property of their families.[36]

Forced to admit that women abetted men's avoidance of Confederate service, many of the same men viewed the torture of deserters' wives as a simple necessity. Torturing the wife of deserter band leader Bill Owens, after all, had resulted in his capture and imprisonment. In some counties, prosecessionist millers also denied deserters' wives government grain, even though there was no official Confederate policy to that effect.[37]

Women who sheltered male kin in the nearby woods eagerly told their side of the story. In separate letters to Governor Vance, Phebe Crook and Clarinda Crook Hulin, daughters of a Montgomery County Methodist schoolteacher and kin to numerous deserters, blasted their Confederate occupiers. Clarinda, who had three "outlier" brothers-in-law (she did not mention this in her letter), implored Governor Vance to consider the plight of farm women. "I hav three little children to werk for and I have werk[ed] for ever thing that I have to eat and ware," she wrote. But military men sent to the region to restore order were "destroying every thing they can lay hans up on." Troops had taken her "last hog" and poured her molasses all over her floor. "It ant only Me they air takeing from," she added; "they take the women'[s] horses out of the plows," she explained, for their own use.[38]

Ten more months of armed warfare between militia and deserters brought a more detailed letter from Clarinda's sister, Phebe. As a single woman, Phebe Crook could not anchor her protest in the time-honored trope of the soldier's wife or mother. She seemed eager, however, to describe herself as "a young lady that has Neather Husband, son, father, no[r] Brother in the woods" (although she did have male kin hiding in the woods). Invoking the moral authority of republicanism rather than motherhood, Crook informed Governor Vance of the "true" conditions of her community. Calling on him to "protect the civil laws and writs of our country," she denounced the militia and magistrates of her county for arresting "poore old grey-headed fathers who has fought in the old War and has done thir duty."[39]

Enraged by home guard who, Crook insisted, had no intention themselves of fighting in the war, she condemned their physical abuse of women and children and their burning of barns, houses, and crops, all done in the name of fulfilling the governor's directive to force deserters out of the woods. Following such orders was merely an excuse, she wrote, for pro-Confederate men to "take their guns and go out in the woods and shoot them down Without Halting them as if they war Bruts or Murder[er]s." Once again, Crook emphasized rights of citizenship rather than victimhood by assuring the governor that her motive for writing was that "I always like to [see] people hav jestis."[40]

Despite the sisters' separate appeals to Governor Vance, they could not prevent the killing of their three brothers-in-law, on 28 January 1865. Jesse, John, and William Hulin were executed, along with James Atkins, who had been identified as a draft evader by the hated Sheriff Sanders during the previous fall court term. The Hulin brothers, like Martha Sheets, belonged to the county's network of Wesleyan Methodist families who opposed slavery and refused to fight for the Confederacy.[41]

Was it mere coincidence that Sheets's threatening letter to Sheriff Sanders was dated only one day before the executions, probably on the very day that the Hulin brothers and Atkins were thrown in jail? Not likely. It would also appear that ten women from the Wesleyan community charged with rioting at the Sanders Mill in May 1865 had revenge as well as the acquisition of grain on their minds.[42]

In an 1867 letter to Colonel M. Cogwell, commander of the military post at Fayetteville, Hiram Hulin described how two county justices of the peace had delivered his captured sons and their companion, James Atkins, into the hands of "murderers who were home guard troops." Rather than taking the men to prison to await trial for evading Confederate service, the home guard "deliberately shot and beat to death with guns and rocks my three sons and Atkins while tied with their hands and handcuffed together." Although the elder Hulin pleaded for justice for his sons and their companion, the Reconstruction government failed to convict anyone for the murders.[43]

The persistent claim by Confederate leaders that the war was fought on behalf of the South's "fair women" clearly was meaningless rhetoric to plain farm women of the Randolph County area. Jesse, John, and William Hulin left behind numerous kinfolk, including wives, children, and father. James Atkins left behind his widowed mother, Sarah, who had been charged the previous fall with harboring him as a deserter. The trauma of so many deaths likely explains why Nelson and Clarinda Crook Hulin moved to Kentucky shortly after the war, along with numerous members of the Crook family. Jesse Hulin's widow, Caroline, who had long aided her husband in hiding in the woods, remained with their children in Montgomery County. Carefully saving the shoes, socks, and cap that he wore on the cold morning of his death, Caroline passed them on to descendants, for whom they became grim reminders of a war that turned Southerners, sometimes even neighbors, into cold-blooded killers of one another.[44]

Governor Vance's policies in regard to deserters and those who harbored them found their harshest expression in orders issued by Lieutenant Colonel Alexander Carey McAlister, commander of a detachment of soldiers assigned to break up deserter bands in the Randolph County area. In March 1865, McAlister directed his forces to scour the country for seven miles around for "deserters, absentees, and recusant conscripts," adding that "you are empowered to impress citizens for guides." If citizens (who inevitably included women as well as men) refused to obey orders, the soldiers were told to administer "punishment as you may think necessary to protect you from betrayal." Toward any who resisted their authority, or the authority of the government, McAlister advised his soldiers that "no quarter will be shown; they will be shot down wherever found."[45]

What did McAlister mean by these words? Did he actually intend for soldiers to shoot down civilian women as well as men? Probably not. The dilemma faced by Confederate occupiers, epitomized by vigilante Adams Brewer's insistence that Captain Ramsey's soldiers shoot Franny Jordan's female accomplice, emanated from contradictory attitudes about "womanhood." Typically, lower-class and black women were considered dissipated and potentially dangerous, while women of the white propertied classes were imagined to be timidly reposing in their homes. In forming their poli-

Caroline Hulin, widow of Jesse Hulin, one of three brothers murdered by vigilantes in Montgomery County, North Carolina, for refusing to fight for the Confederacy. Photograph courtesy of Elaine Reynolds.

cies, Confederate leaders had difficulty imagining the wives, mothers, and daughters of propertied white men on the front lines of home front "battle-fields." But there they were. And there, too, was Adams Brewer, "ordering" Captain Ramsey's soldiers to shoot a female civilian suspected of treason. Although no woman accused of disloyalty appears to have been executed by the Confederacy, arrests and tortures of Unionist women were regularly reported throughout the war.[46]

On the one hand, Governor Vance regularly deplored the ill-treatment of women and children by militia, magistrates, and home guard. On the other hand, as Phebe Crook's letter made clear, such abuses were a predictable result of his proclamations and policies in regard to deserters and those who abetted them. Just three weeks after Crooks wrote her letter, prominent lawyer Thomas Settle, a supporter of peace candidate William Holden, informed Vance that roundups of disloyal women in the Randolph County area had "terrified" some pregnant women into having "abortions almost under the eyes of their terrifiers." Yet it was Governor Vance who ordered the arrest and detention in prison camps of all citizens, irrespective of gender and age, who harbored deserters or evaders.[47]

In line with the Confederacy's policy of detention, Major J. G. Harris, headquartered at Asheboro, requested on 27 March 1865 that Lieutenant Colonel McAlister send Mary Jane Welch and Christiana Wilson to him "under guard," since Welch had admitted that she and Wilson had participated in two robberies committed by deserters.[48] But McAlister, who lamented on 16 March that deserters "possess so generally the sympathy of the inhabitants [that is, women] that we are laboring under great difficulties," now had an about-face in regard to detaining women. On 30 March, just three days after the arrests of Welch and Wilson, he advised Major Harris that extorting confessions from captured women and children was "productive of more evil than good" and ordered the practice ended. Of course, by that time the war was almost over.[49]

Deeply felt class, cultural, and religious values animated women's resistance in the Randolph County area, presenting Confederate authorities with a qualitatively different home front than that of Orange County. No inner war raged in Orange County, although civil disorder increased dramatically during the final year of the war. The obvious cause of that disorder was abject poverty. By 1864, many women of Orange County were stealing from their wealthier neighbors and merchants, but none dared openly threaten a Confederate official, as did Martha Sheets of Montgomery County. Although both classes of women struggled for personal survival, women like

Sheets also fought to restore the justice they believed was threatened by the Confederate government.

As discussed earlier, Nancy Carroll and Elizabeth Gilbert were among the Orange County women driven to theft by the war. Such women and their families often became the maligned "poor white trash" of the so-called New South, as wartime devastation ushered in postwar impoverishment. Nancy Carroll kept house alone in 1870; her eighty-seven-year-old father, widower Archy Carroll, lived with three grown women (perhaps Nancy's sisters) in a propertyless household. Sixty-two-year-old Betsy Gilbert, who lived in Hillsboro in 1870 with Louisa Gilbert Pearson, a propertyless widow with two children, is likely our Elizabeth.[50]

Although it did not constitute an inner civil war, Orange County's breakdown in civil order did revitalize political opposition to the war. As more and more soldiers deserted their units, local peace candidates emerged to challenge Confederate policy. After the war's end, pro-Confederate Conservatives would vie with pro-Union Republicans for local power. By 1868, a fiercely violent white supremacy campaign would dominate that struggle throughout the Quaker Belt, as the Ku Klux Klan terrorized white Republicans, black citizens in general, and even poor people who dared cross the color line. The New South would institutionalize segregation and rewrite the Confederate Lost Cause as a noble effort by the Southern "people" to resist the tyranny of the North.[51]

As for the Randolph County area, well into the twentieth century both professional and amateur historians portrayed Confederate occupation of pro-Union regions of the South in positive terms. In 1901, Captain Ramsey wrote a brief history of North Carolina's 61st Regiment in which he described the very expedition that resulted in the kidnapping of Franny Jordan's teenaged son. Using the language of the Confederate Lost Cause, Ramsey lauded his troops for their unsurpassed bravery in battle and gave special credit to Company D for having "restored peace" to the citizens of Chatham and Moore Counties, where they were sent to protect "life and property against lawless deserters and conscripts." To Ramsey, and to Confederate leaders in general, Southerners who resisted or defied the authority of the Confederacy were lawless bandits to be hunted down. If a few of their "leading spirits" were killed by his men, well, so much the better for the larger community.[52]

Captain Ramsey could not conceive of white Southerners who opposed the Confederacy on principle or of women who did not seek his soldiers' "protection." Southern Unionists appear nowhere in his narrative, and white married women were subsumed within his reference to protecting communities. Other Lost Cause historians regularly presented such women as damsels in distress, threatened on all sides by Yankees, runaway slaves, and deserters—but never by Confederate forces. Thus, women who fought against the Confederacy, as did those of North Carolina's Quaker Belt, rarely appeared until recently in Civil War accounts as anything other than the deluded female arm of a "lawless gang of marauders."[53]

PART II   Reconstruction and Beyond

THE UNION'S DEFEAT of the Confederacy in 1865 should have been a time of jubilant celebration for pro-Union Southerners and newly freed slaves. And so it was, at least initially. Victory over the Confederacy produced heady, hopeful times for Union men, many of whom gained unprecedented political power. But before the decade's end, the tide had turned against both white and black Republicans. Chapters 3 and 4 reveal the interrelated yet distinct struggles of two communities of dissenters in the post–Civil War South: poor white and African American citizens of Orange County, North Carolina, and white pro-Union deserters of the Confederate Army in Jones County, Mississippi.

For citizens of African descent, the burning question during Reconstruction was whether they would be allowed to exercise the social, economic, and political freedoms granted them by the Republican-dominated U.S. Congress. Economically and politically, antebellum free black men were more prepared than most slaves to assume leadership roles in the postwar South. Thus, in Orange County, North Carolina, a number of male descendants of interracial unions were politically active in the immediate aftermath of Union victory.

Despite societal taboos and economic barriers, Orange County whites and blacks, rich and poor, had regularly interacted with one another, socially and sexually, long before the war. Most obviously, sexual exploitation of enslaved women, a white male prerogative exercised throughout the antebellum South, had contributed to a large population of light-skinned African Americans. Not so obviously, white women also crossed the color line, although it was not their prerogative to do so, especially in older regions of the South with diverse populations.

Chapter 3's Lydia Bowers was such a woman. Like numerous unmarried white women from respectable yeoman families, Bowers was hauled before court magistrates after she became pregnant. Publicly shamed, such women's chances for prosperous marriages typically plunged. But how were unmarried mothers to make a living? Many took jobs as domestics or field workers and lived quiet, obscure lives. Others became locally renowned "public women," not necessarily prostitutes but members of interracial enclaves in which drinking, gambling, and informal exchanges of favors took place. Lydia chose the latter path.

Chapter 3 traces the effect of Lydia's pre–Civil War socioeconomic descent on the life of her daughter, Ann Bowers Boothe, a woman of ambiguous racial identity, in post-Reconstruction North Carolina. Interracial mingling produced many such people in Orange County. After the war, poor whites and their African American kin contributed to a fragile biracial political coalition, which was relentlessly targeted by former Confederate leaders in their vicious counterrevolution against Republican Reconstruction.

In overwhelmingly white Jones County, Mississippi, however, no such biracial political coalition developed. Jones County's prewar population included virtually no free people of color; thus, there was no biracial free community such as that in Orange County on which to build. The lack of such a base, combined with racism, prevented most whites from even considering a postwar political alliance with former slaves. Yet harassment of former Unionists and freedpeople often emanated from the same white supremacist terrorists. Morgan Valentine, a former member of the Knight band, perhaps provided a clue to his decision to move his family to Colorado, where they embraced Mormonism, when he recalled the "Ku Klux" that "after the surrender . . . we had to contend with."[1]

Despite the different racial compositions of the above counties, ordinary whites in both feared that racial equality would undermine their own precarious status. At Mississippi's 1865 constitutional convention, Jones County delegate Thomas G. Crawford expressed such concerns when he spoke for the suffering yeoman farmers of Jones County, while expressing disdain for racial reform.

Crawford framed his objections to political and social equality for African Americans in class-based rhetoric. Arguing that neither former slaves *nor* slaveholders ought to receive congressional funds, he condemned efforts by several legislators to compensate former slaveholders. Crawford called on the state first to address the needs of impoverished white widows and children. At the same time, he objected to legislative debates over freedpeople's status when so many whites in his district were suffering. "In honesty to this convention," he implored his colleagues "to remember the white race [that is, the white yeomanry] and not be wholly absorbed in Africanism."[2]

The "white race" that Crawford deemed more worthy of legislative aid was epitomized by Jones County's Unionist rebels against the Confederacy. In 1895, thirty years after he gave the above speech, Crawford testified on behalf of Newt Knight's appeal to Congress for compensation for Knight Company survivors, widows, and children. Chapter 4 provides the full story of Newt's decades-long effort to convince the U.S. government that his band of guerrillas had fought on behalf of the Union Army.

Throughout the years, Newt justified his petitions for compensation with the same basic arguments, although national and local shifts in political power affected how those arguments were presented and received. His first claim was read before three Republican-dominated Congresses between 1870 and 1873, whereas his second and third claims were reviewed between 1888 and 1891, after the resurgence of the Southern Democratic Party. Chapter 4 analyzes the changing political scene, bureaucratic delays, misplaced evidence, changing legal strategies, and fading memories that all contributed to the final defeat of Newt Knight's claim.

Newt's long legal battle demonstrates how difficult it was for a Southern white man to prove he had supported the Union during the Civil War. With the Myth of the Lost Cause firmly entrenched by 1900, most Northerners as well as Southerners generally assumed that all respectable Southern white men had revered the Confederate cause since its earliest inception. But the depositions of Newt Knight, his co-Unionists, and their adversaries simultaneously illuminate and complicate our understanding of the role of ordinary white men and women in the Civil War.

CHAPTER THREE

Disordered Communities

Freedpeople, Poor Whites, and "Mixed Blood"
Families in Reconstruction North Carolina

White people, wrote Colonel Samuel Thomas in September 1865, "still have the ingrained feeling that the black people at large belong to the whites at large, [and] . . . will cheat a negro without feeling a single twinge of their honor. To kill a negro they do not deem murder, to debauch a negro woman they do not think fornication, to take property away from a negro they do not consider robbery." With those words, Colonel Thomas, assistant commissioner of the Freedmen's Bureau for Mississippi, captured the essence of why the decade of Reconstruction to follow would be one of the nation's bloodiest and most divisive.[1]

Writing only two months after Colonel Thomas filed his pessimistic report for Mississippi, Clinton A. Cilley, superintendent of the bureau's West District in Salisbury, North Carolina, offered a similarly bleak assessment of race relations in that state.[2] Superintendent Cilley estimated that about three-fourths of blacks were willing to work, while the rest made their livings by stealing and prostitution. Although he estimated that three-fourths of whites were likewise willing to employ blacks, he thought that only two-thirds were willing to pay fair wages—and that even they would not treat blacks fairly except for the "advice and authority" of the Freedmen's Bureau. Were the bureau discontinued, he concluded, "blacks would be no better off than before the war."[3]

It is not surprising that Southern white men, especially former slaveholders, would rage against their loss of political authority and racial dominance. For a brief few years, their world was turned upside down, and most did not doubt that their diminished power signaled the destruction of civilized society. But more than political and racial dominance were at stake. At its most fundamental, day-to-day level, slaveholding men's right to dominate their households was also challenged. To better understand their struggle to maintain power, we must examine gender as well as race and the lives of poor as well as propertied whites.[4]

African Americans formed an important but fragile alliance with white Unionists. Early in the war, local and state Confederate leaders had cracked down hard on Orange County citizens who opposed secession. From Chapel Hill, William Lloyd, Cannon Bowers, and Joseph Ivey were said to be the only men in their neighborhood who dared vote against secession. But open dissent against the Confederacy resurged among many Southern whites, especially in the yeomanry, during the final two years of the war. The stage thus was set for showdowns during Reconstruction over which political party would prevail in the wake of Confederate defeat. Orange County's Unionists were from various backgrounds, but the greatest levels of dissent came from neighborhoods made up mainly of nonslaveholding farmers and laborers.[5]

Durham's best-known Unionist was William W. Guess, a wealthy Whig slaveholder. As a result of his opposition to secession, Guess's grain mill was boycotted by disgruntled Confederates during the war. Old Sam Cole, who continued to patronize Guess's mill, was another outspoken Unionist. Neighbors worried for his safety, but Sam may have escaped harassment because of his advanced age (he was over eighty years old) and because three of his grandsons lost their lives in service to the Confederate Army.[6]

If it was dangerous for propertied white men to express Unionist views, it was doubly so for African American women. Nelly Stroud, of Chapel Hill, remembered that "colored people" like her did not discuss the politics of the war, at least not publicly: "A still tongue made a wise head." As a washerwoman, Stroud's livelihood depended upon the willingness of whites to hire her; she dared not shoot off her mouth about politically charged issues. Even her friend Nancy Brewer, unusual as an economically independent black woman who owned her home and had purchased her husband out of slavery, agreed with Stroud that blacks generally kept quiet. She felt compelled to add, however, that they always sympathized with the Union cause, believing it was "God's will for the colored race to be free."[7]

Freedom did come, but it was quickly followed by the Ku Klux Klan's reign of terror. In the eastern portion of the state, blacks were too numerous and too necessary a labor force to be cowed into submission. In the western mountain counties, where few blacks lived and where Unionism had flourished during the war, poor white farmers joined the Republican Party in droves. Two strongholds of state Republicanism, then, eastern blacks and western white voters, were not easily swayed before 1875 by white supremacist threats or rhetoric.[8]

The situation was quite different in the state's Piedmont region, where both whites and blacks joined the Republican Party in substantial numbers. In 1867, with former governor William W. Holden as their leader, the North Carolina Republican Party endorsed Congress's Reconstruction Acts, pledging its support for military supervision of the South's reentry into the Union. It agreed as well to hold a convention at which a new state constitution would be framed that ratified the Fourteenth Amendment and conferred rights of citizenship upon African Americans. A new day seemed to be dawning.[9]

The Republican coalition was powerful, but the Conservative Party had a trump card that it did not hesitate to play: the deeply engrained disdain that most whites felt for blacks, especially newly empowered blacks, described so succinctly by Freedmen's Bureau commissioner Samuel Thomas. Klan violence soon erupted in response to ratification of the state constitution of 1868, which provided for free public schooling for black and white children as well as universal male suffrage. Conservatives railed against the inevitable mixing of races they predicted would follow, blasting the biracial Republican Union Leagues as proof that blacks intended to rule the South.[10]

Klan terror was widespread throughout the Piedmont but was less effective in some counties than in others. Randolph, Moore, and Montgomery Counties, which had large Unionist yeoman populations and a small but devout community of Wesleyan Methodists, were less responsive to white supremacist tactics. This region, considered the "heart" of the Quaker Belt, remained more strongly attached to the Republican Party throughout Reconstruction than the counties of Alamance, Caswell, and Orange, where Klan terrorists mounted a culture of intimidation.[11]

That culture lasted well into the twentieth century. In March 1961, North Carolina's *State* magazine still insisted that the Ku Klux Klan "became active" during Reconstruction in response to "roaming ex-slaves" who "robbed, raped, and killed." Many Southern white editors simply took at face value the words of white supremacists (many of them Klan members themselves) from almost a century earlier.[12]

Superior court judge and Klan member David Schenck, for example, claimed in his diary that "a negro was made to be governed with severity—and nothing else will answer the purpose," after witnessing ex-slaves celebrating the Christmas season of 1868 with a lavish use of alcohol. Jacob Alson Long, a lawyer and chief of the Alamance County Order of White Brotherhood, attributed Klan terrorism to oppression of whites by idle, shiftless black men who were bent on forcing white women to become their brides. Men such as Schenck and Long were respected members of society whose words were treated as authoritative long after the Klan was discredited.[13]

Schenck embodied the white upper-class assumption that former slaves, and black people in general, must not wield power and could not direct their own affairs. His complaints about black "drunkenness, theft, cheating, and lewdness" reflected his deeply ingrained racism, for excessive celebrations of freedom and lawbreaking among some blacks was inevitable, as most were free for the first time, although, at the same time, impoverished.[14]

A long, devastating war followed by the sudden end of slavery had upended Southern society and thrown its communities into chaos. Court records between 1865 and 1868 are filled with accounts of theft, affrays, and drunkenness among both whites and blacks, testimony to the profound disorder and threat of starvation that accompanied political turmoil. Although racism blinded many whites to these facts, yet some did perceive the conditions that led to desperate acts. After freedman Green Durham, for example, was sentenced in late 1867 to eighteen months in jail for stealing bacon, thirty-three citizens of Chapel Hill, most of them white, petitioned Governor Jonathan Worth on Durham's behalf. Citing his three children and the "delicate health" of his wife, they called on the governor to remit him from jail.[15]

Despite Conservatives' insistence that "dissolute" blacks must be forcibly controlled for the protection of society and white womanhood, they and the Klan were after far more than black criminals during Reconstruction; they wanted no less than to drive the Republican Party out of the state and blacks back into submission. In Orange County alone, local courts were too overwhelmed and intimidated to adequately punish Klan crimes.[16]

Squire Alston discovered the limits of local justice in March 1869. Alston, a black citizen, swore before an Orange County justice of the peace that about a dozen masked men had broken into his home two days earlier and dragged him and his wife from their beds and ordered them from their house. The armed men proceeded to torch the house, fire off guns, and throw rocks at Alston as he struggled to extinguish the flames. Although Alston identified three of his attackers, the accused men never appeared in court to answer charges of assault and battery.[17]

From Hillsboro, S. B. Williams, a black pastor and freedman school-teacher, informed Governor William Holden, on 16 September 1869, of the murders of two black men, one of whom was forcibly removed from jail and shot; the other was found with his tongue cut out and his throat slashed. Williams, afraid for his and others' lives, asked the governor to provide either a police force or arms for the citizens.[18]

That same month, four masked men with pistols seized Wright Malone from a coal kiln and hanged him. Cold-blooded murders such as these also led concerned whites, particularly Republicans, to report Klan outrages to the governor. Six days after Pastor Williams addressed his letter, James B. Mason, of Chapel Hill, reported five Klan raids in that town in the space of two weeks. Klansmen were "rowdying up & down" the streets late at night, and Mason, like Williams, called on the governor to send aid. Fearing for his own safety, he, too, asked that his name not be revealed.[19]

William W. Holden, elected governor for a second term in 1868, explained to Chief Justice Richmond Pearson that the civil courts "are no longer a protection to life, liberty, and property; assassinations and outrage go unpunished, and the civil magistrates are intimidated." Under the Shoffner Act of 1870, Holden imposed martial law on Alamance and Caswell Counties, declaring each to be in a state of insurrection and ordering state troops into both under the direction of Union officer George W. Kirk. For his efforts, he became entangled in the "Kirk-Holden War." Local leaders, members of the Conservative Party and often of the Klan as well, whipped up support among the local populace by denouncing Holden's suspension of civil rights and his choice of a Union officer to head the intrusion into their counties.[20]

Although over 100 arrests were made during Holden's war on the Klan, its controversial nature led President Ulysses S. Grant to deny federal support for the governor's crackdown. Emboldened by federal timidity and popular opposition to marshal law, the North Carolina Assembly impeached Holden in December 1870, and in March 1871 he was convicted. At the behest of beleaguered Republicans and African Americans, Holden had risked his political capital and lost. Again and again, racism and a sense of outrage at an intrusive government would lead white North Carolinians to privilege white supremacy and local autonomy over efforts to protect African Americans and white Republicans from terror and outright murder.[21]

Despite Governor Holden's impeachment ordeal, Republicans continued their struggle to gain control over the Klan. On 10 January 1871, in preparation for federal investigations of the Klan, James B. Mason coauthored a lengthy report of Klan outrages, which provided names, political affiliations, and details of abuses. Thomas Kirby, a "leading Republican" among blacks, had been threatened; Jerry Reeves, Sampson Atwater, and James Morgan, black Republicans, were beaten up. The Klan also attacked two men named Morrow; one was beaten and the other was shot to death. Several white men of Orange County were also reported to have been threatened, beaten, or whipped. Nathaniel King, described as an "old man," left the county after being beaten up because of his political views. When the wife of Neverson Cates, who was also harassed, declared aloud that they should have the Klan arrested, her husband told her to hush, that the Klan was too strong.[22]

The wives of black men were frequently assaulted or harassed by the Klan. In contrast to supposed reverence for white womanhood, no deference was paid to black women who got in the Klan's way. Sampson Atwater's wife reportedly suffered a severe gash to her forehead after being knocked to the ground for begging the Klan to spare her husband's life. That same year, the court charged the Atwaters with fornication on unspecified grounds. The charges did not stick and seemed designed only to harass the couple. The wives of Madison Nunn and Dick Cotton, who shared a household, were beaten up by Klan members who came looking for their husbands. Klan members "abused and cursed" the wife of black Republican activist Henry Jones for similar reasons: Jones was not at home when they came looking for him.[23]

Those Orange County freedmen who kept their heads down may have saved their own lives, but they still made little economic progress during Reconstruction. Only 14.1 percent of black male household heads owned real estate in 1870, and the average size of their farms was only one-quarter that of white farms. By 1880, three-fourths of the county's black farmers, compared to one-fourth of white farmers, were sharecroppers. Planters and former slaveholders continued to enjoy wealth despite their loss of capital in slave property. Among the yeoman class, on the other hand, farm sizes decreased after the war, and one-third of all white farmers owned no land at all.[24]

In this class-bound and racially divided society, not all violence was perpetrated by the Klan or was necessarily premeditated. Violence often resulted from the assumption of many whites that it was their duty and right to police blacks. The 1867 killing of Bill Fuller, a freedman, is a case in point. On the day he died, Fuller attended a corn shucking at Bill Faucett's home, located in the Cedar Grove neighborhood on the land of Catlett C. Tinnin, a sixty-year-old former slaveholder. The friends gathered to work, but also to play music and sing songs together, creating a festive atmosphere that infuriated Tinnin. Perhaps he was irritated by the sounds of blacks enjoying their freedom, or perhaps the noise just got to him. Whatever the case, he angrily entered Faucett's house and confronted the men, threatening to "blow out their brains." The black men, who dared not take lightly such threats from white men, quickly scattered. Tinnin then walked to a window and fired his gun. Bill Fuller, who had just exited the same window, took the bullet in his leg.[25]

The injured man, who was not discovered for almost half an hour, died from his wound. During the court's investigation, witnesses seemed to agree that Tinnin did not intend to kill Fuller but had fired indiscriminately through the window without seeing him. Tinnin, they pointed out, was "very much hurt" when he discovered what he had done and immediately called for a doctor.[26]

Perhaps Tinnin was innocent of premeditated murder, as he and his witnesses claimed, or perhaps the black men who testified in his defense were too scared to say otherwise. Either way, Bill Fuller died because of the right claimed by white men to patrol black men and regulate their behavior. Significantly, Tinnin told Bill Faucett that had he known Faucett was hosting a corn shucking rather than an ordinary frolic, he would not have interfered. As during slavery, white men would "allow" black men who gathered together to work white men's land (rather than simply to revel in freedom) to engage in a bit of merriment along the way.[27]

Political images of Republican-mandated racial equality helped to convince white voters that African Americans were the greatest threat to their prosperity and moral values. Conservatives regularly warned that free schools would bring racial integration and lead to miscegenation. In reality, the mixing of races had a long history among Southerners. What Conservatives really feared was *voluntary* mixing among white and black citizens, for mixed-race children born to unmarried free women had long been a troublesome class in slaveholding society.[28] Unlike in the case of enslaved children fathered by white men, the behavior and labor of free mixed-race children was far less easily controlled. In antebellum North Carolina, criminal offenses such as fornication, prostitution, and bastardy were prosecuted by the county courts as a means of regulating the reproductive behavior of poor whites and free blacks. In the wake of emancipation, the same laws now applied to freedwomen.[29]

No longer slaves, but hardly free from sexual exploitation and economic dominance, unmarried freedwomen were now summoned to court when suspected of being pregnant. Before the war, white men might treat slave quarters as brothels in which the services were free of cost and without social consequences. Now the courts expected them to provide support for children born to such liaisons. Furthermore, court charges of bastardy brought public exposure of men's behavior.

Orange County's Pattie Ruffin, a former slave of North Carolina chief justice Thomas Ruffin, was seventeen in 1865 when the Thirteenth Amendment to the Constitution abolished slavery. When she became pregnant the following year, she was accordingly summoned to appear in court to identify the father of her bastard child.[30] Pattie's predicament was complicated by the fact that her child's father was a white man who wished not to be identified as her sexual partner or as the father of a mixed-race child. No doubt from a prominent family, he soon received crucial intervention from prominent state politician and lawyer John W. Graham. On 19 August 1866, Graham explained in a letter to Colonel Hugh B. Guthrie that "negro testimony is rather inconvenient to some who have been prowling around too promiscuously." He directed Guthrie to inform Pattie that she had a "right" to refuse to name the father as long as she paid the court five dollars and posted bond assuring that her illegitimate child would never become a charge upon the county. In closing, Graham expressed his hope that "we might let the young fellows go for what was done before negroes were allowed to testify" against white people.[31]

Graham clearly thought nothing of coercing a black seventeen-year-old domestic servant into forgoing support payments for her child in order to protect the identity of a young scion from an elite family. Adhering to the maxim "boys will be boys," Graham personally intervened on behalf of the "young friend of mine" who was "quite uneasy" about the prospect of being charged as "Papa" of Pattie Ruffin's baby. For her part, Pattie did as she was told. On 21 August 1866, she refused to name her child's father in court.[32] Ruffin was left to raise her child alone with only her biological kin to assist her. But what about those children suddenly freed from slavery whose parents were less easily identified and whose networks of kin were fractured by generations of enslavement? For them, the courts turned to its apprenticeship system. Apprenticeship laws had been drawn up for North Carolina during the seventeenth century as a means to support indigent, illegitimate children. Under this system, children were bound by contract to work for propertied adults of the county, who in turn fed and clothed them.[33]

Apprenticeship not only supported indigent children, but it had also long supplemented slavery by providing state control over the labor of mixed-race children. Particularly in counties such as Orange, with high numbers of free people of color, the apprenticeship system functioned to control free children of African ancestry, whether born to white or to African American women. In the decade preceding the war, 61 percent of Orange County's apprenticed children were designated "black" or "mulatto," although free black women made up only 9 percent of female-headed households.[34]

In the wake of emancipation, some former slaveholders evicted freedpeople who did not leave of their own accord; other ex-slaves signed labor contracts under the direction of Freedmen's Bureau agents. Simultaneously, many formerly enslaved children were bound to white landowners, usually their former masters, as apprentices. And, just as before the war, apprenticeship effectively denied parents custody over their own children, as well as control over their labor.[35] Ratification of the Fourteenth Amendment to the Constitution in 1868 gave African American parents the tools to fight for custody of their children. Between 1868 and 1870, the Republican-dominated courts of North Carolina aided many parents who sued for release of their children from apprenticeship contracts. In Montgomery County, in 1869, Lila McDonald successfully regained custody of her children after her Republican lawyer filed a petition citing apprenticeship of former slaves as "contrary to the provisions of the Fourteenth article of the United States [Constitution and] . . . the spirit of the Reconstruction Acts of Congress."[36]

Successful challenges to the apprenticeship system by blacks occurred throughout the state during the period of Radical Reconstruction, contributing to the slow demise of apprenticeship, beginning in 1873. Most black parents who sought to rescind apprenticeships appealed to provost marshals or agents of the Freedmen's Bureau. Others, such as Lila McDonald, initiated court suits during an era in which black men briefly wielded political power.[37]

Despite Republican judges' sympathy for freedpeople's civil rights, they did not always rule in favor of those seeking custody of former slave children. The difficulty of proving paternity complicated cases that involved fathers rather than mothers. A slave father often could not live near his child or form a permanent, stable relationship with the child's mother. Allen Compton's lawyer took full advantage of such factors in 1871 when the former slaveholder's right to custody of fourteen-year-old Green Compton was challenged by Alexander Corbin, who claimed to be the boy's biological father.[38] Compton's lawyer emphasized that Corbin himself admitted that he barely knew the boy he now called "son" and that he had not sought custody of him in the immediate aftermath of the war. Nor had Corbin challenged the apprenticeship of Green to Compton back in 1866. The lawyer also took an easy shot at the character of Green's deceased slave mother, Minerva, describing it as "very bad" since "most all her children" had different fathers, making it impossible to know if Corbett was one of those fathers.[39]

Judge George Laws ruled against Alexander Corbin in probate court. Corbin's lawyer, Republican Isaac R. Strayhorn, appealed Judge Laws's decision to the Seventh District Superior Court. Citing testimony from witnesses who claimed that Minerva and her master, Allen Compton, had casually stated on separate occasions that Corbin was Green's father, Strayhorn also reminded the court that under slavery, Minerva could not have married any of her children's fathers. Superior court justice Albion Tourgee, although a Republican and courageous defender of freedpeople's rights, nevertheless upheld Judge Laws's decision.[40]

Two pieces of evidence may have compelled Tourgee to rule against Corbin. First, certain testimony indicated that Minerva had a free black husband (although her marriage would not have been legally valid) from around 1857–58 until the time of her death in 1861 and that this husband had recognized Green as his son. Second, Corbin's failure to seek custody of Green before 1871 raised suspicions. Was it merely coincidental that Green was by then a strong teenage boy, capable of contributing valuable labor to a household? In this crucial era of history, struggles over children were simultaneously struggles over labor.

When freedman Ben Harris appealed to the Freedmen's Bureau with a plea that "surly the Law doe Not Call for Children to be bond out when their peapel is Abel to keep them," his former master told Colonel John R. Edie of the Freedmen's Bureau that Harris only wanted his children's earnings and would keep them in "rags and half-starved" if granted custody. Of course, freedpeople did desire such earnings, which were essential to black postwar household economies, as well as the company of their children.[41]

Certainly, most former slaveholders were not primarily concerned with the welfare of black children when they sought apprenticeship contracts. Most were interested in employing and apprenticing strong, able-bodied freedpeople. Even the paternalistic concerns that D. C. Parrish of Orange County expressed for his former slave John could not mask his economic interest in regaining the teenaged boy's labor. While pulling fodder in Parrish's cornfield, John was "carried off" by a freedman claiming to be his father. "I call it stealing," complained Parrish to Freedmen's Bureau officer Isaac Porter. John, he explained, was a "favourite boy" whom he had even sent to Sunday school. After admitting that John was not much interested in Bible study, however, Parrish got to the point: the boy's father wanted him now that "I have raised him to be larger enough to be of good service to me."[42]

Dependent, helpless former slaves were a constant concern for bureau authorities. On Christmas Day 1865, Lieutenant E. A. Harris of the Freedmen's Bureau of Morgantown wondered what was to be done with "very young orphans, blind and infirm—totally dependent Negroes." Not only were former masters loath to care for crippled and infirm freedpeople, he wrote, but there were many children "so young that no one will take them for any consideration. . . . Masters wish them removed from their plantations at once."[43]

For black men, gaining custody over children, including the right to reap the benefits of their labor, was essential to claiming authority over one's household, a basic male prerogative denied them under slavery. But for other freedmen, the desire to build a new life and prosper economically discouraged efforts to unite with biological families. In June 1866, Benjamin Markham, of Orange County, received a letter from his brother, G. R. Marcom, expressing fears of a labor shortage on account of so many black men moving west and leaving women and children behind, "strowling about" the streets. "I think some of them is bound to starve," he wrote, "but they are free."[44]

Black women remained politically and legally the South's most powerless group, but, like black men, they exercised their freedom by asserting themselves both personally and politically. Some, for example, refused to be treated like slaves by masters who were now their employers. One Orange County black servant flew "into a rage" when her mistress scolded her for arriving late to work. Another responded to the condescending airs of her employer's daughter by reminding her that "her own hair [was] nearly as straight" and that she was "quite as free" as herself.[45]

Lila McDonald's challenge to the apprenticeship system and Pattie Ruffin's bastardy case are particularly instructive about connections between politics and issues of gender and reproduction. McDonald lived in the heavily Unionist county of Montgomery, located in the heart of the North Carolina Quaker Belt. She won custody of her children from their former master by engaging the services of a Republican lawyer who had opposed secession. Ruffin, on the other hand, was summoned to court for breaking the law, that is, giving birth to an illegitimate child. But there was more to it than that. She had entered into an interracial affair with a well-connected member of Orange County society who could call on a prominent political leader for aid. And that leader, John W. Graham, was no friend to freedpeople. A member of the Conservative Party by 1868, he introduced the bill in the General Assembly, passed by the State Senate in January 1873, granting amnesty to members of the Ku Klux Klan.[46]

Freedmen's Bureau agents were sometimes the only recourse for desperate freedwomen suffering abuse and neglect by former masters or husbands. Charles Yarboro, of Lexington, bluntly informed W. F. Henderson of the bureau in early 1867 that he would no longer supply "vittles & clothing" to Harriet, his former slave, now that she was pregnant with her second child. He ordered Harriet to seek new employment and a new home, which she did. But she soon returned to Yarbro's plantation after being denied work at a nearby factory. "If she don't get a place by Monday I shall set her out in the road," Yarbro warned agent Henderson.[47]

Sometimes black women escaped exploitation by white men only to encounter abuse at the hands of newly empowered black husbands. J. Cowles, of Hamptonville, referred the case of a former slave named Clary to the bureau after she requested protection from her husband, freedman Rufus Blackburn, who, she claimed, had violently forced her from their home, taken up with another woman, and kept the furniture, pots, and quilts left to her by her master. Clary wanted the bureau to intercede and force Blackburn to return her goods. Similarly, Dillie, a field hand described by W. H. Worden as "an industrious woman," complained to the bureau that she and her six children were being turned out of their home by her husband.[48]

Some women sought the aid of the bureau in order to escape husbands who viewed them as their property now that slavery was abolished. After Alfred Gray's wife refused to live with him in their High Point home, he showed up at her new home, claiming "she was my wife and I had a right to her." When Mrs. Gray refused to go home, the two came to blows. She then told agent Dilworth that she intended to divorce her "cruel and unkind" husband. But Mr. Gray reiterated rights of ownership: "I consider her my property and thus I have a right to her." Within a month, he had reportedly convinced his wife of his "written authority" to take possession of her, and she returned home with him. White men had long denied black men the prerogatives of household hegemony that they assumed for themselves; small wonder many were now eager to exercise them fully.[49]

Although the Freedmen's Bureau mediated domestic disputes between husbands and wives and at times provided immediate relief or advice, it had neither the funding nor the power to change the societal conditions that produced ongoing personal crises. Sometimes the bureau was forced to mediate conflicts in which both the plaintiff and the defendant were ultimately victims. This was certainly the case when Linda McQueen, a freedwoman of Montgomery County, named freedman Harry Butler as the father of her infant after allegedly being coerced into hiding the identity of the child's white father.[50]

Butler's attorney, Benjamin F. Simmons, argued that Butler, who had fathered two of McQueen's previous children, was, like McQueen, a "pure-blooded African" and therefore could not be the father of her mulatto infant. But a jury found Butler guilty and ordered him to pay $75 child support in three installments over a year's time. That, and additional court costs, forced Butler to indenture himself to Spencer Haltom, a white man, for three years in exchange for Haltom's paying his debts.[51]

Butler was rescued from his dismal fate by his lawyer's appeal to the Freedmen's Bureau. Responding to Simmons's claim that his client's apprenticeship amounted to "secondary slavery," the bureau granted him a new trial and Butler was soon acquitted. Linda McQueen, however, like Pattie Ruffin and countless other freedwomen, was left to support her child as best she could after suffering a humiliating trial. Untouched by the scandal was the child's alleged white father, who was never identified in court.[52]

Before the Civil War, Southern lawmakers discouraged interracial liaisons between white women and black men but tolerated the relatively few interracial marriages that occurred. After 1872, Conservatives sharply curtailed the rights of freedpeople under the banner of white supremacy. The intensity of white attacks on interracial relationships, including marriages, increased dramatically; neither social nor sexual congress between black men and white women was to be tolerated.[53] So desperate was the quest for racial purity among Southern white lawmakers that in 1884 Dicey McQueen Williams, a white woman, was forced to file a deed in county court swearing that her daughter, Mary Ann McQueen, was "purely white and clear of any African blood whatever." Mary Ann's father, white soldier Calvin McQueen, had died in 1862 fighting for the Confederacy.[54]

Since no one questioned that Calvin and Dicey were white, why were there suspicions that their daughter might have "African blood?" The reason was simple: shortly before the war began, the McQueens' marriage had ended and Dicey had entered into an interracial union that was accepted in Montgomery County during the 1860s as a legal marriage. Dicey and her second husband, Wilson Williams, had several children together, meaning that Mary Ann McQueen, a white child, lived among "black" (no matter how light their skin) siblings. Her own whiteness would be forever suspect.[55]

It was this environment that enabled several members of the Hopkins family of Granville County to initiate a property suit against Ann Bowers Boothe, the widow of their uncle, Nash Boothe, of Orange County. Citing rumors that Ann Boothe was part black, the Hopkinses challenged her right to inherit her husband's land. Lawyers for the Hopkinses cited Ann Boothe's immersion in Orange County's interracial subculture as evidence for their claims. Ann's Durham neighborhood included white yeoman farmers and laborers, a few former slaveholders, and many blacks. Like most of her Bowers kinfolk, including her mother before her, she farmed a small plot of land. As in the case of her mother, too, some of her associates were people of color who had been persecuted by the Klan two decades earlier. Ann, then, was part of an interracial underclass linked to the social revolution so feared by Conservatives during the early days of Reconstruction.[56]

Ann claimed to have married Nash Boothe on 30 May 1876, three years after his wife, Mary Jane, divorced him on charges of adultery and abandonment. She was well acquainted with him, since he and her mother, Lydia Bowers, had cohabited before he married Mary Jane. In 1870, Nash lived in Lydia's home in Durham, where sixteen-year-old Ann also resided. In 1872, soon after the courts charged Nash and Lydia with fornication, their relationship ended, perhaps because Lydia had died. In February of the following year, Nash married Mary Jane, who was probably pregnant. His relationship with Ann, barely out of her teens in 1874, followed soon after.[57]

Nash Boothe, a womanizer and brawler, was well known in the town of Durham for his escapades. In 1854, he and Dr. Bartlett Durham, for whom the town was named, were separately charged with assaulting and battering one another. Similar charges against Boothe are scattered throughout Orange County's criminal action papers. Jailed in 1870 for another assault and battery, he petitioned the court to release him early because he had a family to feed and a crop on hand. Katy Carroll, a defense witness for Ann Boothe who knew Nash well, described him as a "bad, hard drinking, fussy man."[58] Ann's mother, Lydia, had her own reputation for misbehavior in the town of Durham. She had given birth to at least two illegitimate children, and Ann was rumored to have "black blood" from the time of her birth. Neighborhood gossip had it that Lewis "Red" Pratt, a slave, was her true father. Whether or not the gossip was true, Ann was born free because her mother was free.[59]

Suspicions of racial impurity among poor white women went hand-in-hand with charges of sexual impropriety because white women were key to maintaining separation of the races. In the slaveholding South, the mixing of blacks and whites potentially destroyed social and legal constructions of whiteness, creating a class of people lumped together as mulattoes. Thus, although Ann's mother, Lydia, was at least nominally a member of the white yeoman class, her illicit affairs automatically lowered her status and that of her daughter. In fact, Lydia's interracial associations were enough to convince two trial witnesses that she, too, was of "mixed" blood.[60]

Lewis Pratt, rumored to be the father of Ann Boothe, was a light-skinned man with kinky red hair (earning him the nickname of "Red") who worked as a blacksmith for his master, William N. Pratt. Pratt, one of the richest slaveholders in Orange County, freed his slave before the war for "meritorious" service. Lewis, then, belonged to that enclave in which blacks and whites, enslaved and free, interacted on a regular if distinctly unequal basis. Strong evidence supported the claim that he had been intimate with Lydia Bowers. According to Lewis's own brother, he had once described Lydia as a "fine sweetheart" who was hard to break away from.[61]

Still, there was no evidence that Lewis Pratt was Ann Boothe's father. Defense witnesses claimed that Lydia Bowers had sworn in court that Alexander Copley, a white man, was the father of her bastard daughter and that Copley had paid the requisite court fine and visited with Ann over the years. Katy Carroll claimed she heard Copley say that "he intended to take the child home and make it work for him when big enough." Plaintiff witnesses countered that Copley had been furious at Lydia for swearing a Negro child to him and that her friends had locked her away to keep Copley from whipping her.[62]

There was no documentation for either version of Ann's entry into the world. She testified that her mother had always told her that Copley was her father and denied that Copley had ever tried to whip her mother. Ann also claimed never to have seen Lewis Pratt face to face.[63]

Katy Carroll's deposition on behalf of Ann demonstrated the absurdity of the court's discussion of racial categorization. Carroll, age fifty-six, who had long known both Lydia and Ann, knew them as white women. A poor white woman from the same Durham neighborhood, she also understood the lives of single and married women who worked for their living.[64] Ann worked hard, she pointed out, "ploughing, hoeing, and doing other outdoor work," so of course her skin was dark. Lewis Pratt, Nash Boothe, and Alex Copley, she added, were all about the same color (although only one of them was "black"), and Ann's skin was "brighter than any one of the three."[65]

In spring 1890, the Superior Court ruled in favor of Ann Boothe and her children. The plaintiffs, however, were granted a new trial, and this time, in August 1892, they won. The defendants immediately filed for an appeal to the state supreme court but were denied. On 25 February 1893, they filed a petition to be reheard and were denied again. As a result of spurious claims regarding her racial identity, Ann Boothe lost the lands that she had plowed and hoed alongside her husband for almost two decades.[66]

Mixed-race women and women who socially or sexually crossed the color line demonstrated the intimate connections between women's personal lives and the politics of race before, during, and after the Civil War. In the end, it was not Ann's paternity, which was based on hearsay, but her frequent associations with black people that were enough to convict her of being black. As plaintiff lawyers noted, she was currently living on land owned by John Johnston, a black man. Ann Boothe was thus decreed, by reputation and association, to be a "low, dissolute, colored women" who had no rights to a white man's property.[67]

The attorney who prosecuted the case against Ann Bowers Boothe was none other than John W. Graham, who also prevented Pattie Ruffin in 1866 from either identifying or collecting child support from the white father of her child and who supported white supremacy and amnesty for the Klan. Graham personified the white men described by Samuel Thomas in 1865: "To debauch a negro woman they do not think fornication, to take property away from a negro they do not consider robbery."[68]

During Reconstruction, Southern white politicians and lawmakers rose up against the social as well as political revolution that confronted them in the wake of their battlefield defeat. They were determined that no matter what level of violence was needed, black men must not become the equals of white men, either as statesmen or as patriarchs of independent households. Nor were black women to assert their sexual rights or think that they, like white women, might claim the prerogatives of domestic security. Yet simply being white was never enough. Poor whites were to keep their place, politically, socially, and sexually, or risk being equated with the degraded black race.

CHAPTER FOUR

Fighting a Losing Battle

Newt Knight versus the U.S. Court of Claims, 1870–1900

In 1873, on the eve of Southern "Redemption," former Mississippi congressman John F. H. Claiborne described defeated Confederates to U.S. attorney general George Henry Williams as "bitter and unforgiving" of Southern Unionists. Specifically, he objected to the government's plan to publish a full digest of the names of Southern Unionists seeking compensation for support of the Union during the Civil War. Claiborne, who years earlier had written an essay extolling the simple virtues of life in rural Jones County, an infamous Unionist stronghold during the Civil War, now warned the attorney general that it was a mistake "to suppose that Southern men who were true to the national government during the war, now repose on a bed of roses, and that that period may now be safely disclosed."[1]

The same year that Claiborne made his appeal, Newt Knight's petition for compensation as a Unionist was buried in committee by the U.S. Congress. Like the vast majority of Southern Unionists, he would never receive a dime from the federal government.[2] Still, Newt refused to give up. On the morning of 29 January 1895, twenty-five years after filing that first petition, he appeared at a hearing held in Ellisville, the Jones County seat, for his third effort to convince agents of the U.S. government that his Knight Company had fought for the Union Army during the late war.

By this time, the political and literary battle over the meaning of the Civil War had been won by a "redeemed" Democratic Party that extolled the noble Lost Cause of the Old Confederacy. The same year that Newt provided his deposition, J. F. "Frank" Parker, editor of the Jones County Democratic newspaper *New South*, condemned the Knight Company as a band of traitors and murderers. With a rhetorical flourish that had become standard by 1895, Parker revered the "memories of noble, chivalrous deeds achieved by [the] noble, heroic dead, who sacrificed their lives for love of country." The "bitterness" toward Unionists that Claiborne described in 1873 now appeared as smug contempt for men guilty of the rankest disloyalty to their "country."[3]

Seemingly undaunted by an inhospitable political climate, Newt pressed on. His second and third claims, initiated in 1887 and 1891, were subsequently merged and litigated by the U.S. Court of Claims until 1900, when they were finally rejected, once and for all. Newt Knight's petitions of the government then faded into oblivion, practically lost to historians despite the unparalleled insights they provide into the South's most famous Unionist uprising.[4]

Newt's first claim (1870–73) was prepared by him and his Free State of Jones allies. No lawyer oversaw the process, although B. A. (Benagah) Mathews, a probate judge and close associate of Newt, functioned as one, gathering materials and contacting the appropriate congressmen to gather support for submitting a bill to Congress. The materials that Mathews sent to Congress included Newt's signed affidavit, certified by Justice of the Peace T. J. (Thomas Jefferson) Collins, which summarized the contributions of the Knight Company to the U.S. government during the Civil War. This affidavit stated that the band was "organized and equipped at a battleground known as Sals Battery, Jones County, Mississippi, on the 13th day of October A.D. 1863." Calling themselves "Knight's Company of the United States Infantry," the men elected Newt Knight their captain and performed the "duties" of an infantry, obeying "any and all orders from United States Officers," while furnishing their own "armes, ammunition, and rashens," until officially disbanded on 10 September 1865.[5]

The affidavit said nothing about an ordinance of secession from the Confederacy, nor did it mention any oath of allegiance to the U.S. government. Rather, Newt focused on proving that he, as captain of his company, had worked directly with Union military forces in the immediate aftermath of the war. To document this assertion, he submitted first a U.S. government requisition form, dated 16 July 1865, that listed large amounts of staples to be transferred at government expense from Meridian to Shubuta. Signed by Captain O. S. Coffin, U.S. quartermaster of Meridian, the form specified that "Mr. Newton Knight" or his assignees would receive the goods.[6]

Also included as evidence were several handwritten military orders Newt had received from U.S. officers during July and August 1865. Among the tasks he performed on behalf of Union forces were the return of two illegally held black children to their father and assistance provided to a "Mrs. Davis," described by Union captain J. Fairbanks as destitute. Several of the letters further revealed that Newt had seized a supply of wool and "jeans" cloth from Amos Deason, Jones County's former Confederate congressman, in response to orders issued on 31 July 1865, from 2nd Lieutenant H. T. Elliott, commander of the 50th U.S. Colored Troops.[7]

A reproduction of Newt's Knight Company roster, copied by hand from the original he kept throughout the war, accompanied the affidavit. The original roster had apparently been a work-in-progress, regularly updated during the war, on which Newt listed each man's rank, date of enlistment, and length of service and noted whether wounded, captured, or executed by Confederate soldiers. Following Colonel Lowry's raid on Jones County, for example, Newt dutifully recorded all executions and also the "reenlistments" of those who fled to New Orleans. Echoing the words in Newt's affidavit, the roster submitted to Congress was titled "A List of the Company Organized and Equipt at Sals Battery in Jones County, Mississippi, on the 13th day of October, 1863, and Styled as Knight's Company of United States Infantry."[8]

The packet of materials that accompanied Newt's first claim contained a testimonial of support signed by several local citizens. This was a highly personal affidavit, its signatories all closely connected by kinship and politics to the Knight band, although none appear to have been members. John Mathews, H. L. (Harmon Levi) Sumrall, Allen Valentine, James Hinton, and Madison Herrington affirmed Newt's opposition to the war and emphasized the horrific treatment he received from Confederate forces for refusing to take up arms against the United States. "The Rebels was determined to make him fight or kill him," the men agreed.[9]

The certified letter went on to describe how Confederates destroyed or appropriated Newt's household goods, including horses and mules, leaving his family destitute. Its author then described how Confederates tortured Newt after he returned home to aid his family: "They got holt of him and they tyed him and drove him to prison and there cruelly treated him for some length of time." After Newt escaped and again returned home, in May 1863, he "immediately tuck measures to rase a company to oppose the Rebels."[10]

In this letter was also the first written assertion that members of the band had taken an oath of loyalty to the U.S. government. On 13 October 1863, the signatories agreed, Newt and other disaffected men from the region organized the Knight Company, electing officers and taking a "sollomn vow to be true to each other and to the United States and to fight on behalf of the United States during the war." Like Newt's affidavit, the letter was witnessed and certified by T. J. Collins, justice of the peace, and Prentice M. Bynum, clerk of the Jones County Circuit Court, both of whom were closely associated with the Knight Company.[11]

B. A. Mathews wrote a cover letter for Newt's packet of materials and, on 8 December 1870, sent it to Mississippi's Republican representatives, Legrand W. Perce and George C. McKee. In the packet, he included the mailing address of Union brevet brigadier general William Linn McMillen, who, he explained, "had an interview with Capt. Knight shortly after the surrender." It was McMillen who reportedly ordered the 16 July transfer of staples from Meridian to Shubuta that Newt received. Mathews ended by assuring Perce and McKee that the men of the Knight band were "as good citizens as the county afforded" and asked that the congressmen let him know when they received the package and what they thought of the claim.[12]

Two days before Mathews mailed the file, Richard Simmons of Jasper County, a former Paulding sheriff and Republican nominee for the State Senate from Mississippi's Ninth Congressional District, sent a letter of support to Representative McKee, calling Newt a "true Union man." On 10 December, Republican judge William M. Hancock, known for keeping a derringer within handy reach while serving the circuit court during these dangerous times, likewise wrote a letter to Representative Perce, vouching for Newt Knight as an "honest & clever man" and a "staunch Republican."[13]

For the next three years, Newt Knight, his associates, and the families who hoped to be compensated by the federal government waited in frustration as their bill was read before three Congresses, only to languish in committee after each reading. On 16 January 1871, the bill was read before the House, which then referred the bill to the Judiciary Committee. Meanwhile, Perce requested more testimony "showing services rendered" by the Knight Company to the U.S. government, which Mathews apparently sent. Despite these efforts, Perce informed Mathews in July that Congress had adjourned that spring without acting on the bill. A new bill would be necessary. Perce was still hopeful of success, assuring Mathews that he had heard "no opposition from your section in regard to the claim" and promising to introduce a new bill as soon as possible.[14]

Fifteen months later, on 16 April 1872, Perce informed Mathews that the bill had been read a second time and referred to the Committee on Military Affairs. He advised Mathews to write directly to committee member George Harris, to whom he had handed the claim papers. He also advised Mathews to write again to Representative McKee, since, because of redistricting, McKee would "probably" represent Jones County during the next Congress.[15]

Mathews followed Perce's advice but likely was not satisfied by the response he received from McKee. On 20 June 1872, Representative McKee apologized for being so late in answering Mathews's letter, admitting that "as to the actual condition [of the bill] in the committee, I know nothing." Since Jones County was to be added to McKee's district, he promised to "take the matter in charge." Yet, in his next sentence, he counseled Mathews that the district court magistrate, however, "must look after the interests of his own constituents." This ambiguous statement suggested that Jones County claimants should not expect energetic representation from their new congressman.[16]

Representative McKee, a conservative Republican who opposed "Negro rule" within his own party, would hold power in Mississippi far longer than most Republicans by cooperating with Democrats on issues of race. The only indication that he acted on behalf of Newt's claim is a note he scrawled on the back of Richard Simmons's letter of support affirming that Simmons was a "prominent Union man" and "reliable." Perhaps in frustration at McKee's lackluster response, Newt Knight and B. A. Mathews appealed to former governor Adelbert Ames, now Senator Ames (1870–74), who agreed to press their claim. On 21 November 1873, Mathews sent a packet of claim materials to Ames, informing him that the accompanying papers should be available from the House Committee on Military Affairs where Representative Perce had filed them. Perhaps more as a courtesy than a request, Mathews added, "Say to . . . McKee we still solicit his aid in the case." One week later, Mathews wrote again to Ames: "We are anxious to know whether they have been received or not. Pleas write soon."[17]

Senator Ames did not let the Jones County men down. He replied that he had received Mathews's letters and was waiting on the accompanying papers still held by the House Committee on Military Affairs. On 18 December

1873, Ames introduced the bill before the Senate of the 43rd Congress, and Representative Albert R. Howe of Mississippi read it before the House of Representatives. Despite this promising turn of events, the Senate referred the bill to the Committee on Military Affairs and the House referred the matter to the Committee on Claims. Newt Knight's claim now lay dormant in the graveyard of two committees.[18]

The U.S. Congress, inundated by individual claims after creating the Southern Claims Commission in 1870, allowed Newt's petition to die in committee. By failing to act in the critical years before 1875, Congress denied Newt and his men their best chance at winning compensation. After that year, the political tide shifted dramatically at the national as well as the state levels. Representative Howe was defeated in his bid for reelection; Senator Ames was elected governor in 1874, only to resign in 1876 in the face of violent efforts by Democrats to impeach him. Finally, no election more chillingly demonstrated for Newt Knight the shifting political tide than that of his band's old nemesis, Robert Lowry, as governor in 1882.[19]

On top of all that, by the 1880s Newt Knight was the patriarch of an extensive mixed-race community in a state that excoriated and forbade interracial marriage. One might have expected him to retire to private life, but Newt was nothing if not audacious. Despite the changing political environment and his controversial living arrangements, in 1887 he reinstituted the Knight Company's request for compensation. No doubt heartened by Congress's passage of the Bowman Act in 1883 and the Tucker Act in 1887, which allowed resubmission of formerly rejected or tabled Southern Unionist claims, Newt now employed a team of lawyers to put forth his claim once again.

In the wake of the Bowman and Tucker Acts, lawyers eager to represent such claims may have first contacted Newt rather than vice versa. So now they, rather than local leaders such as B. A. Mathews (deceased by 1880) who knew the story of the Free State of Jones firsthand, would shape the contents of his claim. The Washington, D.C., firm of White & Bailey submitted Newt's latest petition to Congress on 22 November 1887. Although this new version provided much the same narrative as to how and when the Knight Company came to be formed, the fingerprints of lawyers were visible. The "Knight Company" suddenly became the "Jones County Scouts," suggesting that Newt's lawyers believed that a name reminiscent of typical Civil War units might better convince the government of the band's legitimacy, especially since it had never officially been mustered into the Union Army.[20]

Probably for the same reason, a specific example of the Union Army's attempt to muster the "Jones County Scouts" into military service was inserted into the petition's narrative. General Ulysses Grant, it read, had sent an officer into Jones County for that very purpose in 1864, but the officer was "killed by the Rebels at Leaf River Bridge." The word "Leaf," had been crossed out and replaced with "Rock", changing the skirmish's location from the Leaf River Bridge to the "Rock River" Bridge. In later testimony, Newt Knight would assert that this skirmish occurred at the "Rocky Creek" Bridge.[21]

Not only did Newt now rely on out-of-state lawyers to press his case, but he was also forced to present his claim in a pro-Confederate political climate, both locally and nationally. In 1887, John H. Bynum, clerk of the Jones County Court, certified Newt's new petition, as had his distant cousin, Prentice M. Bynum, in 1870. But unlike the first Bynum, a former member of the Knight Company, the second Bynum had supported the Confederacy during the Civil War and actively opposed the political appointments of Newt Knight and his men during Reconstruction.[22]

Once again, on 9 January 1888, Newt's bill was read before both the House and the Senate, and, once again, it was referred to the Committee on Military Affairs. The committee in turn asked the War Department to search its records for evidence that a company headed by Captain Newton Knight had served the Union Army during the Civil War. Ignoring altogether that Newt's petition asserted that his company was never officially mustered into U.S. service, Congress may have treated the claim in this pro forma manner because of the overwhelming number of claims flooding its chambers. Based on the War Department's inability to find a nonexistent record, the Committee on Military Affairs then recommended the bill be "indefinitely postponed."[23]

The bill's swift demise may have motivated Newt to obtain new counsel. On 3 August 1889, fifty-five-year-old Gilbert Moyers, of Memphis, Tennessee, took over the case. Moyers maintained an office in Washington, D.C., and specialized in prosecuting private claims against the government (especially those of Civil War Southern Unionists). Originally from Michigan, he had fought with the 3rd Michigan Cavalry during the Civil War, participating in the Vicksburg Campaign of 1863, which had caused so many Jones County soldiers to join the Knight band after their parole by General Grant.[24]

For a third time, a narrative of the Knight Company's origins and actions during the war was drawn up. The new petition briefly mentioned the efforts by Senator Ames and Representative Perce before the 42nd Congress on behalf of Newt Knight's claim. The narrative was also expanded to explain that in 1861 Jones County voters had sent an antisecession delegate to Mississippi's convention to decide whether the state would leave the Union. In dramatic language, it described able-bodied men who refused to join the Confederate Army (or leave the region) as having been "hunted with dogs and run down like wild beasts, and either hung like felons or forced into conscript camps and compeled [*sic*] to perform the most menial services." In resistance, the men who formed the "Jones County Scouts" took "a solemn oath to defend and protect the cause of the United States, before an officer authorized to administer an oath." What had initially been described in 1870 as a simple "vow" of allegiance taken among the men had now become an official oath.

The new claim included a freshly copied version of Newt's wartime roster. Data concerning the executions, captures, and escapes of men were restored, and a new title and preamble were added to the roster: "Company Roll of Jones County Scouts—Vols. (Miss.) U.S. Vols., Mar 1861," it read. "Organized and went into the service of the United States Oct. 13, 1863. Disbanded and turned over arms to U.S. authorities at Ellisville, Miss., Sept. 10, 1865." Step-by-step, as Newt's lawyers attempted to strengthen the Knight Company's case, new "facts" were added to petitions.[25]

This latest bill was referred to the Committee on War Claims. In the meantime, attorney Moyers obtained additional written support, including a petition signed by twelve male citizens who were *not* former members of the band (although easily identified as kin to members). Emphasizing the Knight Company's commitment to the well-being of families, this petition claimed that a large number of Union men from Jones and surrounding counties had organized themselves at a "mamoth [*sic*] mass meeting" in 1863, not merely to avoid Confederate service, but to protect the community against the "thefts, robberies, and rapes" that accompanied the chaos inflicted by war.[26]

In November 1890, Moyers's cocounsel, Thomas B. Johnson, collected depositions from Newt Knight and several key players in the Jones County uprising. For reasons that are not clear, between August 1890 and March 1891, Moyers applied twice to the Court of Claims, resulting in two claim numbers that then were merged. Bureaucratic wrangling delayed the process for over three years, stalling the process of obtaining depositions. Although scheduled to resume in August 1894, the second phase of interviews did not begin until 29 January 1895 and was not completed until 8 March 1895. In all, fifteen men were deposed. Five, including Newt, testified on behalf of the claimant; ten, including five former members of the Knight band whose testimony contradicted Newt's, testified on behalf of the defense, the U.S. government. In several cases, there was no clear reason why one side rather than the other called a witness. The interviews were conducted much like a trial, with witnesses being interrogated and cross-examined by each side.[27]

After providing personal information such as age, address, and occupation, the men were asked pointed, specific questions that frequently varied according to each man's relationship with the Knight Company. Fifty-eight-year-old Newt was first to be interviewed. Much of what he said was by now familiar: The "Jones County Scouts" had been formed at Sals Battery, in Jones County, on 13 October 1863, by men from Jones, Smith, Covington, and Jasper Counties. Although no mustering officer was present, the men "pledged ourselves to stay together and obey all orders from the government of the United States." Promised by General Grant that they would be mustered into U.S. service, that promise was never fulfilled. The men disbanded on 10 September 1865.

U.S. attorney John C. Dougherty's cross-examination of Newt was occasionally condescending and sarcastic. For example, he asked, did Newt not know that Jones County's pro-Union delegate to the state convention had voted *for* the secession ordinance, suggesting that voters had not, after all, elected a Union man? The testiest exchange occurred when Dougherty asked Newt if he had submitted an earlier claim for compensation to one of Mississippi's governors. Newt replied that he had not but offered that he *had* met with provisional governor Adelbert Ames, who "thought our claim was just and ought to be paid." He added that Ames "commissioned me as Colonel of the Militia of Jasper County." Questioning Governor Ames's high regard for Newt, Dougherty snapped back, "If Governor Ames thought the claim was correct and just, why did he not pay it?" Shot back Newt, "I don't suppose that he thought that *he* was the government." At this point, the court adjourned for lunch.[28]

In hindsight, Dougherty's vague reference to Newt's 1870–73 claim hinted that the hard evidence provided by Newt and B. A. Mathews in 1870 had not been transferred to the current claim. Although attorney Moyers requested all original papers pertaining to Newt Knight's earlier claim from the clerk of the House of Representatives in March 1891, the papers apparently were not found. Given the passage of so much time and the Knight Company's transformation into the "Jones County Scouts," perhaps this is not surprising. Further obscuring identification of the claim was a secretarial error that listed Scott County as the location for the Jones County Scouts.[29]

Despite the missing evidence, during his interview Newt again identified H. T. Elliott and William L. McMillen as Union officers from whom he had received and obeyed orders and, again, cited battles fought against Confederate forces led by Lieutenant Hensley, Colonel Maury, Colonel Lowry, and Captain Gillis. When asked to give an example of the Union Army's efforts to muster the Knight band into service, he returned to the story of how a "detail" of Union soldiers, sent to Jones County to muster the Knight Company into service, had been "followed by Rebel forces and shot into at Rocky Creek Bridge," near Ellisville. During this attack, he said, the detail's commanding officer was killed and several soldiers were captured by the Rebels and made prisoners. Now, not only had Newt testified to contacts with Union officers for which the evidence was missing, but he had described an event that was easily disputed by the defense.

An ambush of federal soldiers by Rebel forces at Rocky Creek Bridge did indeed take place, but in June 1863, three months before the Knight Company was formed. General Grant had directed a detail of forty men, detached from the 5th Illinois Cavalry and commanded by Captain Calvin A. Mann, to tear up the New Orleans, Jackson, and Great Northern Railroad at Brookhaven, Mississippi, and then move on to Winchester and destroy the Mobile and Ohio Railroad Bridge over Buckatunna Creek. This mission was short-circuited when Captain Mann and his forces were routed by Rebels after departing Brookhaven, following an eighty-five-mile chase that ended six miles from the Leaf River and two miles from Ellisville, at the Rocky Creek Bridge. Captain Mann was not killed, although four of his men were. He and his surrendered forces were transported under guard to Jackson. Four badly wounded soldiers were left behind in Ellisville.[30]

This certainly sounded like the skirmish Newt had described. Had he somehow confused Rocky Creek Bridge with another skirmish? Or were there two Rocky Creek Bridge skirmishes, the second one less well known than the first? There is plenty of evidence that Yankees visited Jones County in 1864, as Newt claimed. On 29 March 1864, Confederate captain W. Wirt Thomson commented to Secretary of War James Seddon that Yankees were said to be "frequently among" Jones County citizens, who had raised a federal flag over the county courthouse. On 7 April 1864, Daniel P. Logan reported that large numbers of deserters from Jones County, Mississippi, were "openly boasting of their being in communication with Yankees." Finally, on 14 August 1864, Brigadier General W. L. Brandon complained to Major

General D. H. Maury that a Yankee lieutenant is "entertained and protected" in Jones County by deserters.[31]

Significantly, Newt's earlier 1870 claim never mentioned the Rocky Creek Bridge skirmish. Only later, perhaps under pressure by lawyers to provide *specific* examples of Union efforts to muster the band into U.S. service, did he describe such a battle. Under questioning, however, he was unable to provide the name and rank of the Union officer that he claimed had been killed there, making it easy for the defense to fill in the true facts of Rocky Bridge, which totally refuted Newt's version of the story.[32]

Especially damaging to Newt's testimony were government witnesses who accurately recounted the 1863 battle of Rocky Creek Bridge. Joel E. Welborn and C. M. Edmonson, Confederate stalwarts during the war, were apparently among the local men who had assisted Lieutenant W. M. Wilson in capturing the Union cavalry. Eighty-four-year-old Joel E. Welborn correctly placed the Rocky Creek Bridge skirmish in June 1863, identified Calvin Mann as the cavalry's commander, and correctly "conjectured" that Mann's mission had been to reach the Mobile and Ohio Railroad in Buckatunna and "tear it up." He, himself, he added, had housed two of the four wounded soldiers. C. M. Edmonson and E. M. Devall echoed Welborn's account. So perfect were these men's memories of a skirmish that had occurred thirty-two years earlier that one assumes they had carefully prepared for this question.[33]

Newt's lawyers were on surer ground when they focused on whether the Union Army had provided arms and aid to Jones County Unionists. Under cross-examination by attorney Johnson, sixty-seven-year-old Jasper Collins testified that, in early summer 1864, his "old friend" James Welch had traveled to New Orleans to gain arms for the band, but that those arms were captured en route by Confederates. According to Jasper, however, success was nonetheless achieved after he assumed the task of intercepting arms in Meridian provided by General William T. Sherman. Jasper claimed that he camouflaged a wagon trip north by traveling first to Shubuta, where he obtained "family supplies," before continuing on up to Meridian. But "I was too late with the wagons," he explained, and "the [Knight] Company, I think, got old man Mark Bynum and old man B. A. Mathews to go on horseback for the ammunition & my understanding was that they got it. I know [because] I got some of the ammunition."[34]

Lending credence to Jasper's words was a letter from General Sherman, dated 29 February 1864, just after his Meridian Campaign, to Major General Henry Halleck. Sherman closed his letter by mentioning a "declaration of independence by certain people who are trying to avoid the Southern conscription, and lie out in the swamps. I promised them countenance and encouraged them to organization for mutual defense." Troublesome, however, is Jasper's reference to this event as having occurred "at the close of the war." Either he was mistaken about Sherman's role in providing the arms, or, quite possible, the passage of time had dimmed his memory of exactly when this event happened.[35]

In 1864, Jasper Collins was the band's major link with Union forces. Newt Knight testified that Jasper made a personal visit to Nashville, where he appealed directly to General Grant's army for aid. Jasper confirmed this, although he claimed to have traveled to Memphis, not Nashville, before backtracking to Vicksburg and then returning home, between March and July 1864. Newt and Jasper did agree on the salient point: that Jasper traveled to Tennessee in 1864 to plead with Grant's army to come to their aid.[36]

Jasper's memories of this important trip at times faltered. At one point he stated that the trip occurred "in 1863 or 1864" but later settled on 1864. Struggling to recall the name of the U.S. general in Vicksburg who questioned him "right smart" about the Knight Company, Jasper first identified the general as "Hudleston," then as "Hurlbut." He further described him as "the officer commanding the forces of the U.S." and claimed that the general had a list of the Knight Company men "that had been taken to him by a man by the name of Lewis." Hurlbut also told Jasper that he was serving under General "Grant, I think," and that he said "he would send up a statement of the matter and if he got orders he would come to our relief."

There is no record of a U.S. Civil War general named Huddleston, but it is plausible that Jasper spoke with U.S. general Stephen Hurlbut, commander until November 1864 of the 16th Army Corps, formed from troops under the command of General Grant. If he did speak with General Hurlbut, however, it was in Memphis, where Hurlbut was quartered between March and July 1864, and not in Vicksburg. Possibly Jasper confused a conversation that occurred in Vicksburg with one in Memphis.[37]

The defense called Jasper as a witness seemingly to contradict key aspects of Newt's testimony, for there is no evidence of friction between the two men. Unlike Newt, Jasper claimed that the main reason for seeking federal aid was to protect the community, specifically its women, rather than to muster into U.S. service. He also contradicted Newt's testimony that T. J. Collins, Jasper's nephew, had administered an oath of allegiance to the U.S. government to the Knight Company. The defense based much of its case on whether or not this oath was ever administered, and, if so, by whom.[38]

Meanwhile, attorney Moyers sought to strengthen Newt's claim by using bolder, more specific, language, and apparently Newt did nothing to dissuade him. Not only was the statement that the "Jones County Scouts" had collectively vowed before "an officer authorized to administer oaths" to defend the U.S. government inserted into the claim's petition, but also the preamble to the band's muster roll was again revised in early 1895. It now stated that the Scouts had been "sworn into the service of the United States" (but stopped just short of stating *military* service) "by T. J. Collins, a Justice of the Peace in and for Jones County." These changes weakened rather than strengthened Newt's case. Defense lawyers could now aggressively press witnesses to verify the name of the "officer" who had sworn them into "service."[39]

In their answers, most of the men appeared tentative, confused, or in disagreement about the very event that brought the company into existence. Contributing to confusion and disagreement was the defense's habit of conflating the question of whether an oath had been administered with that of whether the band had ever been mustered into Union military service. In his cross-examination of Newt, for example, attorney Dougherty asked him to reconcile his petition's assertion that an authorized officer had administered an oath of allegiance to his men with his verbal testimony that the Knight Company was never officially mustered into the Union Army. Newt replied that he did not remember "ever making a statement that we were sworn in [to the military] by a proper officer."[40]

Simply put, swearing allegiance to the U.S. government was an entirely different matter from having been mustered into military service to the Union. Under redirect, Newt's attorney clarified this point, asking him to name the officer who had administered the men's oath of allegiance to the U.S. Constitution. Newt replied that Justice of the Peace T. J. Collins had done so, near Smith's Store, in Jones County, on 1 October 1863.[41]

The defense continued to mix the two issues, despite being corrected. Dougherty, interrogating Harmon Levi Sumrall that same day, asked whether T. J. Collins was the official who allegedly had sworn "Knight and his men into *service*." Sumrall, who signed the 1870 affidavit that first alluded to the band's "vow" of allegiance, replied that he had never heard that such an event occurred. Yet, when the defense asked the same question of former band member William M. Welch, Welch unwittingly accepted the two issues as one and the same, stating that "old man V. A. Collins" (T. J. Collins's uncle) "administered the oath; he swore us into the service of the U.S., I think." Dougherty's merging of two separate issues had confused Welch. As witnesses struggled to recall details of an event that had occurred thirty-two years before, the distinction between pledging loyalty to the United States and being mustered into U.S. military service was clear to some and not so clear to others. This confusion played right into the hands of the defense.[42]

The defense varied its wording of the above question, causing witnesses' responses to vary as well. When asked to identify who had sworn the men "to bear true allegiance to the U.S. government and to defend the cause of the Union," Morgan Valentine agreed with Newt that a justice of the peace by the name of "Collins" had done so, though "my memory is bad [and] I cannot state the exact date." Former band member Montgomery Blackwell, asked only if he remembered taking "an oath" and, if so, "before whom, and when, and at which place," specified that the oath was "to support the Constitution of the Union." He agreed with Newt that it was taken at Smith's Store. But, like William Welch, he thought it was V. A. Collins, a justice of the peace, who had administered the oath.[43]

Jasper Collins offered yet a third response to questions about the oath. Asked whether "the company was sworn into any *service*, and, if so, what was the nature of the oath, and by whom was it administered," Jasper formed his answer with care. Avoiding the word "service," he said that the men had signed an oath that "we should be loyal to the *Government* of the U.S. — but I cannot state this positively." He agreed with others that the action took place "somewhere in the vicinity of Smith's Store, which was our rendezvous."[44]

Who did Jasper believe had administered this oath? If anyone might have ended the confusion over which of the Collins men had delivered the oath, surely the uncle of one and brother of the other would have done so. But Jasper offered yet another name, answering that "it seems to me that B. A. Mathews drew up some sort of oath that we all signed." His brother, V. A. Collins, he explained, did administer an oath of allegiance to the U.S. government, but only *after* the war, when he was appointed probate judge. Furthermore, his nephew, T. J. Collins, did not live in Jones County during the war. He became its justice of the peace only afterward.[45]

Given that both of the Collinses received political appointments immediately following the war, it is possible that the passage of years had merged some witnesses' memories of their official actions between 1865 and 1870 with that of the October 1863 oath ceremony. It is also plausible that Jasper remembered correctly that B. A. Mathews had delivered the oath. Although it is unlikely that Mathews, a Unionist deeply enmeshed with the Knight band, held office during the war, he was literate and by 1869 he was a probate judge. His close ties to the band were emphasized by Jasper's response to Dougherty's question of whether Mathews was a member: "I will make this statement: Mr. Mathews was with us so often that I cannot tell whether he was or was not a member of the Company; he was with us a great deal."[46]

Despite the general consensus among former Knight Company members that they had taken some sort of oath, the defense raised doubts about their testimony by focusing on a less essential feature of the event—who had administered the oath. As all the lawyers knew, that question could not be answered definitively, since V. A. Collins and B. A. Mathews were both dead and T. J. Collins was living in Texas.[47]

Doubts about the Unionist sentiments of band members were further strengthened by negative testimony from their wartime adversaries. Throughout the South during the Civil War, folks like those in Jones County engaged in bloody inner civil wars in which neighbors murdered neighbors in the name of either the Union or the Confederacy. After the war, festering resentments erupted in renewed violence.

Several men who testified were directly involved in wartime efforts to quell the Knight band and postwar efforts to prevent its members from holding political office. Prominent in such efforts were Edmond M. Devall, Charles M. Edmonson, Joel E. Welborn, and Ausberry B. Jordan, all from an intermarried circle of slaveholding merchants/politicians who had supported the Confederacy during the war. These men were now asked to evaluate the validity of Newt Knight's claims.[48]

Newt's lawyers summoned Edmond M. Devall, sheriff of Jones County throughout the war, to testify on behalf of their claimant. Perhaps they reasoned that, as former sheriff, Devall would have to acknowledge Newt's anti-Confederate stance and behavior, but Devall did no such thing. Rather, he disingenuously claimed to have no firsthand knowledge that Newt Knight had opposed the Confederacy. In regard to an oath of allegiance to the U.S. government, he testified that no Jones County officer could legally have administered one, since all had been allied with the Confederate state. When asked if there had ever been a mass meeting of Jones County citizens for the purpose of "taking defense against the Confederates," he claimed never to have heard of such a meeting.[49]

Devall had either forgotten or chose to ignore a letter he had written to Governor Charles Clark during the war. That letter, dated 24 March 1864, revealed that the sheriff was quite attuned to the activities of local deserters; he even described a meeting "by deserters of this county" in which "they resolved not to pay any tax, neither state, county, nor Confederate." Desert-ers had gone so far, Devall reported to Clark, "as to press wagons" and haul away "a good deal of the tax-in-kind from . . . the adjoining counties." They had even "ambushed, shot, and killed dead" those government agents who attempted to drive stock out of the county. But now, in 1895, the former sheriff recalled none of these events.[50]

Defense witness Ausberry B. Jordan, who was married to the daughter of former Confederate congressman Amos Deason, attempted to further weaken Newt's claim. Not surprisingly, he characterized the men of the Knight Company as mere deserters, not defenders of the U.S. government. During the war, Confederate officer Amos McLemore was murdered in Representative Deason's home, almost certainly by Newt Knight and his men. Then, immediately following the war, federal officers empowered Newt to seize Confederate goods from Deason. Thus, although Jordan claimed never to have met Newt Knight, given his connections to Amos Deason he surely knew him by reputation.[51]

Newt's lawyers, recognizing that several witnesses for both sides belonged to the local Confederate clique that had most directly clashed with Newt Knight's men, suggested to Jordan that he and his Confederate associates harbored deep prejudices against the Knight Company. Jordan denied this, pointing out that he himself had opposed secession before the war. In Jones County, however, it was not so much whether one opposed secession be-fore the war that mattered—voters preferred the cooperationist candidate over the prosecession one, 166 to 89—but whether or not one embraced the Confederacy after secession was accomplished.[52]

Although Jordan's insistence that former Confederates had no prejudices "at all" against Newt Knight rang hollow, it may be that political prejudices had died down by 1895. One defense witness, a former loyal Confederate soldier, actually supported Newt's claims. Oquin C. Martin described him-self as "a right smart secessionist until I was converted." Perhaps this strug-gling farmer was less influenced by romantic images of the Confederate Lost Cause than by the poverty that engulfed so many Southerners after the war ended. Unfortunately, none of the lawyers expressed interest in learn-ing when or why Martin had "converted." Unlike Devall and Jordan, Martin testified he had often heard—and believed—that Newt Knight "raised a company of infantry in opposition to the Confederacy and in favor of the Union." On cross-examination, attorney Johnson asked him whether there was "in this county at that time a strong prejudice, and is there yet a strong prejudice, against Capt. Newton Knight and his men." Martin's response was telling: "Yes there was then, but I haven't heard much of it in later years."[53]

The passage of time and kinship almost certainly contributed to the remarkably sympathetic testimony provided by defense witness Joel E. Welborn. One of Jones County's wealthiest slaveholder merchants, Welborn commanded the Mississippi 7th Infantry Battalion from which many men of the Knight Company had deserted until early 1863. The father-in-law of Sheriff Devall, he had clearly "moved up" in the decades preceding the war from the humbler, nonslaveholding status of many of his Welborn relatives. His support for the Confederacy during the war clearly put him at odds with those relatives.[54]

While commanding the 7th Battalion in November 1862, Major Welborn personally alerted Confederate authorities that many of his men were AWOL following the battles of Iuka and Corinth, prompting more aggressive pursuit of Jones County deserters by Confederate forces. Several of his Welborn kin were among the AWOL and were subsequently paroled and returned to the military; two of them promptly joined the Knight Company. After the war, Joel Welborn was an unpopular man among the common folk. Bankrupt as well, he moved away from Jones County in 1868. One would expect harsh words about the Knight Company from such a man.[55]

The defense wasted no time eliciting those harsh words from Welborn, questioning him first about the Rocky Creek Bridge skirmish to which Newt had alluded five weeks earlier. Yet, beyond describing the 1863 skirmish at Rocky Creek Bridge and testifying that, to his knowledge, neither T. J. Collins nor V. A. Collins had held office during the war, Welborn affirmed the sincerity of Newt's motives for deserting the Confederate Army and forming his own band of men. After describing the "terror" inflicted by the Knight "crowd" and several of its skirmishes with Confederate forces (thus verifying Newt's own testimony), he was asked whether Newt and his men "bonded together for the purpose of entering into the service of the U.S. government, or was [their] true object simply to protect themselves from being arrested?"

Welborn's answer cannot have pleased government defense lawyers. "My understanding," he replied, "was that they were Union soldiers from principle." This belief, he explained, was based on "acquaintance with several of his men," on "intimate neighborship," and, finally, on the word of "Gentlemen" known for their "honest conviction." Not only had two of Welborn's cousins joined the Knight Company, but he was also a distant cousin to Newt's wife, Serena. He reported with authority that the entire Knight family was "anti-secession, including Newton Knight." Under cross-examination, he even qualified his use of the word "terror" to describe the behavior of the Knight Company. Newt "made no predatory incursions" into the community, he explained, but "was a terror to those who were in arms against him." For Joel Welborn, who died less than nine months after giving his testimony, the bonds of kinship and neighborhood had clearly, if belatedly, triumphed over the divisions wrought by war.[56]

In 1900, the U.S. Court of Claims made its final judgment on the Newton Knight case after considering briefs submitted by the government and the claimant's counsels. On behalf of the government, Assistant Attorney General Franklin W. Collins (no relation to the Jones County Collinses) charged that Newt's claim was based wholly on hearsay and pinpointed its most glaring weaknesses. First, former band members disagreed about who had administered the alleged oath of loyalty. Collins made much of T. J. Huff's and T. G. Crawford's statements that they had no memory of having taken such an oath, as well as former sheriff Devall's statement that no meeting of Union men had ever taken place in Jones County. Newt's testimony about the Rocky Creek Bridge skirmish was dismissed as factually incorrect. Finally, the roster for the Jones County Scouts was characterized as a likely fraud—where was the original, the defense asked?[57]

Attorney Gilbert Moyers argued that the simple act of having fought the Confederacy in the swamps of the Leaf River, with the knowledge and approval of the federal government, was proof that the Jones County Scouts had aided the Union and ought to be compensated. And they had done more than merely fight, he argued; they had organized themselves to "wage offensive and defensive war on the rebellious forces at every opportunity and by all means at their command." As for confusion over who administered the oath of allegiance, that was a "natural" result of the passage of years. Moyers also defended Newt Knight's roster as a faithful rendering of the original and speculated that "the attorney for the Government who conducted the cross-examination had seen or knew of the existence of the original muster roll." Significantly, he was silent in regard to Newt's Rocky Creek Bridge story, which the defense had discredited by assuming that Newt referred to the 1863 skirmish that had taken place at the same location.[58]

Clearly, the thirty years that had passed between Newt Knight's submission of his first claim and the government's final review of the evidence doomed the claim to failure. A simple bureaucratic act, the filing of the 1870–73 claim documents separately from those gathered between 1887 and

1895, played a major role in defeating the claim. In fact, the defense indicated no knowledge of claims submitted by Newt Knight prior to 1890, as well as no knowledge of the crucial evidence submitted in 1870. Lacking such evidence, the defense described Newt's testimony as "uncorroborated by a scintilla of documentary or record[ed] testimony."[59]

Assuming as he did that Newt's claim was first filed in 1890, attorney F. W. Collins pointed out that Union officers who might have corroborated Newt's testimony, specifically Grant, Sherman, Butler, McMillen, and Elliott, were conveniently dead. But none of the generals had died before 1884, and at least one, William L. McMillen, was still alive in 1900. Furthermore, Lieutenant Elliott's letters to Newt were extant but were buried in a separate government file. Nor was Newt's roster a fraud, as attorney Collins alleged, although its preamble and title were doctored in subsequent copies more than once. The original roster is today still in the hands of Newt's descendants.[60]

Newt Knight and his lawyers deserve blame, too, for the final defeat of his claim. Remember that the first claim, assembled by B. A. Mathews, not only offered irrefutable evidence of Newt's actions on behalf of Union forces but was notable for what it *did not* attempt to argue. Newt's 1870 petition never mentioned the Rocky Creek Bridge incident and never referred to the band as the "Jones County Scouts." Finally, although its accompanying affidavit, the one signed by six witnesses attesting to the Knight Company's efforts on behalf of the Union, *did* cite a "vow" of allegiance to the U.S. government, it made no claim that the vow was administered by an officer of any sort.

Only after Newt reinstituted his claim in 1887, with the aid of lawyers not previously familiar with wartime events in Jones County, did the errors and confusion that so weakened his case begin to appear. Combined with the government's misfiling of Newt's core evidence, the insertion of untrue or undocumented "facts" proved fatal to Newt Knight's claim. In the end, it was not so much Newt's Confederate wartime enemies who defeated his claim as it was a plodding government bureaucracy, lawyers unfamiliar with Jones County's history, and aging men's fading memories.[61]

Nor was the U.S. government much interested in handing out money to Southern Unionists, especially by 1900. At the national level, slavery was no longer trumpeted by either Northern or Southern elites as the cause of the Civil War. The nation had reconciled its differences with comforting images of a tragic war fought by honorable men over abstract principles of constitutional right. At the same time, industrialization of the rural South enriched entrepreneurial businessmen both north and south of the Mason-Dixon Line in a time of deep economic depression. Ironically, such changes may have influenced Joel Welborn to assist his kinfolk and neighbors in gaining government pensions in their old age (from the government, after all, that he had fought against) rather than to refight his community's inner civil war.[62]

THE CIVIL WAR was the defining moment in Newt Knight's life, reshaping his political view of the world and propelling him to forever assert his independence from conventional authority. For the rest of life, he would revisit the years 1863 to 1865, filing claims until the close of the century in a vain attempt to gain compensation for his and his band of men's loyalty to the U.S. government. Ironically, the Southern white man who fought with such ferocity against Confederate forces on the battlefield spent much of his old age battling the U.S. government he had defended.

In 1892, or shortly thereafter, Newt bluntly assessed the war that had dominated his entire adult life. Southern nonslaveholding farmers, he told an interviewer, should have risen up and killed the slaveholders rather than agree to fight their war. For it was slaveholders, he proclaimed, who clambered for war in order to protect their peculiar institution against "preachers" up north and women who "wrote books" against slavery. The northern abolitionist movement, he claimed, had stimulated Southern "common people" to steal slaves and lead them to freedom via the Underground Railroad, but slaveholders "could not take this, and so they brought on war." In the process, they had tricked Southern common men into fighting their war for them.[63]

Such words were heresy to most white Southerners by 1892, but Newt seemed not to care. The lessons of the past twenty-five years had not been lost on him. Being on the winning side did not assure one a place at the table; the fruits of victory were routinely denied to "little men" such as him. With his suit dismissed once and for all in 1900, it was hardly surprising that Newt would conclude that only a massive uprising of the common people could have prevented the travesty of a slaveholders' war.

PART III Legacies

ONE WOULD BE HARD-PRESSED to find a white person of the turn-of-the-twentieth-century South who, at least in public, did not proclaim undying devotion to the Lost Cause of the Confederacy and to the superiority of the white race. Indeed, most New South leaders lauded such beliefs, which came to appear timeless, as at the very core of white Southern identity. Yet there were other Souths that could never quite be buried, including the politically dissident South that struggled to find its voice in third-party movements. And there were multiracial communities in which people defied racial categorization as white, black, or Indian. These alternative Souths contradicted images of a united white citizenry or of a society of distinct races in which people could be ranked and ordered according to their bloodlines.

In recognition of these other Souths, chapters 5 and 6 analyze two legacies of Southern wartime dissent and postwar struggle. The rise of dissident political movements that challenged the hegemony of the Southern Democratic Party is the subject of chapter 5. Chapter 6 examines the growth of a multiracial community born of the Civil War collaboration between Newt Knight and Rachel Knight in the Jones County region of Mississippi.

Despite Mississippi's long history of political conflicts, it is often portrayed as a "one-party-state" before the 1950s, Texas less so after 1928, when national Republicans began to convince many white Southerners that they, rather than Democrats, represented the true party of social conservatism as well as economic progress. Until that time, the Southern wing of the Democratic Party used a states' rights philosophy to successfully bill itself as the guardian of racial segregation, sexual chastity, and Christian social values.

Yet, between 1877 and 1902, Republicans, Greenbackers, Independents, Prohibitionists, and Populists all challenged the seemingly invincible Southern Democratic Party. After 1902, Socialists, Progressives, and Republicans continued to offer alternatives to the Democratic Party, but with ever-dwindling success in convincing voters to abandon the "party of their fathers."

From Mississippi and Texas, respectively, Jasper J. Collins and his brother Warren J. Collins were central figures in dissident political factions from within their separate communities. Between 1894 and 1920, they and their cohorts espoused radical agrarian views, successively joining the Populist, Progressive, and Socialist Parties during these years.

Religion joined third-party movements to challenge the prevailing political order. As conservative Democrats "redeemed" the state from Republicans, a circle of Jones County Unionists, including Jasper Collins, helped to found a Universalist Church in rural Mississippi. Universalism's fundamental tenet of God's universal goodness and salvation for all humankind distanced these Southerners from their opponents, religiously as well as politically.

We have seen that dissent was a Collins family tradition. At least three generations of Collinses, most of whom intermarried with other equally feisty family lines, rejected conventional political parties and religious denominations. What can we learn from the half-hidden, often distorted, history of these families of southeastern Mississippi and East Texas? In telling the stories of their resistance, chapter 5 suggests the potential for a very different South than that which emerged from the ashes of war.

In Texas, Warren J. Collins proved to be a magnet for kinfolk hoping to make a fresh start after the war. Jasper, however, did not join his kinfolks' caravans west but remained in Jones County, where he participated in state and local politics. And what about Newt Knight, the ultimate New South dissident? Newt does not appear prominently in chapter 5 because his political career was short-circuited by his open embrace of his mixed-race descendants.

Chapter 6, however, explores the legacy of Newt's rejection of the color line. There was nothing unusual about Southern white men having sexual relations with black women, forced or consensual, right under their wives' noses, particularly before slavery was abolished. But Newt's post-Reconstruction interracial homestead was quite unusual. He lived openly in the community he had founded, among his interracial kin, for the rest of his life.

Not only Newt, but also his white wife, Serena, broke the social rules of southern segregationist society. Although Serena left his household sometime between 1880 and 1900, she did not completely leave the racially mixed Knight community, even after several of her grown children married white partners and left. Rather, she lived with her daughter Mollie and son-in-law Jeffrey (Rachel's son) until her daughter's death around 1917. Even after Mollie's death, Serena remained close to Jeffrey and her grandchildren. They were, after all, a family—a multiracial one that Serena, as well as Newt, embraced.

Chapter 6 extends the multiracial Knight saga into the twentieth century by focusing on several Knight women—especially the sisters, Anna, Grace, and Lessie, who personified the struggles and triumphs of being female as well as multiracial in the segregated South. The centerpiece of this chapter is Anna Knight, who carved out a remarkable international career as a teacher and Seventh-Day Adventist missionary, spending many years in India.

Anna's steely determination shaped the course of her kinfolks' lives as well as her own. In 1898, she established an Adventist-sponsored school and two Sunday schools in the Knight community. Under her tutelage, many of her relatives gained educations and converted to Seventh-Day Adventism. Although education and religious faith were important tools for combating racial prejudice and segregation, other Knights, including Anna's sister Lessie, opted instead to identify with their European or Native American heritage and to ignore or deny their African ancestry. Under segregationist terms, they were "passing," but under their own terms they were choosing the ancestry that suited their self-image and afforded them the same opportunities for self-fulfillment that "white" Americans enjoyed.

CHAPTER FIVE

Civil War Unionists as New South Radicals

Mississippi and Texas, 1865–1920

By 1895, sixty-seven-year-old Jasper J. Collins, aging warrior of the Free State of Jones and the man who allegedly set Mississippi's infamous Newt Knight on the road to opposing the Confederacy's "rich man's war and poor man's fight," had become a Populist. He never forgot (or repudiated) his years in the Knight Company, in which he served as 1st Sergeant to Captain Newt Knight and fought against Confederate forces from the swamps of Piney Woods Mississippi. A spirited dissenter all his life, he now moved on to fight new battles, this time for the rights of the common man against a new enemy—the corrupted Democratic Party.

Populism emerged from the South's agrarian reform movements of the 1880s. Mississippi's preeminent agrarian reformers, Thomas P. Gore, the "blind orator" from Webster County, and Frank Burkitt, a former captain in the Confederacy from Chickasaw County, helped galvanize state support for the People's Party in 1892. From Marion County, southwest of Jones County and bordering Covington County, Nevin C. "Scott" Hathorn Jr. was elected to the state legislature in 1895 on the People's Party ticket. He also served that year as proxy delegate from Covington County to the state People's Party convention.[1]

Although Hathorn was a decade younger than Jasper Collins and Newt Knight, he was probably acquainted with both. Hathorn's father, raised in Covington County, was a staunch Unionist likely related to Robert C. Hathorn, the husband of Newt Knight's sister Keziah. Two of Robert and Keziah Hathorn's sons ran with the Knight band during the Civil War. Scott Hathorn had yet another connection with the Free State of Jones. In 1895, he and Prentice M. Bynum, former member of the Knight Company and nephew of Jasper Collins, served together as officers of the Marion County People's Party.[2]

Whether or not connections to the Free State of Jones influenced Hathorn, by 1895 Populism flourished enough for Jasper Collins to entertain his greatest hopes for the small farmers of Mississippi since the brief era of Radical Reconstruction. In Texas, his brother, Warren Jacob Collins, enjoyed a similar political evolution. Like Jasper, Warren grew increasingly disaffected with the political establishment in the years following the Civil War. His East Texas county of Hardin boasted significant Populist and Socialist minorities, and by 1910 he himself was an enthusiastic member of the Socialist Party, extolling the virtues of Eugene V. Debs.[3]

The Collinses' Civil War Unionism was a direct result of the decision by their father, Stacy Collins, not to own slaves. None of the sons owned slaves either, although all were prosperous farmers who could have purchased them had they so chosen. In contrast, Scott Hathorn and Newt Knight were both descended from large slaveholders. Their grandfathers, Samuel Hathorn and Jackie Knight, were veterans of the War of 1812 who traveled to southeastern Mississippi as soldiers and returned there to live around 1817–18. Both men settled in Covington County, bought slaves, and passed them on to the next generation. Samuel died before the Civil War, but his son, Nevin C. Hathorn Sr., also owned numerous slaves. Even so, Hathorn Sr. and Jackie Knight both opposed secession in 1861.[4]

The elder Hathorn's and the elder Knight's Unionist principles remind us that Piney Woods Mississippians' opinions about secession were not drawn neatly along class lines, at least not in 1861. The ravages of war, however, stimulated class resentments. One story remembered by Hathorn descendants was that of Nevin Sr. chiding his prosecessionist brother-in-law, Alex Harper, for having kept his sons out of the Confederate Army while two of Nevin's sons served despite his own opposition to secession. Harper replied that his boys refused to join the local Confederate company because it was filled with the "rag tag and bob tails of the county." Nevin reared up for a fight, ready to avenge this brazen insult. Only the intervention of Alex's wife, Patsy, prevented a "regular dog fight" between the men. Such conflicts, coupled with policies that favored well-placed families, accelerated disaffection with the Confederacy. The war not only threatened lives but also educated younger men like Scott Hathorn and Newt Knight about the prerogatives of class. Both men would apply their dawning class consciousness to postwar and New South Mississippi politics.[5]

The Collins brothers' support for agrarian political movements was perhaps more deeply rooted in their family history. In both Mississippi and Texas, branches of the family lived in overwhelmingly rural areas where stock-raising accompanied, even prevailed over, farming. These were Piney Woods folks from families that had deliberately chosen forests over fields and family labor over slave labor. So, just as they had rejected the slaveholders' war, the Collinses and associated families resisted the imperatives of postwar commerce and agriculture, which threatened their way of life even more than plantation slavery had. And, as wartime Unionists, men like Jasper and Warren more easily rejected the political parties of their youth. The Democratic admonishment to Southern white voters to reject thirdparty challenges and "vote the way you shot" must have brought smiles to their faces.[6]

But the economic conditions they faced as small farmers were nothing to smile about. The plight of farmers in the postwar South is well documented. High cotton prices and expanded railroads in the immediate aftermath of war made growing cotton the fastest way to pay for much-needed farm improvements and the high taxes imposed by Reconstruction state governments. Accordingly, many farmers cut back on food crops, converting their fields to cotton in the hope that the cash crop would enable them to recover from the devastating effects of war.[7]

Most did not recover sufficiently. Cotton prices fell as farmers went into debt for food and fertilizer, putting them at the mercy of merchants and creditors. Here were the seeds of the infamous crop lien system. The merchant who extended credit, with all its attendant fees, to the cash-poor farmer protected his investment by obtaining a lien on the farmer's future crop. And so began the farmer's endless cycle of indebtedness. Too often, he could not settle up with his creditor and thus began the year further in debt, gripped by the fear of losing title to his land.[8]

For many farmers, fears became reality. In both Mississippi and, particularly after 1900, Texas, growing numbers of small farmers slipped from being landowners to being land renters, their tenant status heralding corporate capitalism's final assault on Jeffersonian independence. The East Texas

Piney Woods offered hope of recovery to beleaguered Mississippians, perhaps even a return to open field stock-raising and self-sufficient farming.[9]

Such hopes were particularly appealing to the Collinses of southeastern Mississippi because they had relatives in the Big Thicket of East Texas. Becoming part of a larger exodus of farmers "gone to Texas," several of Warren Collins's cousins, nephews, and in-laws pulled up stakes around 1872 and joined him there, building yet another bridge between the Mississippi and Texas branches of the Collins family. But the way of life they hoped to preserve was about to give way to the entrepreneurial dreams of land speculators and lumbermen.

Chief among the Mississippi kin who joined Warren Collins in Hardin County, Texas, were the widow and sons of his late brother, Simeon, a former member of the Knight band who died within four months of his release from Camp Morton prison after being forced back into the Confederacy. For Lydia Collins, mother of their twelve children, at least five of whom were minors, her husband's death capped off four horrific years. During the war, she had tended home and farm while Simeon and their four oldest sons hid in the woods, coming in when they could to tend crops and stock. In 1862, she buried her youngest child; in 1863 and 1864, she gave birth to two more: Laurence Yeager and the aptly named Patience.[10]

Before the war, Simeon Collins had been a prosperous farmer whose total property was valued at $8,000. By 1870, his widow claimed just over $1,000 in property. Various kinfolk in households surrounding hers claimed even less. Small wonder several of these families decided to take their chances in Texas. In addition to Lydia, five of her grown children, Matt, Frances, Jeff, Frank, and Morgan, moved with their families to Polk and Hardin Counties in Texas around 1872. Other migrants to East Texas associated with Mississippi's Knight Company included Bill Holifield, whose wife, Sarah, was Lydia Collins's sister, and Tom Loftin, whose brother Giles hid out during the war with the Knight Company. By the mid-1870s, participants in both the Mississippi and the Texas deserter bands were living in close proximity to one another. In 1873, for example, the widow and sons of Simeon Collins lived in the Fifth Congressional District of Hardin County, alongside Simeon's brother, Warren Collins.[11]

Making a fresh start in East Texas proved difficult for these migrants as stock-raising and farming gave way to timber cutting and lumber mills in the postwar industrial economy. During the 1870s, Northern and British businesses began buying vast acreages of fertile timber and ranch lands, referred to by historian James R. Green as "the picnic grounds of one of the juiciest barbeques of the Gilded Age."[12]

By 1885, the Democratic Texas legislature had transferred some 32 million acres of state lands, much of it wilderness, into the hands of entrepreneurs and railroad corporations. Railroad and lumber companies proceeded to raze the brush and fell the seemingly endless trees that forested the Collinses' beloved Piney Woods. As a result, many of the children and grandchildren of Simeon and Lydia would live in drab, smoky mill towns, working for wages rather than farming the land.[13]

One of the earliest Knights to leave Jones County was Newt's brother Frank, who headed for Texas. With his wife, Jane, their children, and two of his brothers-in-law, Frank moved to Cherokee County around 1866, only to return to the Jones County area ten years later. At some point in his travels, Mormon elders visited Frank's household and piqued the interest of the family. After remaining another six years in Jasper County, Mississippi, Frank Knight, his wife, and his Turnbow brothers-in-law converted to Mormonism and moved to Colorado. Around the same time, Morgan Valentine, 1st lieutenant of the Knight Company and brother-in-law of Warren Collins, decided to do the same. Several families of Knights, Turnbows, and Valentines thus moved to the San Luis Valley of Colorado, where they settled in the Mormon colonies of Manassas and Sanford.[14]

By embracing Mormonism, Frank Knight joined multitudes of Southerners who chose alternative religious faiths as they struggled to re-create a sense of community in the wake of the Civil War. Public reactions against those who rejected traditional Protestant Christianity in the late nineteenth-century South were fierce and frequently violent. Like political third parties, dissident religious groups threatened the reconstituted order over which the Democratic Party reigned supreme.[15]

In seeking a new community, Frank Knight also escaped association with his infamous brother Newt and the Free State of Jones. His and Jane's descendants, many of whom remain Mormons today, were told next to nothing about their uncle (except that he was a bad man) or about the Jones County Civil War uprising. By contrast, Morgan Valentine remained in touch with his old partner Newt and his Jones County relatives. After his first wife died, Morgan returned to his old community and married Newt's niece, Mary Mason Knight. In 1890 and 1895, he provided depositions at the Jones County courthouse on behalf of Newt's petition for compensation for the Knight Company from the U.S. government. Before his death in

1901, Valentine returned for good to Jones County, reportedly no longer a practicing Mormon.[16]

For those who remained in Mississippi, political struggles continued. With national "reconciliation" between the North and the South the order of the day, conservative Mississippi Democrats capitalized on the alleged horrors of "black Republicanism" to help bring Confederate elites back to power. In response, agrarian radicals employed reactionary as well as progressive tactics to challenge Democrats during the 1880s and 1890s. Just as the Ku Klux Klan had used terror to control freed blacks, Republicans, and Unionists in 1868, angry white farmers practiced "whitecapping" in the 1890s.[17]

In both Texas and Mississippi, bands of whitecappers, typically white farmers who had lost their lands because of debts, ganged up on merchants who had assumed control over their foreclosed farms and who often worked those lands with black labor. Whitecappers were particularly brutal in their attempts to drive blacks off the lands.[18]

Some Populist leaders made strenuous efforts to focus farmers' attentions on the political system itself rather than on black laborers. In 1892, Tom Watson of Georgia vigorously denounced acts of racial terrorism, blaming the Democratic Party for pitting the races against one another. "You are deceived and blinded," he warned farmers, "that you may not see how this race antagonism perpetuates a monetary system which beggars both."[19]

On 7 July 1893, Scott Hathorn indignantly responded to charges that whitecapping was spawned by Farmers' Alliance doctrines (specifically those that excluded blacks from membership). In a letter to the *Pearl River News*, Hathorn insisted that whitecapping was the offspring of the Ku Klux Klan, not the Alliance, and he condemned both terrorist groups for their lawlessness. His strong words left him politically vulnerable to Democratic charges of hypocrisy when less than a year later he served on a jury that acquitted a man accused of whitecapping. Hathorn then fired off another lengthy letter to the *Pearl River News* defending the jury's decision as based entirely on the evidence presented and in no way signaling his approval of such violence.[20]

Did Hathorn vote to acquit whitecappers because he believed the state failed to prove its case? Perhaps. Certainly, his Unionist family background gave him ample reason to oppose vigilante groups, which had harassed Unionists as well as blacks in the aftermath of Confederate defeat. But he may also have sought politically to have it both ways—that is, to win support from an important, if lawless, element of rural Mississippi while defending the reputation of the Alliance, seedbed of Populism, as lawful and responsible.

Although most Populists embraced racist views typical of American white society, there were instances of interracial cooperation among them. In the town of Anderson, located in Grimes County, Texas (not far from Warren Collins's Hardin County), blacks were murdered or driven from the county in 1900 for daring to participate in a biracial Populist coalition. In Nacogdoches during the 1890s, white Populist Andrew Jackson Spradley encouraged blacks to join the People's Party. Later, as sheriff (1900–1904), he risked his life defending blacks against whitecappers.[21]

And, of course, in Mississippi, Newt Knight presented a notable exception to typical forms of Southern white racism by living openly and without apology among his multiracial descendants. Socially, Newt lived as he chose, even though the "white Negro" community offended many friends and relatives (such as his brother Frank), who turned against him after the war. Politically, his career was short-circuited by the era's shrill white supremacist rhetoric and racial violence.[22]

Nevertheless, three years after Newt refiled his Unionist claim in 1887, he briefly enjoyed the support of a Democratic congressman.[23] As political allegiances shifted in response to severe economic depression, former Unionists and Confederates tentatively rallied around interests of class. Newt Knight now drew more sympathy from Democratic agrarians sympathetic to Populist ideals than from probusiness Republicans. On 23 January 1890, Representative Thomas R. Stockdale, a former Confederate officer and Democrat from Mississippi's Sixth District, sponsored Newt's Unionist claim for compensation before the 51st U.S. Congress.[24]

But this conciliatory moment was brief. Stockdale's agrarianism soon doomed him to political exile by conservative Democrats. Agrarians, however, retaliated by throwing their support to none other than Democrat Scott Hathorn. Hathorn moved further yet from the mainstream of Democratic Party politics when he converted to Populism in 1892.[25]

During the same period, Jasper Collins not only embraced Populism; he changed his religious affiliation as well, thanks to the early groundwork laid by Rev. John C. Burruss, a Universalist minister. Around 1875, Burruss was preaching sermons near Jasper Collins's community of Moselle, in a grove near the home of Sherod Sholar, who had invited him to the area. Although Burruss remarked that "the opposition was very mean in those days," Universalist preachers continued to visit the community, conducting services under trees or in homes of local citizens.[26]

The Southern branch of Universalism traces its origins to the German Dunkers of North Carolina, who moved into South Carolina during the revolutionary era and then onto the southwestern frontier. Antebellum Southern Universalists tended to be well educated, even wealthy, admirers of Jeffersonian culture and principles of tolerance. Though many were slaveholders, Unionist views were common among them. In the Southwest, particularly after the Civil War, their churches tended to be small, rural gatherings of families related by marriage and kinship.[27]

The backgrounds of Jones County Universalists reflected these geographic and political patterns. The Collinses and the Herringtons, who traced their ancestry back to colonial North Carolina and revolutionary South Carolina, where Dunkers enjoyed a strong presence, had migrated into the Southwest during the early nineteenth century. Throughout his life, Stacy Collins, father of Jasper, exhibited strong republican tendencies as well as religious irreverence. Orange Herrington's grandfather reportedly disdained conventional, organized religion altogether. Orange was a freethinker who subscribed to the magazine *The Jeffersonian* (published by Populist Tom Watson) before he embraced Universalism.[28]

The Sholars and the Kirklands were Universalists in Alabama before migrating to Mississippi. In 1889, the Sholar family organized a small Universalist church in Moselle. After Jasper Collins and Andrew Herrington began worshipping with the congregation, a group of Collinses began a Universalist Church at Ellisville. In 1903, these churches united as the Burruss United Memorial Church. Then, in 1906, Orange Herrington of Ellisville offered his own home as the site for what became Our Home Universalist Church.[29]

During the 1890s, Jasper Collins rejected the two fundamental institutions of white Southern orthodoxy: the Baptist Church and the Democratic Party. He and his son Loren and a nephew, Timothy Wyatt Collins, now cooperated with former Confederates who supported the People's Party. When the Mississippi People's Party convened in Jackson on 31 July 1895, Loren and Timothy both served as delegates. Loren also ran on the Populist state ticket for Supreme Court clerk.[30]

Just three months earlier, on 26 April 1895, Jasper and Loren had printed the first issue of their Populist newspaper, the *Ellisville Patriot*. J. F. (Frank) Parker, Jones County editor of the Democratic *New South*, was incensed and greeted the paper with scorn and scathing insults for its cofounder, Jasper Collins. Labeling Jasper a "hump-backed, mosquito-legged, senseless creature" who published "filthy slime," Parker quickly linked Jasper's Populist views to his wartime Unionism. During the war, he wrote, Jasper had belonged to a "gang of houseburners, robbers, and midnight assassins," whereas "true southern people" cherished the "noble" efforts of fallen Confederate soldiers. Jasper's refusal to deny or apologize for his wartime actions in the pages of the *Patriot*, and especially his claim that former Governor Robert Lowry had executed innocent men during the war, further enraged Parker: "We have heard General Lowry say that he never . . . had any innocent men hung and we believe what he says."[31]

Locally and statewide, the rise of Populism generated a firestorm of protest among conservative Democrats. The editors of Jackson's Democratic *Clarion-Ledger* questioned the patriotism of the "disgruntled crowd" that "fumed and fretted" at the state convention of the Mississippi People's Party in Jackson on 31 July 1895. They lost no time in denouncing Populist gubernatorial candidate Frank Burkitt for his "wild assertions" and "false figures." Waving the bloody shirt, over and again the *Clarion-Ledger* falsely linked Burkitt, former Democrat, with the Reconstruction administration of Republican Adelbert Ames.[32]

Clarion-Ledger editors labeled the Populist masses "honest but deluded," using Christian imagery to remind readers that a "real Democrat" "once in grace [was] always so." The Democratic Party, they intoned, was "the real People's Party of this country." Populists employed religious imagery of their own. A resolution approved by committee stated that corrupt land deals between legislators and individual businesses "call[ed] to mind the conduct of money changers and those who sold doves in the temple of the Most High God."[33]

Scott Hathorn opened the Populist state convention of 1896 by denouncing the Democratic Party for its "manifest insincerity, intolerance, and fraud in elections." He called for a free ballot and "honest count of all the votes cast." He then demanded "equitable taxation of all property including bank currency and all forms of security according to their value" and finished by appealing to "just and fair-minded men" to unite in a "supreme effort to restore to the wealth producers and tax payers of this state and nation the government of our fathers."[34]

Despite the passion of its leaders, the Populist movement peaked in 1896 and then suffered a quick demise. In Mississippi, the Democratic Party not only outspent but also demonized the People's Party through its vast network of newspapers. In counties where money and influence were not enough, Democrats resorted to stuffing ballot boxes or miscounting votes. The state's 1890 constitution had effectively disfranchised black voters, leaving the party wholly dependent on white voters for success. At the same time, improved cotton prices in 1895 reduced many farmers' sense of urgency, while state poll taxes discouraged poor farmers from voting at all.[35]

As in Mississippi, physical intimidation, voter fraud, and appropriation of several Populist planks during the 1896 elections aided Texas Democrats' crushing of Populism. Populist leaders, determined to avoid fusion with Democrats, fused instead with the Republican Party and urged voters to support William McKinley for president in return for Republican support for Jerome Kearby, the state's Populist gubernatorial candidate. This desperate strategy, meant to attract black voters, drove many rank-and-file white Populists, who wanted nothing to do with "the party of the Negroes," into the arms of the white supremacist Democratic Party.[36]

One of the Populists-turned-Democrat was Vinson A. Collins, son of Warren Collins. Reflective of the deep political differences that separated father and son, in 1962 Vinson Collins published a family history that criticized his father's very approach to life. Although ninety-five-year-old Vinson remembered the hard lot of ordinary farmers in postwar East Texas, his words were those of a deeply conservative and, by 1962, very wealthy retired lawyer. He made no mention of the railroad and lumber barons who had reshaped the landscape of his parents' world, although he acknowledged that several of his brothers went to work in the saw mills while his father struggled to maintain the traditional life of a farmer and herder. He praised his father as a self-educated, "smart," "brilliant," and "honorable" man, but in the same breath he blamed him for the family's struggles, calling Warren a "very poor businessman and indeed a bad manager."[37]

Throughout his narrative, Vinson attributed the family's fate to individual successes and failures without reference to the larger economic and political conflicts in which his parents were vital participants. Still, the rich detail of his narrative opened a wide window on the lives of plain farmers during this era of change and strife. Though Vinson never mentioned the word "Populist," and certainly not "Socialist," in reference to his father, the conditions that led Warren to become both are evident.

In 1875, wrote Vinson, practically all that Warren and Eboline Collins owned beyond their farm and livestock was an old spinning wheel and loom. Night after night, he observed his mother spinning and weaving cloth to make clothes for the entire family. Although his father produced crops of "grain and sweet potatoes" and repaired fences and killed hogs, it was his mother whom Vinson credited with performing the family's most important tasks. It was she who salted and smoked the meat, because "she could not trust Pa to do it right," and she who milked the cows ("she would not let anybody else milk") and churned the butter and cream and still found time to tend a garden of vegetables. Vinson's resentment of his father's traditional ways ran throughout his narrative. In contrast, he remembered his mother as a paragon of strength, virtue, and hard work, a woman who lived to make others, particularly her children, happy.[38]

Despite his criticisms of his father, Vinson's narrative reveals a man determined to maintain the rural backwoods life he loved while preparing his children for a changing world. In 1877, Warren Collins moved his family from the Big Thicket to the county seat of Hardin in order that the children might be educated. "Pa was always a great mover," wrote Vinson, as though the struggle to make a living had nothing to do with such moves. Next, the family settled on Cypress Creek in Woodville. The land was poor, reported Vinson, but provided a wonderful range for raising hogs and cattle, Warren's beloved and traditional occupation. A changing economy dictated that his older sons now worked at nearby saw mills, while Vinson, age sixteen, farmed, planted, and raised hogs with his father.[39]

Although Eboline's life was, as ever, defined by the demands of motherhood, her work patterns changed as a result of the family's move. She gave birth to her eleventh child but also became a full-time housewife with indoor duties only. In addition to the farm they owned, in 1880 the family rented another farm, on "very good" land. That year, a household "revolution" occurred, wrote Vinson, particularly for his mother, when the family acquired its first cookstove and sewing machine.[40]

Following these changes, in 1887, a telling break occurred between father and son, one that presaged the dramatically different political paths they would take. During that year, Vinson remembered, his father forced the nineteen-year-old son to slaughter several hogs that he had "raised with great care." It frustrated Vinson that his father always sold his hogs at the first opportunity, even though their price would double if he simply held them another year. Warren's refusal to allow Vinson to hold out for a better price on the hogs also prevented Vinson from purchasing new clothes. Infuriated by his father's old-fashioned, frugal ways, he moved out of the family home and went to work for his cousin Frank. The old traditionalist, it seems, had raised a budding capitalist.

Warren might have been old-fashioned, but he placed tremendous value on his children's education, and Vinson knew that. He soon moved back home, went back to school, and earned a teaching certificate. Determined not to farm and raise hogs all his life, or work in the saw mills, Vinson continued his formal education while teaching school, eventually earning a law degree.[41]

In 1910, Vinson Collins entered politics as a progressive Wilsonian Democrat, the same year that his father ran for Congress as a Socialist. Despite his son's apostasy, Warren was one of many Texas Populists who refused to abandon the radical principles of the Omaha Platform of 1892 and instead moved on to become Socialists. Recognizing the alarming increase of tenancy among Southern farmers, Socialists defined tenant farmers as part of a national working class more thoroughly than had Populists before them.[42]

The Texas Socialist Party, founded in 1903, addressed the problem of growing landlessness, particularly among white farmers, to a degree never attempted by Populists. Indeed, Tom Watson dismissed Socialism, holding that private property was a "law of nature," its origins so sacred that government must not impose regulations, as Socialists demanded, upon the ability of landlords to control their properties, despite their impoverishment of tenants and sharecroppers.[43]

Whereas Texas Populists had tried and failed to build a biracial movement among white and black farmers, the state's Socialist Party discouraged interracial cooperation among landless white, black, and Mexican American farmers on any but a most basic economic level. T. A. Hickey, the powerful editor of Texas's Socialist newspaper *The Rebel*, tried to have it both ways. He frequently emphasized pride of race and white "manliness" as core ingredients for building a successful Socialist state but then would chastise white workers for refusing to organize alongside blacks.[44]

On 19 August 1911, editor Hickey praised Warren J. Collins, the "old fighter from East Texas," for representing one of those families in which a "strain of radicalism runs through the veins." Hickey was pleased that Warren, the "old gentleman" from Hardin County, had run for Congress on the Socialist ticket against Democrat Martin Dies. Although Collins lost that election, Hickey hoped that the Collins clan would "increase and multiply until they cover the earth with the clean, clear water of Socialism."[45]

Warren did his best to fulfill Hickey's hopes. While in his late seventies, he not only ran for Congress as a Socialist but also as county judge with a Socialist slate of candidates from Hardin County. On 9 December 1912, Collins assured Hickey that "I am in the fight [to elect Socialists] up to my chin." He optimistically predicted that "six months of [President] Wilson's administration will make more Socialists than [Eugene] Debs could make in four years of public speaking."[46]

Although Vinson Collins turned toward the Democratic Party after Populism's decline, editor Hickey also praised the younger Collins in 1911 for his progressive political views. In his early years, Hickey noted, Vinson was an "early champion of the farmer and the working man, running variously as a Populist or Democrat" for several offices. But at the same time Hickey applauded Warren, the "veteran fighting Socialist of east Texas," for rejecting mainstream political parties despite his son's career. "Neither his son's politics nor prominence in the Dem[ocratic] ranks have any weight with that brave old Spartan," wrote Hickey.[47]

Mississippi Populists made peace more quickly with the Democratic Party than did the militant Texans. Orange Herrington, leader of the Burruss Universalist Church and a Populist as late as 1900, soon became Jones County's leading Democratic agrarian reformer. In 1905, he began contributing a column called the "Farmer's Page" to the *Laurel (Miss.) Ledger*. In December of that year, he and Jasper Collins were elected secretary-treasurer and president, respectively, of the local branch of the Southern Cotton Growers Association.[48]

It is not clear whether Jasper Collins rejoined the Democratic Party, but he did remain a staunch agrarian. After attending a cotton-growers convention in New Orleans, he proclaimed its highlight to have been the chance to meet his Populist hero, Tom Watson. On 29 October 1909, Jasper attended a political mass meeting that issued a resolution calling on all interested citizens to meet at Ellisville the following Friday "for the purpose of discussing of anything as affects us politically." Citing the "great division" among citizens "along political lines," the resolution advocated "education" as the only means for finding solutions across party lines. Clearly, Jasper and his cohorts were still bucking the political status quo.[49]

Meanwhile, Orange Herrington, another lifelong admirer of Tom Watson, struggled to meet Populist goals within the parameters of the Democratic Party. In mid-1909, he served on the executive committee of the Farmers' Union, an affiliate of the American Federation of Labor, helping the organization's state president build a Jones County chapter. As late as 1936, Herrington espoused Populist views while yet proclaiming loyalty to James K. Vardaman.[50]

Not all Jones County agrarians could stomach the Democratic Party after watching it alternately slander and co-opt the People's Party, most particularly those with kinship ties to the old Knight Company. In 1912, Jasper's nephew, Timothy Wyatt Collins, was elected delegate to the Progressive Party national convention. Jasper's grandson, Buford T. Collins Sr., ran for circuit court clerk on the Socialist ticket in 1913.[51]

In 1915, Jones County put forward a Socialist slate of candidates for the offices of sheriff, circuit court judge, railroad commissioner, and county assessor, none of whom won election. Whereas the county's 1895 Populist slate had been a mixture of former Unionists and Confederates, all of the Socialist candidates were sons, grandsons, or nephews of members of the Knight Company. All had particularly close connections to Jasper Collins.[52]

Jasper Collins died shortly before the Socialist Party took root in Jones County. Interviewed on 10 April 1913, only months before his death at age eighty-five, he continued to pronounce Tom Watson "one of the greatest men the South ever produced." He also spoke openly about his Civil War past to his interviewer, citing passage of the "Twenty-Negro law" in late 1862 as the moment when he and other Jones County soldiers refused any longer "to sacrifice their lives for what they believed to be a hopeless cause."[53]

Twice in the interview, Jasper noted that he was unwilling to fight in order that others might keep blacks in slavery. To insist as he did that secession was an effort to protect slavery and to further suggest that fighting to keep blacks enslaved was an unworthy cause ran completely counter to twentieth-century Lost Cause rhetoric. In 1913, conventional wisdom dictated that the war had not been about slavery at all, and that blacks in any case were happier as slaves than as free people.[54]

When Jasper died four months later, his obituary noted his "independence of action and great force of character" but shied away from specific political references to his past. Although his membership in the Universalist Church was noted, the obituary only hinted at his extraordinary political history by stating that "when he believed that a cause or principle was right, he espoused the same and heeded not public censure or applause."[55]

Warren Collins of Texas received much the same treatment after his death. As his son Vinson became more politically prominent—and conservative—the father's political radicalism was buried. In vague language reminiscent of brother Jasper's obituary, Warren's 1926 obituary reported that he "took a keen interest in politics up until the last days of his life and always took a fearless stand on any issue regardless of its public favor." The word "socialism" was not mentioned.[56]

As nineteenth-century Southern dissenters passed away, there were fewer voices to counter the tide of Lost Cause rhetoric, which routinely portrayed southern Unionists, Populists, and Socialists as cowards and traitors. This new orthodoxy, followed by the crushing of Socialism during World War I and the Cold War, all contributed to a diminished appreciation of the

Jasper J. Collins, 1st sergeant to Newt Knight of the Free State of Jones and brother of Warren J. Collins, leader of the Big Thicket jayhawkers of East Texas, circa 1913. Standing with him are Vivian and Virginia, daughters of his son Loren. Photograph courtesy of Constance Bradley.

politics of dissent practiced by ordinary Southern citizens and exemplified by Jasper Collins, Warren Collins, and Newt Knight.

The ability of the Southern Democratic Party to slander, co-opt, or ultimately crush all third-party challenges demonstrates why the "New South" of 1900 was plagued by poverty, violence, and racial segregation rather than being based on economic cooperation and full political participation by its citizens. By 1920, a simple shorthand sufficed to explain such inequalities: "negroes" must be kept in their "natural" places or all society would be lowered; puny, pale-faced millworkers and tenant farmers were "poor white trash" incapable of elevation; Socialists, reformers, and labor unionists were dangerous radicals who must be driven from society. And, of course, the sacred symbol of Southern greatness had become the Confederate "Lost Cause."

CHAPTER SIX

Negotiating Boundaries of
Race and Gender in Jim Crow Mississippi

The Women of the Knight Family

The Knight family of the Jones County region of Mississippi has long con-
founded notions about race in the United States. Descended from white
Southerners, former slaves, and Native Americans, it did not fit into the
discrete categories of racial identity demanded by Jim Crow laws in the
aftermath of the Civil War and Reconstruction. Furthermore, many of the
family members refused to abide by the South's "one drop" rule, which
demanded that white persons with any degree of African ancestry identify
themselves as black.

The lives of the multiracial Knight women reveal various strategies by
which conventions of gender, class, and marriage might be manipulated to
escape the worst effects of racial discrimination. The daughters of former
slave George Ann Knight—Anna, born in 1874, Grace, born in 1891, and
Lessie, born in 1894—learned early in life that a poor "mulatta" living in the
Piney Woods of Mississippi could hope for little better than the economic
support of a white man in exchange for sexual favors. Neither the mother
nor the grandmother of the sisters ever married, but both gave birth to

numerous children fathered by white men. To the dominant white society, such women were little more than prostitutes whose behavior reinforced a common stereotype that women of color lacked morals.[1] Yet, through travel, education, or unconventional personal choices, Anna, Grace, and Lessie escaped the fate of their female forebears.

The oldest sister, Anna, joined the legion of educated middle-class "black" women who, between 1890 and 1930, worked tirelessly to uplift African Americans by opening the doors to education and health care.[2] Before she could join the ranks of elite African American women, however, she first had to lift herself. Her struggle to escape her mother's fate began early in life. Described as having "blue, blue eyes," Anna had every reason to anticipate the sexual advances of white men as she approached her teen years. Sexual activity would likely result in pregnancy, at which point all avenues to social respectability would close. Had Anna followed the paths of her mother and grandmother, she too would have been disdained by whites for bringing unwanted "white Negroes" into their world. As late as 1963, her grandmother Rachel was described as a "concubine" by many local whites.[3]

Anna might have married a man of color and raised a family, but, instead, she never married at all. While still a teenager, she embraced Seventh-Day Adventism much as a drowning person would grasp a life jacket. She believed with all her heart that God had lifted her from a life of poverty and degradation. No amount of physical risk or intellectual challenge deterred her from following a religious path that simultaneously relaxed the grips of gender conventions and racism. Anna's religious conversion and successful career as a teacher and missionary especially impacted the lives of her sisters. Yet, despite the influence of their older sister, Grace and Lessie followed different paths in life. Like Anna, Grace was identified as a black woman, remained single, and became a schoolteacher. Unlike Anna, however, she lived her entire life within the community of her birth. Sister Lessie, on the other hand, followed yet another path by leaving Mississippi and living as a white woman.

In taking the paths they did, all three sisters avoided much of the social harassment that plagued their kin, particularly those who refused to be defined as "Negroes" and who engaged in illegal marriages or illicit relationships across the color line. During the 1948 miscegenation trial of their cousin Davis, for example, the private affairs of the Knight sisters' long-dead grandmother, mother, and several of their aunts were paraded before the public.[4]

Martha Ann Ainsworth, former slave of Sampson Jefferson Ainsworth, by whom she had several children. Many multiracial Knights claim descent from her as well as from Rachel Knight. Photograph courtesy of Sondra Yvonne Bivins.

On 14 November 1949, Davis Knight's trial again made national head-lines when the Mississippi State Supreme Court overturned his conviction. In reporting the historic decision, newspapers provided not only the facts of the case but also rehashed Mississippi's most famous legend, that of the Free State of Jones. Davis, readers learned, was the great-grandson of Newt Knight, a white man and the infamous "captain" of a band of deserters in the Jones County region who had held the Confederacy at bay during the final two years of the Civil War.[5]

White men who fathered the children of black women were common in Southern society, and Piney Woods Mississippi was no exception. Former slave Martha Ann Ainsworth, another of Davis Knight's ancestors, was sold to a southwestern frontiersman during times when white men scrambled to lay claim to land and human property. With slave markets dotting the landscape, any lonely frontiersman might buy himself a comely woman of color with either cash or animal skins. Such may have been Martha Ann's fate. According to descendant Yvonne Bivins, she was born around 1825 in present-day West Virginia. Bivins speculates that Sampson Jefferson (Jeff) Ainsworth purchased her as a teenager, perhaps in Mobile, Alabama, and then moved her to the place of his birth, Smith County, Mississippi.[6]

Slavery appears to have provided more than a labor force for Jeff Ainsworth. In 1840, one young female slave, almost certainly Martha Ann, lived in the Ainsworth household. By 1850, the Ainsworth household claimed three additional slave children; by 1860, there were five, all the right ages to be Martha's known children. Although Jeff fathered at least ten children with his white wife, Anne, he is remembered as the father of his slave's children as well. Martha Ann's progeny described themselves to later generations as "children of the plantation," denoting their special status on account of being the master's children. The paternity of Martha Ann's children seemed to be an open secret in the surrounding community.[7]

Newt's behavior differed from Jeff Ainsworth's—and that of many other white men of the area who were said to have fathered children with enslaved women—in that he openly embraced both his "black" and his "white" families. Everyone knew that white and black Knights who lived in the vicinity of Soso, on the borders of Jones and Jasper Counties, were kin to each other, although few people publicly said so.[8]

Ethel Knight's depiction of the Knight community in *Echo of the Black Horn* reflected the simultaneous disdain and fascination that many whites felt toward racially mixed people. Her portraits of multiracial Knight women drew freely upon popular literary stereotypes of seductive black "Jezebels" who led white men to personal destruction and "tragic mulattas" who attempted to escape their inferior racial status by "passing" as white. Ethel merged these images in Rachel and George Ann by portraying them as dangerous, desperate women, almost comically craven with desires for the same white man—Newt Knight. She portrayed one of Rachel's younger daughters, Fannie, as a more conventionally "tragic" mulatta. In daring to marry Newt's white son Matt, Fannie transgressed what Ethel considered to be boundaries decreed by God. Interracial marriages, besides being illegal in Mississippi after 1878, created "white Negroes," who, she believed, had no place in segregated society. "There must be two races," she wrote, "a black, and a white, for a mixed race will always be a people without 'place.'"[9]

Long before Ethel Knight published her vitriolic "history," descendants of Rachel Knight and Martha Ann Ainsworth endured social ostracism and racial discrimination. The Knight sisters came of age around the turn of the twentieth century, during the height of white supremacy campaigns throughout the South. Their view of themselves and of their appropriate

Family of Jeffrey and Mollie Knight, circa 1910. Seated are Jeffrey and Martha Ann (Mollie). Standing, left to right, are their children, Altamira, Otho (father of Davis Knight, tried in 1948 for miscegenation), Leonard Ezra, Charlie, Ollie Jane, and Chances Omar. Photograph courtesy of Dianne Walkup.

position in society reflected not only their genealogical descent from Newt, a white man, and Rachel, a woman likely of European, African, and Native American ancestry, but also their descent from Serena, Newt's white wife. Serena was the mother of Matt, who married Rachel's daughter Fannie, and Mollie, who married Rachel's son Jeffrey. As a result, many second- and third-generation Knights knew both of their white grandparents on intimate terms.[10]

Serena moved out of her husband's household sometime between 1880 and 1900, yet she did not move out of the interracial neighborhood. Instead, this white woman lived in the multiracial household of her daughter Mollie, despite having three white sons who, by 1895, were married to white women. Serena apparently rejected Newt because of his philandering, but she did not reject their two children who married across the color line; nor did she reject her multiracial grandchildren. Mollie and Jeff's children hardly knew their enslaved grandmother, Rachel, but they grew up in Serena's daily presence.[11]

The third generation of Knight women, defined by white society as black despite their mixed ancestry and light skin, faced difficult choices. Segregation and violent repression of blacks increased throughout the South after 1889, the year of Rachel's death. Many of her descendants thus sought light-skinned mates and intermarried with cousins and other light-skinned families of color. By the dawn of the twentieth century, the Smiths, the Ainsworths, and the Knights were deeply intertwined through marriage and kinship. All were represented in the so-called Knight community (named for patriarch Newt Knight), located in Jasper County, near the Smith and Jones County borders.[12]

To elevate themselves and overcome limited social mobility, many of Rachel's and Martha Ann's twentieth-century descendants blended into white society, sometimes sporadically, sometimes permanently. Those with darker skin and curlier hair focused on achieving middle-class status through religious training and education. In either case, to be raised in a neighborhood that included white kinfolk meant that many Knights "performed" whiteness simply by being themselves. And, because Southern norms of middle-class behavior were white-defined, familiarity with white culture aided their efforts to achieve gentility. To gain social mobility was no easy task in the Jones County region, however, since most local whites identified "Knight Negroes" by their dark eyes and olive skin and the neighborhood in which they lived. As Davis Knight's trial later demonstrated, most

Knights found it necessary to leave Mississippi in order to live as whites or to achieve middle-class status.

Given the Knight community's strong Euro-American heritage, it is not surprising that many members declined to identify themselves as black, despite the South's "one drop" rule. The presence of a white mother and grandmother in the household further influenced the children of Mollie and Jeffrey to identify as white and, later, to leave the state. After Jeffrey's death around 1932, his son Chances Omar moved his family to Oklahoma, where he made his whiteness official. Chances's brother Otho took a more defiant route by marrying his cousin Addie and remaining in the Soso area, where he too raised his children as white.[13]

Many Knights, whether or not they left Mississippi, explained their olive skin by claiming Native American ancestry. In Oklahoma, Chances Omar's descendants erased their enslaved ancestor, Rachel, from their family history and attributed their Indian ancestry to their white grandmother, Serena, who they claimed was descended from the Cherokee "Trail of Tears." Descendants of Chances's sister, Ollie Jane Smith, offered yet another version of their ancestral roots. They did not deny descent from Rachel but insisted that she was a Sioux Indian who had been kidnapped, transported to Mississippi, and enslaved sometime before the Civil War.[14]

Like many of Mollie and Jeff's children, several of Fannie and Matt Knight's children left Mississippi and identified as white rather than resign themselves to the bleak future they faced as Mississippi Negroes. In 1914, a legal challenge to their right to inherit their deceased white father's property may have hastened that decision. That year, several of Fannie and Matt's adult children filed suit to inherit shares of Matt's meager estate. On 27 January 1914, fifty-year-old Fannie stood before Chancery Clerk W. H. Bufkin and testified in defense of her children's claims.

Whether or not the children could legally inherit their late father's property depended on whether Fannie was black, and thus on whether her marriage to Matt, which had been performed by a white Methodist minister and recorded in the county court's "white" marriage book, was legally valid. The matter was further complicated because Matt had abandoned his wife and eight children in 1894. As Fannie explained to her lawyer, he "just went off and left me [for] this other woman." Because his marriage to Fannie was no longer valid under Mississippi law, Matt was able to marry that "other woman" (a white cousin) in 1895 without bothering first to obtain a divorce.[15]

Matt's decision to end his marriage to Fannie created problems for her even beyond the obvious one of being left alone to raise eight children. On the one hand, if she conceded that her marriage to Matt was invalid, she would be labeled as a kept black woman with a slew of illegitimate children. On the other hand, if she insisted on its validity, she could not legally marry again. Barely thirty years old when Matt left her, Fannie neither obtained a divorce nor remained single. On 20 December 1897, she gave birth to a child (presumably not fathered by Matt) who died before the age of two. In 1904, she married Dock Howze, a minister of the gospel.[16]

Marriage to Dock promised greater economic security and renewed respectability for Fannie. During this era of segregation, however, Mississippi courthouses did not extend traditional courtesies of womanhood to black women. At the hearing for her children's suit, Fannie was peppered with humiliating questions by defense attorney Goode Montgomery. How many children did she give birth to after Matt left her? Why did she marry Dock Howze if she believed that her marriage to Matt was legal? Fannie answered with a logic that made perfect sense in her world but that played into the hands of the defense: "Well, he went off and married and left me," she answered. "I stayed single about ten years; I thought it was all right [to marry again]."[17]

Fannie's admission that she had remarried without first obtaining a divorce from Matt allowed Montgomery to deliver the defense's coup de grâce: "G. M. [Matt] Knight was a white man . . . and you are a negro woman." This Fannie denied. "I am Choctaw and French," she countered. When Montgomery asked her if Dock Howze was not also a Negro, she replied that Dock was Choctaw and Irish. Montgomery then cited evidence commonly used by whites to determine whether people as light-skinned as Fannie and Dock were in fact black. Did not Fannie and Dock live among "niggers," he asked. Like the tragic mulattas of so many novels, Fannie was forced to admit that she and Dock "lived on that side." She was thus stripped of her dignity and her children were labeled bastards because of her "sin" of attempting to cross over into white society.[18]

Such were the experiences that motivated many Knights to leave Mississippi. By 1920, at least three of Fannie and Matt's children were living as whites in Texas. Like their Oklahoma cousins, they erased their African ancestry and told spouses and children that their olive skin and curly hair were the legacy of Native American ancestry. One son, George Monroe Knight, changed his surname to McKnight and told his children that their grandmother, Fannie, had been a "full-blooded Cherokee."[19]

George Monroe's brother, Henry, however, remained in the Soso region and married light-skinned Ella Smith, granddaughter of Martha Ann Ainsworth. Henry and Ella's daughter, Addie, married her cousin Otho Knight. Their son, Davis, would make history in 1948 for daring to identify himself as white.[20]

The humiliation that Addie Knight experienced at her son's 1948 trial was no less than that suffered by her grandmother, Fannie, in 1914. Forced to listen to Tom Knight, her white cousin, testify in court that her son was a Negro, Addie endured more insults outside the courtroom in the immediate aftermath of the trial. There, in the streets, Tom mingled with the crowd, freely labeling the family of Davis Knight as "nigger Knights." He did not recognize Davis's mother as she stood nearby listening to him. Assuming that Addie was white, Tom kindly asked her who she was. Addie spat back, "I'm the nigger mammy of that white boy you are trying to [im] prison."[21]

Addie and Otho Knight's determination to have their family accepted as white, which included refusing to send their children to Anna Knight's Adventist school, alienated them from some of their kinfolk. In the aftermath of Davis Knight's conviction, for example, Nancy Knight, his "copper-colored" cousin, told a reporter that she personally had no use for "white niggers." Neither, apparently, did Nancy's sister, Allie. Almost twenty years earlier, Allie had used her position as midwife to the Knights' family physician to report Otho and Addie's daughter, Louvenia, as a Negro on her birth certificate. Louvenia struggled against the consequences of Allie's act in 1960 when she sought to enroll her two sons in a white school. During an investigation conducted that year into the boys' racial status, Louvenia claimed that midwife Allie Knight had labeled her a Negro at birth "for spite," knowing that her parents "considered themselves white." To Allie and her sister, Nancy, however, Otho and Addie's determination to be white was the problem. Descended from Rachel Knight's son Hinchie, they came from a branch of the family whose members either could not, or chose not to, identify as "white."[22]

In contrast to the family of Otho and Addie Knight, Lessie Knight successfully attained white status, avoiding ugly public scenes and family schisms, by moving out of Mississippi. She enjoyed a successful career as Mrs. Leslie Robertson, the manager of a Hilton Hotel in Beaumont, Texas. No longer burdened by the Knight surname or notoriety, she did not seem unduly concerned that her African ancestry might be discovered. She made regular trips back to Mississippi and remained on good terms with her sisters. As a middle-aged woman, she even sat for a portrait with her "black" sister Grace. When she died of kidney disease in Beaumont on 20 February 1944, her other "black" sister, Anna, was at her side. Lessie's death certificate listed her parents as Newton Knight and George Ann Knight and her race as white.[23]

Not all the Knights who left Mississippi did so to blend into white society. Anna Knight, who had left the state decades ahead of her cousins and her sister, represented the other route to social elevation—through attainment of education and by following middle-class mores. While still a child during the 1880s, Anna yearned for knowledge and respectability. Her intense love of reading led to her discovery of the Seventh-Day Adventist Church, which was proselytizing throughout the South during the late nineteenth century. When an Adventist salesman visited the Knight home, fifteen-year-old Anna convinced her mother to subscribe to *The Home and Fireside Magazine*. Soon after, she established contact with other Adventists by placing an ad requesting that subscribers send her reading material. She soon received a flood of Adventist literature and began an important correspondence with Edith Embree, who worked for the Adventist *Sign of the Times*. Under the tutelage of "Miss Embree," Anna became a devout believer in Adventist doctrine. Before long, her association with the church became her ticket out of Mississippi.[24]

After Anna announced her desire to be baptized in the Adventist Church, Elder L. Dyo Chambers, secretary-treasurer of the Southern Missionary Tract Society and Book Depository in Chattanooga, Tennessee, invited her to attend the Graysville Seventh-Day Adventist Academy. Apparently impressed by Anna's religious devotion, determination, and self-discipline, Elder Chambers and his wife brought Anna to Chattanooga and took her under their wing. At critical points in her religious development, the couple housed her, subsidized her schooling, and arranged for her training as an Adventist missionary nurse.[25]

The investment of the Chamberses in Anna Knight proved a wise one on their part, for Anna gave as much to the church as she received, working at various times as missionary, nurse, teacher, and administrator. As a foreign missionary, she spent six years in India; as a domestic missionary, she worked in Mississippi, Georgia, and Alabama to improve the health and education of Southern black children. In 1971, one year before her death at the age of ninety-eight, the Adventist Church awarded her its thirteenth Medallion of Merit Award for "extraordinary meritorious service" to Adventist education.[26]

Despite her work on behalf of the church, Anna maintained strong ties with the Knight community for her entire life. Because of the school she founded near Soso, generations of Mississippi Knights received excellent educations. In 1963, Quitman Ross, the white attorney who had defended Davis Knight in 1948, commented that mixed-race Knights "have an elementary education quite superior to that possessed by the ordinary graduate of backwoods grammar schools." Until the very end of her life, Anna sent money and encouragement for the education of her kinfolk's children.[27]

Because of Anna's long career, no one else in the Knight community—not even Newt Knight—left behind so extensive a paper trail as she, including a church-sponsored autobiography, *Mississippi Girl*, published as a testimonial to Seventh-Day Adventism in 1952. Anna's religious work and devotion dominate the text. She wrote nothing about the anti-Confederate uprising led by Newt Knight, nor did she mention the relationships and marriages that evolved out of Newt's wartime alliance with her grandmother, Rachel. Yet, in explaining how she became an Adventist and describing her subsequent efforts to uplift her kinfolk, she provided tantalizing glimpses into the Knight community, as well as insights into her own character.

Anna only hinted at the interracial household in which she had been raised and which emerged simultaneously with the Mississippi legislature's mandate for racial segregation. She did not identify either her mother, George Ann, or her grandmother, Rachel, by name, but referred to her mother as a "slave born in Macon, Georgia." Her autobiography alluded to Newt Knight as "one of the younger Knights who did not believe in slavery," but she did not identify him—or any white man—as her father. Although Anna's death certificate named Newt Knight as her father, her autobiography implied that both her parents had been former slaves.[28] Anna's reluctance to name her notorious Knight forebears or to admit that she grew up in an interracial household is not surprising given the course of her life. As the oldest of three sisters, she was also the most publicly visible. Like most black female reformers during this era of intense racial oppression, she was pious, impeccably groomed, and scrupulously chaste. Given the times, she dared not appear otherwise. From within black churches and women's clubs, women such as Anna countered dominant media images that presented the ideal white woman as genteel, sexually pure, and domestic, while stereotyping women of color as seductive Jezebels or maternal Mammies.[29]

In 1952, the year Anna's autobiography was published, Davis Knight's miscegenation trial and Ethel Knight's sensational exposé of the interracial

*Anna Knight, circa 1952. Photograph from collection of
Rachel Watts Green, courtesy of Wynona Green Frost.*

Knight community had made the names of Newt, Rachel, and George Ann Knight synonymous with sexual scandal and racial amalgamation in Mississippi. Since Anna could not keep her family's story out of the public eye, she obscured her own connections to it. Rather than provide more grist for the gossip mills, she emphasized her personal triumph over multiple forces of adversity. A subtle subtext of her story is not only her escape from the worst effects of racism but also her shunning of "feminine" characteristics that would have impeded her professional success. Though religiously pious and unfailingly neat and proper in appearance, as a foreign missionary Anna risked illness, loneliness, and physical assault rather than live the life of domesticity prescribed for proper ladies of the era. Clearly, many conventions of white womanhood held no more attraction for her than those assigned to colored women.

The other striking feature of Anna's personality was her asceticism. In large part, this reflected her conversion to Adventism, a conversion that fulfilled her deep desire for order and self-control. Development of Spartan habits enabled Anna to dramatically transform her life, achieve professional success, and gain social respect. It also left her with little tolerance for human weaknesses that led to vice and addictions—especially those involving sexual promiscuity, alcohol, and tobacco.[30]

Anna's rigid standards were most evident during her tenure at Oakwood College, an African American Adventist School in Huntsville, Alabama, established in 1895 to accommodate segregation without denying an education to black Adventists. Oakwood students remembered Anna as a stern, exacting teacher whom they feared as well as respected. Tiah M. Graves described her as a "very intimidating individual." Rosetta Baldwin recalled that students would walk on tiptoe and "shush" one another when they heard her approaching. Although Rosetta came to emulate "Miss Knight," she never forgot her first encounter with the teacher who barked, "What little girl is that; she can't teach school." Similarly, Natelkka Burrell remembered Miss Knight as a "lady with a commanding voice," whose reprimands earned the "great deference" of her students.[31]

Too many people were "enslaved" by their senses, Anna lamented, because of their unbridled individualism and lack of respect for authority. Like a good seventeenth-century Puritan, she justified her own youthful rebellion against earthly authorities by attributing it to God's will, which overrode the commands of parents. She believed, however, that Adventist leaders and parents drew their authority from the true God; therefore, their will must not be thwarted. Known at times to "correct" students with her black cane, she urged "strict order in the family, the school, and the public assembly." Parents, she counseled, must carefully train their children to resist becoming "the willing slaves of every foolish fashion and disgusting habit that has become popular."[32]

Anna's stern disapproval of unchaste behavior indicated her determination to distance herself from the sexualized images to which many of her female kin were subjected. Twice in her autobiography she condemned "card parties and dancing" as "questionable forms of amusement" from which Jesus had saved her. As a teacher, she forbade such activities, and she also occasionally counseled amorous students to not sit too close to one another lest they crowd out the Holy Spirit.[33]

Anna displayed no romantic notions about marriage and expressed a decided preference for remaining single rather than risking marriage with the wrong man. When questioned by another missionary about why she worked late into the night rather than socialize more, she replied, "I really am in love with my work." Anna's attitude allowed her to sidestep the marital choices common among her kinfolk by the early twentieth century. To maintain their light skin, third-generation Knights generally married partners as light-skinned as themselves—often their cousins—or, like Davis, they ignored the law and married whites. Anna chose instead to supplant marriage and motherhood with service to the Adventist Church. Her life as an Adventist professional spared her from ever becoming the sexual property of a white (or black) man, or from enduring the public insults suffered by her aunt, Fannie Knight Howze, or her cousin, Addie Knight.[34]

Although Anna obscured her kinship ties in her autobiography, she emphasized the struggle of growing up poor, black, and female in rural Mississippi. Poverty dictated that females work in the fields and the house. "There was no rest for women," she lamented. Interestingly, she did not long for a more "feminine" childhood, only a more just one. Given the choice, she preferred masculine work and play over feminine chores, stating emphatically that she "liked fieldwork better than housework." Far more distressing to her than the fact that she never owned a doll was that she was denied schooling on the basis of her race.[35]

Of course, racial discrimination did not end when Anna left Mississippi. Even within the Adventist Church, some objected to Anna's attending a white school. Although white and black Adventists still worshiped together in some regions of the South during the 1890s, increasingly the church was forced to adhere to Southern standards of segregation, particularly within its schools. As a result, Anna's attendance at Graysville Academy in Chattanooga, Tennessee, was halted after the first day of school when several children reported to their parents that they suspected she was black. A group of citizens immediately complained to school administrators that a "nigger" had been admitted to a white school. Anna was identified as a "mulatto," a term that, according to her, she had never heard before that moment.[36]

Until the above event, Anna may have hoped to escape the label of "Negro" altogether. Although that was not to be and she could no longer attend classes at Graysville, administrators stood by her and arranged for the school's matron to privately house and tutor her. Small wonder she returned home after a ten-week semester a "dyed-in-the-wool Seventh-Day Adventist." For the rest of her life, she remained grateful that the Adventist Church, and especially the Chamberses, had helped a "poor colored girl" to obtain an education.[37]

Far less overt racism confronted Anna after the Chamberses sent her to Mount Vernon, Ohio, to complete her education and then to the American Medical Missionary College in Battle Creek, Michigan, where she obtained training as a nurse. In the urban North, being a country girl from the South stimulated prejudices more than did her olive skin and curly hair. Anna, self-described as "truly a child of the forest" before she discovered Adventism, worked hard to overcome stereotypes about rural backwardness. Mrs. Chambers helped her in her transition, symbolically covering Anna's "country dress" with a fine "broadcloth cape with a quilted satin lining" and replacing her "old feathered hat" with one that was more suitable for a Seventh-Day Adventist. Anna also learned class-appropriate behavior, at one point vowing to overcome all the "odd sayings" that marked her as a "green girl from the South." Her successful adjustment to Northern middle-class culture made it increasingly unlikely that she would ever live in rural Mississippi again—at least not permanently.[38]

At the American Missionary Medical College, Anna earned the respect of Dr. John Harvey Kellogg, the famous Adventist health expert who developed the first cereals, which bear his family name. In 1898, Kellogg approved Anna's request to return to Mississippi and found a school for her community as fulfillment of the required field medical missionary work. That year, under the auspices of the college, which paid Anna's transportation costs and provided teaching materials, she returned to the Jones County area to perform her first missionary work in the service of her own kinfolk.[39]

Anna's return to the Knight community precipitated a turbulent period in her life. She devoted almost an entire chapter of her autobiography to describing how a gang of white men reacted violently to her establishment of a school for her Knight kin. She claimed that the men were local "moonshiners" who objected to her teaching of temperance in the name of Adventist morality—and to women preachers in general. Curiously, she said nothing about their likely feelings about an African American woman who proposed to educate children of African ancestry and teach them new religious ideas.

Armed with a revolver "and sometimes a double-barreled shotgun," Anna struggled to maintain order, but the men continued to threaten her, forcing her one day to close the schoolhouse and escape through the woods on horseback. Later that same day, a raucous fight ensued between her drunken attackers and two unnamed Knight men. According to Anna, one or more of the attackers subsequently filed a lawsuit against the Knights, which cost them "a little money." She succeeded nonetheless in keeping the school open, albeit with protection from hired watchmen and by carrying guns with her to class.[40]

Anna's harrowing ordeal with the moonshiners tested her faith in God's protection and may have influenced her decision to accept a call from her church to travel to India as a medical missionary. After agonizing over the decision, in May 1901 she left her fledgling school in the hands of Julia Luccock Atwood and her husband, Parker Atwood, two trusted white Adventist missionaries from Iowa. While she was in India, however, the Atwoods were driven from the school by renewed attacks. Anna was deeply disappointed but too immersed in her duties as a missionary to return home.[41]

Several years passed before Anna returned to Mississippi, during which time her kinfolk were without a school. Finally, her conscience was pricked by a letter from home that asked, "Why don't you come back and teach us yourself? You understand us, and you are not afraid. Why would you stay over there, trying to convert the heathen while your own people here at home are growing up into heathen?" Those words convinced Anna that she could fulfill her dream of bringing Adventist principles, both practical and spiritual, to Mississippi as well as India. She now committed herself to battling the "evils of liquor and race prejudice" that motivated those who attacked her school.[42]

Although foreign missionary work provided an escape for Anna from the unremitting pressures of American racism, around 1908 she returned to the Knight community to educate and preach Adventism to her kinfolk. Building a new school was clearly a collective effort among the Knights. Records show that on 31 March 1909, Jeff and Mollie Knight sold one acre of land to the Southern Missionary Society of Tennessee for $150 for "church and school purposes." Anna's brother John Howard Knight and his wife, Candis, conveyed forty acres to Anna on 13 April 1909. Two days later, Anna, her mother, George Ann, and Newt Knight jointly signed a security bond.[43]

As the Knight family rebuilt its school, Anna also worked to improve black health and education throughout the state. More than one black Mississippian told her that she should never return to India, because "we need you here. Let the white folk go to India, and you stay here and work with us." Anna viewed her calling differently, however. Although she engaged in several Adventist projects dedicated to racial uplift in the South, she ultimately concluded that "while I could see that the colored work in America really did need workers, to me, the needs of India were greater by far."[44]

Despite her feelings, Anna did not return to India but continued to work on behalf of Southern blacks. In 1910, after reestablishing the Knight school and training her sister Grace to take over the teaching, she moved to Atlanta, Georgia, to become medical matron of a sanitarium for colored people. There she joined a successful interdenominational effort to create a colored branch of the YWCA. By 1922, Anna was teaching summers at Oakwood College, which enabled her to aid the Knight community without returning to Mississippi. Oakwood soon became a mecca for her relatives, who traveled there to obtain educations not available to most blacks in Mississippi. Van Buren Watts, the son of Anna's beloved Aunt Augusta, later thanked her for having "stuck with our family all the way. Nothing was too good for you to do for us." According to former Oakwood students, "there was never a time that we could say there was no Knight there."[45]

Anna's ability to serve the needs of her relatives and simultaneously carve out a career for herself elsewhere was greatly facilitated by her sister Grace's willingness to remain in the Knight community. Despite the years and geographical distance that separated the sisters, they remained close all their lives. Grace Knight usually lived alone, farming her land and teaching school. As the community's schoolteacher, she became a pivotal point of contact for the Knights, who lived great distances from one another and who often assumed opposite racial identities.

Communications in 1948 between Grace and T. B. Corley, a Laurel oilman, demonstrate this. Intending to drill for oil, Corley sought to lease farmland from the heirs of Newt Knight, whom he described as having "scattered to the four corners of the country." Unlike in 1914, when Fannie Knight was labeled a "nigger" in a court of law for trying to claim marital property rights, in 1948 Corley gained the right to drill on property willed by a white man to his descendants of color by first convincing the heirs to lease their lands to him and then proving the legitimacy of their land claims.[46]

It was Grace who contacted those descendants and assured them that the lease would serve their interests as well as Corley's. In a letter dated 21 May 1948, Grace advised Ardella Knight Bramwell, her cousin's daughter, that "personally, I don't think there is any harm in signing a lease. . . . You might get something. This fellow doesn't want your minerals[,] just a lease." Ardella took Grace's advice but worried that her right to inherit from Newt Knight was compromised by the illegality of her grandparents' interracial marriage. In a subsequent letter to Ardella, Corley admitted that "there are forces at work trying to eliminate the children of Fannie Knight, who was the first wife of Matt Knight, because of a mixed blood marriage." Corley assured Ardella, their granddaughter, that the descendants of Matt and Fannie Knight were "legitimate and therefore rightful heirs to an interest in the old Newt Knight farm" and that she would receive a "small income" from the lease "for many years to come."[47]

Grace's ability to contact and influence the far-flung descendants of Jeffrey and Mollie Knight and Matt and Fannie Knight, many of whom were living as whites, made her as central a figure from within the Knight community as Anna was from outside it. As Anna acknowledged when she dedicated *Mississippi Girl* to Grace, her sister's willingness to confine her power to the circumscribed world of family, despite the fact that she was an educated single woman, assisted Anna's own escape from that world. Perhaps feeling a bit guilty, Anna thanked Grace, who "stayed at home and carried on there, making it possible for me to travel among our people from place to place, doing the work I have tried to describe in this little story."[48]

Although Anna, Grace, and Lessie led very different lives, and although none of them openly challenged the racial and sexual imperatives of the segregated South, all three escaped the fates of their mother and grandmother. In choosing careers that marked them as "old maids," Anna and Grace avoided poverty, numerous childbirths, and the degraded status routinely assigned to African American women throughout much of the twentieth century. Unlike her sisters, Lessie did marry, but she did so as a white woman. Her life embodied the fear of many white supremacists that numerous "white Negroes" were "passing" for white, while it simultaneously contradicted literary images of the "tragic mulatta." No "tragic" discovery of Lessie's African ancestry ever brought misery and shame to her or her children; nor did identifying herself as white force her to abandon completely her ancestral roots. It was Anna Knight, however, who most successfully manipulated conventions of race and gender to gain that which was routinely denied to black women: respectable social status and professional work.

Fathers and Sons

When the war erupted in April 1861, Newt Knight was a law-abiding white Southerner who, like most Jones County, Mississippi, farmers, owned land but no slaves. Because he turned against the Confederacy, crossed the color line, and became the leader of the Knight Company, he became a living legend. At the same time, he was ostracized by many of his closest associates and relatives and, long after his death, vilified by his grandniece, Ethel Knight, author of *The Echo of the Black Horn* (1951).[1]

Until that moment, Newt Knight had symbolized plain folk democracy, inspiring a novel and movie, *Tap Roots*, which celebrated Southern Unionism. Scholarly studies of the Southern plain folk were also popular during this post-Depression decade. Riding the crest of this wave, in 1946 Newt's son Thomas Jefferson Knight published his version of the Free State of Jones, one that emphasized Newt's Unionist principles and community loyalty. To maintain his father's honor in a segregated white society, Tom ignored Newt's interracial family. But in 1951 Newt's image was forever altered. Tom, who died in 1956 at the age of ninety-five, lived just long enough to witness his cousin Ethel's replacement of his heroic portrait of his father's Civil War exploits with that of a lawless, murderous traitor who she claimed betrayed his race by taking a black woman as his lover.[2]

A less notorious but equally important member of the Knight Company was also the subject of a son's twentieth-century biography. Newt's 1st sergeant, Jasper Collins, had no interracial relationships to complicate his Unionist reputation and, thanks to descendants such as his son Loren, is remembered today as a respected community patriarch. During his old age, Jasper's participation in a guerrilla deserter band during the Civil War was usually politely ignored, and his Unionism was obliquely referenced as political "independence."

It was not that Jasper was ashamed of his past. As certain of the righteousness of his Civil War stance on the day that he died as he was in 1862, Jasper spoke about his guerrilla days without apology. In 1895, as a result of his candor, he was viciously attacked in print by his Democratic rival, J. F. (Frank) Parker, a *New South* editor, when he and son Loren published Ellisville's only Populist newspaper, the *Ellisville Patriot*. To discredit the People's Party, Parker heaped scorn on the old Unionist for having fought against Lowry's forces, the "true gallants" of "mighty, majestic manhood," thirty-one years earlier.[3]

Notwithstanding Parker's attack, Jasper's Civil War exploits were usually overshadowed by writers' fascination with its captain, Newt Knight. Over and over, folklorists and journalists debated the legend of secession-within-secession and whether Newt was a Unionist or an ordinary bandit. Around 1942, retired lawyer Loren Collins defended his father's Civil War adventures in an essay entitled "The Free State of Jones, or, Two Ways to Tell a Story." Tales about the Free State had grown mighty tall over the years, and Loren was determined to correct the historical record once and for all. He denounced "wild" accounts of the Knight Company that ranged from insistence that its men had drawn up documents of secession from the Confederacy to claims that the deserters' Leaf River swamp headquarters was the site of a new generation of deserters during World War I.[4]

In certain ways, Loren was far better equipped to defend the Knight Company than was Tom Knight. Many more of his kinfolk had been directly involved, and he had enjoyed a closer relationship with his father than Tom had had with the notorious Newt Knight. Born in 1860, Tom had parted company as a young man with his father over race, unwilling to sacrifice respectability by living in a mixed-race community during an age of white supremacy. At the same time, Tom remained close to his mother, Serena, who left the household of her husband late in their marriage. Given the turmoil that Newt's extramarital relationships likely caused for Serena,

Tom's sympathy for his mother may have further fueled his resentment of his father's interracial affairs.

Loren Collins had endured no such conflict within his family. His childhood memories were dominated by images of family and friends gathered around the fireplace as they rehashed the "perilous and exciting times" they had shared during the war. Other Mississippi children might listen to tales about Confederate bravery, but Loren thrilled to tales about the inner civil war that had raged at his family's very doorstep. Not only had his father, two uncles, and scads of cousins joined up with Newt Knight to form the Knight Company, but his Aunt Sally had also provided food and refuge for the men. As a result, her farm became the site of a pitched battle between the Knight Company and Confederate forces in 1863, just two days before Christmas. Furthermore, Loren's maternal grandfather, John H. Powell, had served as the county's antisecession delegate to the state convention that voted to take Mississippi out of the Union.[5]

Quite simply, the Collins family epitomized the depth of Unionist sentiment in Jones County. Loren's political views thus were shaped by his family as well as the times in which he grew up. Not only did he defend his father's Civil War stance in his old age, but as a young man during the 1890s he had joined Jasper in trying to establish a new political order. Father and son, who served as delegates to the state Populist conventions, were also cofounders of the county's Populist newspaper. After the demise of the People's Party, Loren became a Republican rather than join the hated Democratic Party, which had alternately slandered and co-opted the political movement that he and Jasper had worked so hard to build in the 1890s.[6]

Well into the twentieth century, several of Jasper's descendants supported political parties of dissent. In 1913, Jasper's grandson, Buford T. Collins Sr., ran for circuit court clerk on the Socialist ticket. In 1920, his son-in-law, Thomas J. Lyon, was the Socialist candidate for the U.S. House of Representatives from Mississippi's Sixth District. Like Loren's, Buford's and Thomas's political views were nurtured within a family environment in which Jasper Collins was a central figure. Lyon, who married Jasper's daughter Theodocia, considered Jasper a surrogate father, his own having died in the Civil War. At the time of his death, in 1938, Lyon remained a Socialist, as did the Methodist minister who delivered his eulogy.[7]

Although apparently no daughters wrote histories about their Knight Company fathers, one of Jasper's granddaughters, Betty Myrick Burrow, tried her hand at doing so. According to family members, Burrow's account preceded that of Ethel Knight, who, they contend, appropriated many of her stories. This may well be the case, but there are even greater similarities between Burrow's manuscript and that of Tom Knight, who first copyrighted his in 1935. Since Tom later gave his research materials to Ethel, the question is, who first completed their manuscript, Betty Burrow or Tom Knight? Whatever the answer, Burrow, like Knight, defended the honor and motives of the Knight Company men, but she also addressed more thoroughly the Collinses' role in building the Free State of Jones.[8]

Tom Knight and Loren Collins had very different personal relationships with their fathers, but they defended their fathers' wartime actions along similar lines. Both emphasized that "leading citizens" joined the Knight Company because they were principled Unionists unwilling to fight against their own government in the name of preserving slavery. Furthermore, both insisted that their fathers deserted their units to protect women and children from the dangers and starvation brought on by an ill-conceived war. Like good patriarchs, their fathers' first loyalties were to their families.[9]

One Collins descendant, Keith Lyon, notes that the Knight Company symbolized primal honor to its plain folk defenders, as opposed to the elite code of gentility represented by Confederate officers Robert Lowry and Amos McLemore or by Confederate representative Amos Deason. By killing Major McLemore during the war and shaming Deason during Reconstruction, Lyon contended, Newt Knight heroically triumphed over illegitimate figures of authority who served what plain folk considered to be an illegal, corrupt government.[10]

To demonstrate that Colonel Lowry and his forces were not men of honor, Tom and Loren provided numerous anecdotal examples of women and children who suffered at their hands. High on their list of Lowry's atrocities was his unleashing of bloodhounds on the civilian population. Lowry's forces were also accused of threatening the lives of children in efforts to learn where their fathers were hiding. Allegedly, the men put a rope around the neck of Loren's oldest brother, Henry Clay Collins, whom Loren described as twelve years old, and swung him from a tree until he nearly lost consciousness. So hated was Colonel Lowry in Jones County, Loren insisted, that he never dared reenter the county after the war, even while campaigning for governor during the 1880s.[11]

Two states away, in Hardin County, Texas, Warren Jacob Collins, Loren's uncle and Jasper's brother, led his own guerrilla band, the Big Thicket jayhawkers. Unlike Newt, Warren was not a living legend before his death,

Alzada Courtney, center of middle row, circa 1926. Probably the oldest living adult participant in the Free State of Jones, she was close to 100 years old when Tom Knight interviewed her in the 1930s for his book, Life and Activities of Captain Newton Knight. *Photograph courtesy of Ralph Kirkland.*

and, unlike his brother Jasper, he did not share a close political partnership with the son who later profiled him.

Vinson Allen Collins, a prominent lawyer and Texas state senator between 1910 and 1917, portrayed his father in far more ambivalent terms than Tom Knight and Loren Collins did theirs. Just as Tom ignored Newt Knight's interracial relations, so also did Vinson ignore Warren Collins's Socialist views. Like his cousin Loren, Vinson had once been politically allied with his father, but that changed after 1910 when he abandoned agrarian Populist ideals for more mainstream Democratic Party principles.[12]

Vinson's political evolution represented a steady journey away from the traditions of the parents who named him after his Unionist uncle of Jones County, Mississippi, and later nicknamed him "Yank." Elected senator in 1910, his political move to the right was not completed overnight, however. In 1911, T. A. Hickey, editor of the Socialist newspaper *The Rebel*, in Hallettsville, Texas, praised Senator Collins for supporting restrictions on child labor, an eight-hour workday, and woman suffrage. Vinson demonstrated particular regard for working men by writing the state's first workmen's compensation law in 1913, an action considered so radical during its time that he could not find a colleague willing to cosponsor it.[13]

Still, despite his early progressivism, Vinson's Unionist forebears and Socialist father were distinct liabilities in his quest to build a political career, particularly since that career emerged simultaneously with the Myth of the Lost Cause. Like many of his Democratic cohorts, he anchored his progressive views within profoundly conservative social goals that contrasted with his support for labor legislation. A devout Baptist, his endorsement of woman suffrage was connected to ardent support for prohibition and reflected popular images of women as moral saviors of society.[14]

After beginning his political career as a progressive Democrat, Collins ended it as a conservative Democrat who supported the presidential campaigns of two Republicans, Herbert Hoover and Dwight Eisenhower. During the 1920s, he joined the Ku Klux Klan and ran for governor against the anti-Klan, antiprohibition candidate, Miriam "Ma" Ferguson. His son, Carr P. Collins, and Carr's sons, Carr Jr. and James, continued the family's migration toward conservative Republican politics. As Baptists, they condemned socialism as godless and antithetical to American values, unlike Grandpa Warren, who had argued back in 1911 that the Bible itself espoused socialist principles—something too few wealthy "corn-fed" preachers understood.[15]

Patriotic chauvinism, loyalty campaigns, 100 percent Americanism, and

"Red Scare" fears in the era of World War I further complicated Vinson's relationship with his politically left-wing father. In fact, Warren's political activism and lifelong pride in having opposed the Confederacy seemed to create problems for several of his Mississippi nephews as well, who sought to bury their past affiliations with Newt Knight and the Free State of Jones after they moved to Texas in the 1870s.

Twentieth-century Confederate pension files provide a revealing footnote to the tangle of memory and politics that dogged the Collins family from Mississippi to Texas. In 1925, Warren's nephew, eighty-year-old Morgan C. Collins of Polk County, applied for a Confederate pension. Although the state granted the pension based on Morgan's documented service at Kennesaw Mountain, Georgia, the matter did not end there. On 9 September 1926, W. T. Hickman Sr., of Corrigan, questioned state comptroller S. H. Terrell about whether Morgan was related to those Collinses who "were well known in our county as Bushmen, or who hid out in what is known as [the] Big Thicket [in the] south part of Polk & upper part of Hardin County." In a follow-up letter, Hickman warned Terrell that the United Confederate Veterans of Polk County planned to investigate the "soldiership" of Collins. "We would like to know," he explained, referring to Warren and his brothers, because "all the Collins here but one were deserters." Hickman intimated that legal action would be taken against Morgan Collins if his claim of Confederate service was not "genuine."[16]

Hickman apparently dropped the matter after it was made clear to him that Morgan Collins had served the Confederacy from Mississippi, not from Texas. Authorities seemed to assume that Morgan Collins was not even kin to the Big Thicket Collinses of jayhawker fame. In fact, however, Hickman's suspicions were well founded. Morgan was indeed the nephew of Warren Collins but had been a member of the Knight band in Mississippi rather than a jayhawker in East Texas. He had been forced into the Confederate Army in lieu of arrest and possible execution by Colonel Robert Lowry and his forces.

Nevertheless, both Morgan and the widow of his brother Matt, also a member of the Knight band during the war, were granted Confederate pensions by the state of Texas. Apparently no one, not even the suspicious Mr. Hickman, realized that, although the brothers were not Big Thicket jayhawkers, they had belonged to an even more notorious deserter band back home in Mississippi. The connections between the Big Thicket jayhawkers and the Free State of Jones remained the Collins family's well-kept secret.[17]

In part, this was because the Free State of Jones received far more press, particularly before World War II, than did the Big Thicket jayhawkers. Mississippi's more central position in the Civil War and the Knight Company's more frequent and deadly encounters with Confederate forces brought national attention to the legend of the "Republic of Jones." Over time, in the hands of both Northern and Southern journalists, familiar images of ornery stubbornness and poor whites' penchant for violence were cited to explain the uprising.

Stripped by journalists of his political principles and reduced to a stubborn backwoodsman, Newt Knight appeared as merely suspicious of all government, reacting against authority (usually with fists) in a knee-jerk way without clear thought. In the process, he became a caricature of the Southern man of honor, fighting for the same principles that had led to creation of the Confederate government in the first place. Isolated within his Piney Woods world, he was presented as too provincial to realize that the Confederacy represented his true interests.

Much the same treatment was accorded Warren Collins after his death in 1926. Journalist Dean Tevis interviewed local residents of Beaumont in 1930, who remembered him far more for his fighting prowess than for his political views. As published tales about Warren and the Big Thicket uprising appeared, his son Vinson was embracing ever more politically conservative views. Still, the democratizing effects of World War II and the diminished force of the Lost Cause myth may help to explain the family history that Vinson sketched in 1949, in which he briefly acknowledged his family's Unionist past. Indeed, this short unpublished essay meshed very well with those produced by Tom Knight and Loren Collins from Mississippi during the same decade. After laying out the genealogy of the Collins family, Vinson ended by describing them as "people of convictions; few ever held office, because they had opinions and dared to express them. They were all opposed to slavery and to concession [secession]."[18]

Those sentences were omitted in Vinson's published 1962 history of the family, perhaps in deference to his children and grandchildren. Son Carr P. Collins and Carr's sons were entrepreneurial businessmen who found the emerging Southern wing of the Republican Party more to their liking. In 1959, Carr P. Collins Jr., a politically prominent conservative, published his own genealogical study of the Collins family. In it, he emphasized Warren's pioneering role in the rugged backwoods of Texas but sidestepped his political history altogether.[19]

Carr Jr.'s account made no mention of Warren Collins's hatred of slavery and the Confederacy. Instead, great-grandpa Warren was simply "the Daniel Boone of Eastern Texas." And in case anyone might suspect that grandfather Vinson's nickname, "Yank," reflected Yankee sympathies of Warren and Eboline Collins, Carr Jr. assured readers that Vinson earned his nickname only because he was so "roly-poly" and "pink-faced" as a boy that "no one but a 'Yankee' could be that fat and well-fed."[20]

Vinson Collins's history of the family followed soon after. Like his grandson, he omitted Warren's antislavery and anti-Confederate principles. Instead of praising his ancestors for having the courage of their political convictions, as he had in 1949, in 1962 Vinson repeatedly criticized his father's lack of business sense. By then the aged, wealthy patriarch of a prominent Dallas family, Vinson attributed his impoverished childhood to his father's poor business skills rather than the effects of rapid industrial change.[21]

The younger Collinses were certainly not poor business men. Building on the financial success of their father, insurance magnate Carr P. Collins Sr., the younger generation of Collinses enjoyed millionaire status among the social and economic elite of Dallas. As the title of Carr P. Collins Jr.'s family genealogy, *Royal Ancestors of Magna Charta Barons*, revealed, Warren's great-grandson preferred to claim a dubious descent from illustrious Scottish covenanters of the seventeenth century rather than acknowledge certain descent from a jayhawker of the Big Thicket.[22]

Although Vinson Collins's biography lauded his parents for their struggles and hard work, he had long shed the progressive labor views he had championed as a young senator. On 24 June 1950, the *Houston Chronicle* reported that "although he did much while a senator to help labor, Mr. Collins says labor now is too demanding." Sounding more like a Cold War Republican than a Democrat, Vinson complained that "since the New Deal, we've lost far more than we've gained. Government extravagances and socialistic tendencies are destroying the self-reliance of the American people, and unless it is stopped we're headed for disaster."[23]

In a culture that increasingly blamed Southern white poverty on laziness and inferior genes, Vinson was defensive about his parents' modest resources. He assured readers in 1962 that he did not come from "poor white trash," despite the hard times of his early years. Sidestepping any discussion of his father, he credited his mother's hard work and devotion to child-rearing: "She did not raise a weakly family of children, 'pale faces,' or 'hookworm victims,'" he wrote; "she raised a husky bunch."[24]

More positive images of Warren Collins emerged in the 1970s as the Big Thicket became an important region of study among local historians and folklorists. Lively stories about Warren's band of jayhawkers were routinely recounted as the Big Thicket rebellion became a staple of Texas backwoods lore. As leader of the Big Thicket jayhawkers, Warren personified the hardy East Texas pioneer—yet there were tensions in the images of him. Sometimes he was portrayed as a class-conscious iconoclast and other times as a stubborn backwoods individualist.[25]

Scholars occasionally interviewed descendants and friends from outside Vinson Collins's family circle who still admired Warren's Unionist principles and devotion to preindustrial values. Bud Overstreet, for example, remembered that his grandfather Warren called the Civil War a "rich man's war and a poor man's fight." "That's the reason they wouldn't fight," Overstreet elaborated; "they didn't own nothin'." Before the Civil War, he explained, "the poor white people was just like slaves, too, no better off than the colored man." As another East Texan put it, Big Thicket jayhawkers were "just sensible people. They knew what would happen if the slaves were not freed. . . . Men who had money to start a business of any kind would buy slaves for his labor and poor whites would be left out."[26]

Most accounts, however, highlighted the ever-popular backwoodsman stereotype. Warren Collins was described as a "short, square-set, long-armed and hammer-fisted sort of man who ruled his own roost." He "fought anything that had gall enough to cross him," including the Confederacy, simply because "he didn't reckon the war between the North and South was any part of his 'plan of life.'" Despite more positive and respectful images, he, like Newt Knight, was cast as a stereotypical backwoods brawler, forever ready to fight rather than take orders from anyone. Like Newt, he appeared to be a hardheaded backwoodsman who simply wanted to be "left alone." Not surprisingly, then, Warren Collins is rarely mentioned in scholarly histories of Civil War or New South Texas.[27]

Placing Southern Unionists within the trope of the backwoodsman—or hillbilly—allowed both author and reader to revere the Confederacy while indulging a certain style of anti-Confederate behavior. There were even efforts to reconcile the guerrilla bands' leaders with their worst enemies, much as the nation itself had reconciled in 1877. After the war, according to Tevis's interviewee, Warren Collins shook hands and made up with Captain Charles Bullock, the Confederate officer who had ordered that the Big Thicket be burned during the war in a failed effort to capture the jayhawkers. Likewise, Tom Knight claimed that Newt Knight made peace with Confederate colonel Robert Lowry. No evidence was offered to support either story.[28]

The absurdity of some popular depictions of Southern Unionists reached its nadir in 1946, when one magazine article portrayed Newt Knight as a working-class miscreant who hunted rabbits in a "blue work-shirt," "blue jeans," and "heavy work shoes," an image suggestive of post–World War II labor unionists rather than Civil War Unionists. In an obvious rip-off of journalist Meigs O. Frost's 1921 interview with Newt, this version pretended to draw from the same interview but dramatically altered the original dialogue to suit conservative ideals and hillbilly stereotypes of the 1940s.[29]

Unlike the real Newt Knight of Frost's interview, this reincarnated Newt talked about his Civil War past only when plied with plenty of "likker." He disavowed all political principles, especially that of Unionism. When asked why he and his men had fought against the Confederacy, he expressed no objections to slavery, other than resentment of his rich neighbors. "Hell, no. We ain't Union," a drunken Newt Knight asserted. "We ain't fightin' [for the Confederacy] less'n we got a real reason to fight. Yo'-all want nigrah slaves, help yo'selves. We don't own none." This Newt Knight had nothing against slavery—he was simply too poor to buy one. Reduced to an entertaining hillbilly, Newt personified deviant Southern manhood and poor white jealousy of one's "betters."[30]

Until the ends of their long lives, Newt Knight, Jasper Collins, and Warren Collins refuted contemporary "Lost Cause" histories that portrayed Southern secession and the formation of the Confederate nation as a noble effort to protect state sovereignty. With mixed success, several of their descendants struggled to do the same. Although Tom Knight, Loren Collins, and Vinson Collins attempted to explain their iconoclastic fathers to the public, the political and racial environments in which they lived limited their perspectives. Tom insisted that Newt Knight was a virtuous, law-abiding man of honor but clearly would have preferred that he had supported the Lily-White Republican Party instead of breaking the South's most solemn rules of race.

Loren Collins's decision to join the Lily-White Republicans after the demise of Populism reflected his hatred of the Southern Democratic Party and seemed to be an effort to remain true to his father's politically independent spirit. Over time, however, he seemed unable to find a comfortable political niche in the party that attracted his Texas cousin, Carr P. Collins Sr., for very different reasons. In the end, racism won the day. Loren, like Tom Knight, ignored Newt Knight's interracial relations in order to praise his Unionism. But soon, both men's works were eclipsed by Ethel Knight's sensational revelations about Newt Knight's "betrayal" of the white race and her blanket condemnation of the Knight Company for having committed what she saw as treason.[31]

In Texas, Vinson Collins's public career in conservative politics and his great wealth left little room for the history of his father, Warren, except as the "Daniel Boone" who pioneered in leading the family from Mississippi to Texas. This Texas branch of Collinses provides a striking contrast with certain descendants of Jasper Collins in Mississippi. Rather than obscure the history of Jasper Collins with appealing images of the hardy white pioneer, B. T. Collins Jr. extended his great-grandfather's philosophy into the present. "The crowd or the majority is seldom ever right," he explained. Otherwise, "why would people who owned no slaves fight a war so others could own slaves," as so many Southerners did during the Civil War?[32]

B. T. then extended that logic to twentieth-century racial dogma. Ridiculing Mississippi politician Theodore Bilbo for his segregationist promises to preserve racial "purity," he countered that Bilbo's argument that "blacks would mongrelize the white race simply appealed to the ignorance of many people" and ignored the fact that "all the races are mixed." The main reason that B. T. would not marry a black person, he declared, had nothing to do with biology and everything to do with the history of Jones County: it was because of "what happened to the [multiracial] Knight people of Soso."[33]

B. T. Collins's words indicate, at long last, that many white descendants of the Free State of Jones now are comfortable in defending the actions of the Knight Company and acknowledging its interracial legacy in the same breath. Such was not the case during the segregated 1940s and 1950s, unless, like Ethel Knight, one sought to discredit the company by exposing its leader's personal life. In Texas, most descendants of Warren Collins now acknowledge his Civil War Unionism but are not aware that his alternative political path led him to embrace the Socialist Party during the last decades of his life. Few histories, it seems, are buried faster or deeper than those of political and social dissenters.

Notes

ABBREVIATIONS

The following abbreviations are used throughout the notes.

Bynum files   Victoria Bynum files, San Marcos, Tex.

Freedmen's   Records of the Bureau of Refugees, Freedmen, and Abandoned
Bureau Papers   Lands, RG 105, National Archives, Washington, D.C.

MDAH   Mississippi Department of Archives and History, Jackson, Miss.

ML-USM   McCain Library and Archives, University of Southern Mississippi,
Hattiesburg, Miss.

NA   National Archives, Washington, D.C.

NCDAH   North Carolina Department of Archives and History,
Raleigh, N.C.

Newton Knight   Claims of Newton Knight and Others, #8013 and #8464,
Claims   Committee on War Claims, Records of the U.S. Court of Claims,
1835–1966, RG 123, National Archives, Washington, D.C.

Newton Knight   Newton Knight Folder, box 15, Records of the U.S. House of
Folder   Representatives, RG 233, National Archives, Washington, D.C.

Official Records   U.S. War Department, *War of the Rebellion: A Compilation of the
Official Records of the Union and Confederate Armies* (Washington,
D.C.: Government Printing Office, 1880–1901)

RG   Record Group

SCC-NA   Records of the General Accounting Office, Third Auditor's
              Office, Southern Claims Commission, RG 217, National Archives,
              Washington, D.C.

SHC-UNC   Southern Historical Collection, University of North Carolina,
              Chapel Hill, N.C.

TSLAAC   Texas State Library and Archives and Archives Commission,
              Austin, Tex.

USM   University of Southern Mississippi, Hattiesburg, Miss.

WPA-MDAH   Works Projects Administration, RG 60, Mississippi
              Department of Archives and History, Jackson, Miss.

INTRODUCTION

1 Samuel L. Holt to Gov. Zebulon Vance, 24 May 1863, Governors' Papers, Vance,
   NCDAH.
2 Important early studies of conflicts on the Southern home front that centered on
   loyalty and opposition to the Confederacy include Lonn, *Desertion during the Civil
   War*; Tatum, *Disloyalty in the Confederacy*; Beals, *War within a War*; and Degler, *Other
   South*. During the past two decades, such studies have again flourished. See especially
   Pierson, *Mutiny at Fort Jackson*; Weitz, *More Damning Than Slaughter*; Wetherington,
   Plain Folk's Fight; Williams, *Bitterly Divided*; Storey, *Loyalty and Loss*; Sutherland, *A
   Savage Conflict*; Bynum, *Free State of Jones*; Inscoe and Kenzer, *Enemies of the Country*;
   Pickering and Falls, *Brush Men and Vigilantes*; Baum, *Shattering of Texas Unionism*; Mc-
   Caslin, *Tainted Breeze*; and Crofts, *Reluctant Confederates*.
3 Diary of Samuel A. Agnew, 27 Sept. 1863–30 June 1864, *Documenting the American
   South*, Electronic Edition, SHC-UNC.
4 R. W. Surby, a native of Canada, belonged to the 7th Illinois Cavalry, one of several
   units under the command of Col. Benjamin Grierson during this Mississippi mission. According to a map tracing Grierson's daily movements, on the day described
   above the men were just above the Smith County seat of Raleigh, a few miles from
   the Jones County border. Surby, *Grierson's Raids*, 53–54.
5 Ibid., 54, 55.
6 Ibid., 56.
7 The Richmond riot took place on 2 April 1863. The true identity of "Agnes" was kept
   secret by her friend Sara. Quoted in Pryor, *Reminiscences of Peace and War*, 237–39.
   On elite Southern women's criticisms of the war, see especially Faust, *Mothers of
   Invention*.
8 Quoted in Pryor, *Reminiscences of Peace and War*, 292–94.
9 Ash, *When the Yankees Came*; Blair, *Virginia's Private War*. For an argument against the
   idea that internal dissent was a major cause of Confederate defeat, see Gallagher,
   Confederate War.
10 On the history of the Free State of Jones, see especially Bynum, *Free State of Jones*;
   Leverett, *Legend of the Free State of Jones*; Ethel Knight, *Echo of the Black Horn*; Thomas

J. Knight, *Life and Activities*; and Jenkins and Stauffer, *State of Jones*. Ethel Knight's and Tom Knight's books must be read with special care due to the authors' biases and objectives. Tom Knight, Newt Knight's son, focused primarily on defending his father's reputation as a Unionist and ignored Newt's interracial family altogether. Ethel Knight was a disgruntled pro-Confederate member of the Knight family who presented Newt Knight as a shrewd but demented man who ruined the lives of his children by forcing two of them to marry across the color line. Because Jenkins and Stauffer rely heavily and uncritically on the works of Tom Knight and Ethel Knight, their book must also be read with care.

11 The migratory patterns of the Collins family are discussed in Bynum, *Free State of Jones*, 30–37, 60. On Warren J. Collins and the jayhawkers of the East Texas Big Thicket, see Pitts, "Civil War and 'Kaiser's Burnout'"; Wooster and Wooster, "A People at War," 3–16; Loughmiller and Loughmiller, *Big Thicket Legacy*; Abernethy, *Tales from the Big Thicket*; House, *Big Thicket*; and Zuber, "Fire at Union Wells," 28–29, 62.

12 Payne, "Kinship, Slavery, and Gender." On the importance of kinship ties to Southern history, see Billingsley, *Communities of Kinship*. On Newt and Rachel Knight's relationship, see Bynum, *Free State of Jones*; Bivins, "Open Secret"; Sumrall and Welch, *Knights and Related Families*; and Ethel Knight, *Echo of the Black Horn*.

13 Crofts, *Reluctant Confederates*, 133, 147, 154.

14 The best source of information on William "Bill" Owens is William T. Auman's dissertation, "Neighbor against Neighbor," 151–52. See also Auman's article of the same name, "Neighbor against Neighbor," 59–92.

15 On the influence of Hinton Rowan Helper, see especially David Brown, *Southern Outcast*. On the North Carolina Civil War home front, see Beatty, *Alamance*, 72–105; Bynum, *Unruly Women*, 111–50; Durrill, *War of Another Kind*; Bolton, *Poor Whites of the Antebellum South*, 139–60; Auman, "Neighbor against Neighbor" (dissertation); Kenzer, *Kinship and Neighborhood*, 71–96; and Escott, *Many Excellent People*.

16 Kenzer, *Kinship and Neighborhood*, 6–9, 25–27, 32–33; Bynum, *Unruly Women*, 46–47, 122–25.

17 Escott, *Many Excellent People*, 154–55. For an excellent recent overview of Reconstruction, see Fitzgerald, *Splendid Failure*. On postwar relations between former slaves and masters, see O'Donovan, *Becoming Free*; Bercaw, *Gendered Freedoms*; and Edwards, *Scarlett Doesn't Live Here Anymore*. On Reconstruction in North Carolina, see Zipf, "Whites Shall Rule the Land or Die," 499–534; Edwards, *Gendered Strife and Confusion*; and Trelease, *White Terror*. On the Civil War origins of the state's Conservative Party, see Kruman, *Parties and Politics*, 230–32.

18 The newspaper editors claimed that Crawford delivered his words before the Constitutional Convention of 1865, but the speech does not appear in the published proceedings of that convention. Reported in *Adams Sentinel*, 26 Sept. 1865; *Journal of the Proceedings and Debates in the Constitutional Convention of the State of Mississippi, August, 1865*.

19 Likewise, the Jones County seat of Ellisville was renamed Leesburg, in honor of Gen. Robert E. Lee. See Petition to Senate and House of Representatives from Jones County Citizens to change name of county to Davis and county seat from Ellisville

to Leesburg, Senate Journal, 16 Oct. 1865, vol. 88, RG 47, MDAH. The names were changed back by provisions contained in Article 13, section 2, of the Mississippi State Constitution of 1868, which specified that "all laws now in force in this state . . . shall continue in operation until they shall expire by their own limitation."

20 On political offices held by former members of the Knight Company during Reconstruction, see Bynum, *Free State of Jones*, 132–41. On Democratic politics during this era, see Bond, *Political Culture in the Nineteenth-Century South*, 156–81; Wharton, *Negro in Mississippi*, 131–215; and Cresswell, *Multiparty Politics*, 13–18.

21 *Long v. Long*, 77 NC 287 (1877). This case is discussed more fully in Bynum, "Refashioning the Bonds of Womanhood," 320–34. On race and the reshaping of Civil War memory, see especially Brundage, *Southern Past*; Whites, *Civil War as a Crisis in Gender*; Fahs and Waugh, *Memory of the Civil War*; and Blight, *Race and Reunion*. For studies of multiracialism in the Old and the New South, see especially Sandweiss, *Passing Strange*; Eubanks, *House at the End of the Road*; Pascoe, *What Comes Naturally*; Wray, *Not Quite White*; Painter, *Southern History across the Color Line*; Hodes, *Sex, Love, Race*; Leslie, *Woman of Color*; Bullard, *Robert Stafford*; and Alexander, *Ambiguous Lives*.

22 Lawyers for the Hopkins family cited a North Carolina statute that prohibited marriages between whites and people with African ancestry beyond the third generation. A hastily scribbled chart appears among case papers demonstrating that this rule of law thus extended back to one's great-grandparents. *John Hopkins, Alexander Hopkins, Sally Hopkins (by Alexander Hopkins), Robert Daniel and wife Emma Daniel, Thomas Adcock and wife Larcena, Jordan Nance and wife Sally v. Ann (Bowers) Boothe and daughters Eliza and Nannie (Bowers) Boothe*, Superior Court, 1888–92, Estate Records, Orange County, NCDAH. On segregation and the New South, see especially J. William Harris, *New South*; Dailey, Gilmore, and Simon, *Jumpin' Jim Crow*; Litwack, *Trouble in Mind*; Hale, *Making Whiteness*; Gilmore, *Gender and Jim Crow*; and Williamson, *Crucible of Race*.

23 For arguments that the Knight band consisted primarily of bandits rather than Unionists, see especially Leverett, *Legend of the Free State of Jones*. If the Knight band did take an oath, it seems likely that it was verbally administered; no such written document has been found. Testimonies of Newton Knight, 29 Jan. 1895, J. M. Valentine, 29 Jan. 1895, W. M. Welch, 6 Mar. 1895, J. J. Collins, 6 Mar. 1895, Newton Knight Claims.

24 On the radical vision of the Omaha Platform, see especially Goodwyn, *Democratic Promise*, passim. Cantrell, *People's Revolt* (forthcoming) promises to shed even more light on Texas Populists.

25 Populism contributed with particular force to the establishment of the Socialist Party in southwestern states like Texas, Oklahoma, and Arkansas. On Texas Socialism, see James R. Green, *Grass-Roots Socialism*, 12–16, 42–44; Foley, *White Scourge*, 92–117, 183–202; and Zamora, *World of the Mexican Worker*, 133–61.

26 My thanks to Ed Payne for suggesting this analogy between the post–Civil War Democratic Party and the Baptist Church. Ed Payne to author, e-mail, 21 June 2007, 24 June 2007, Bynum files.

27 Goodwyn, *Democratic Promise*, 430–36; Kirwan, *Revolt of the Rednecks*; Cresswell, *Multiparty Politics*, 157, 167–69.

28 Kirwan, *Revolt of the Rednecks*; Goodwyn, *Democratic Promise*, 430–36; Miller, "Building a Progressive Coalition in Texas," 163–82.

29 Ethel Knight, *Echo of the Black Horn*, 315.

PART ONE

1 John A. Beaman to Gov. Zebulon Vance, undated, Governors' Papers, Vance, NCDAH. Charges of stealing Malinda Beaman's mare were filed against Romulus F. Sanders, son of Montgomery County sheriff Aaron Sanders, in fall 1864 (Criminal Action Papers, Montgomery County, NCDAH).

2 John A. Beaman to Gov. Zebulon Vance, undated, Governors' Papers, Vance, NCDAH.

3 The torture of Mrs. Owens is described by Judge Thomas Settle in two letters to Gov. Zebulon Vance, one dated 21 Sept. 1864 (Governors' Papers, Vance, NCDAH), the other 4 Oct. 1864 (reprinted from H. L. Carson Papers, in Yearns and Barrett, *North Carolina Civil War Documentary*, 103–5).

CHAPTER ONE

1 For historical accounts of Newt Knight and the murder of Colonel Amos McLemore, see Bynum, *Free State of Jones*, 105–6; and Leverett, *Legend of the Free State of Jones*, 62–68.

2 The fullest biography of Warren Jacob Collins was written by his son, Texas state senator Vinson A. Collins, *Story of My Parents*. For a description of Collins as a backwoods brawler, see especially Rienstra, "A Family Full of Legends," 185.

3 William Auman's work on Bill Owens is excellent, but I disagree with his identification of him in the Federal Manuscript Census Population Schedules of 1860 as William B. Owens of Moore County. By Auman's own account, Owens was lynched in 1865; yet this William B. Owens, whose middle name was Bailey, appears in the 1870 population schedule of Sheffield Township, Moore County, as Bailey Owens, and, in 1880, again as William B. Owens. Living in the same household for all three decades is Mary B. Owens (U.S. Bureau of the Census, Federal Manuscript Census, Population Schedules, 1860, 1870, 1880, Moore County, N.C.). It is likelier that the William Owens, age thirty-two, who lived on the Montgomery County side of the neighborhood with his wife, Adeline, age twenty-two, and five households away from Murphy Owens, whose sons were members of the Owens band, is the deserter/guerrilla band leader of this study. This William Owens is absent from the 1870 Federal Manuscript Census, consistent with Bill Owens's murder in 1865. See Auman, "Neighbor against Neighbor" (dissertation), 151–52.

4 On Unionism in the North Carolina Piedmont, see also Crofts, *Reluctant Confederates*. On Hinton Rowan Helper, see David Brown, *Southern Outcast*; and David Brown, "Attacking Slavery from Within," 541–76. The Heroes of America, also called the "Red Strings," were estimated by newspaper editor and future governor William W. Holden to have had 10,000 members in Civil War North Carolina. On the Heroes of

America, see Auman and Scarboro, "Heroes of America," 327–44; and Nelson, "Red Strings and Half Brothers," 37–53.

5 The religious irreverence of the Knight and Collins families is discussed in Bynum, *Free State of Jones*, 45–46, 77–79; on the Collinses, see also Lackey, "Minutes of Zion Baptist Church," 59–65. Throughout *State of Jones*, authors Jenkins and Stauffer contend that Newt Knight was a devout Primitive Baptist who actively opposed slavery on religious grounds. Newt may indeed have hated slavery, but there is no evidence whatsoever that he was a religious abolitionist.

6 According to family stories, the Confederate Army forcibly conscripted both Joseph Owens and his son Daniel in 1864 because the father refused to let the son serve alone. Both were captured by Yankees at the Battle of the Wilderness in Virginia and imprisoned. Joseph subsequently died at Elmira Prison of chronic diarrhea. Joseph Owens's wife was Matilda Queen Northcutt, further suggesting the family's kinship ties to the Owens band, which included several Owens men and one Benjamin Northcutt ("The Owens Family," ⟨http://freepages.genealogy.rootsweb.ancestry.com/jentaylor/Owens.htm⟩).

7 Civil War guerrilla warfare was especially fierce in Missouri; see Fellman, *Inside War*. Anthologies that emphasize diverse locations of Unionism and guerrilla warfare throughout the South include Inscoe and Kenzer, *Enemies of the Country*; Sutherland, *Guerrillas, Unionists, and Violence*; and Noe and Wilson, *Civil War in Appalachia*.

8 For a study of the importance of kinship networks to the migratory patterns and ideological coherence of Southern communities, see Billingsley, *Communities of Kinship*.

9 The names of these fifty-five core members were taken from the Knight Company roster that Newt Knight prepared for his 1870 petition to Congress for compensation for Unionist service during the Civil War (Newton Knight Folder). Birthplaces and migrations of Jones County families were traced through federal censuses, tax and land records, and court files. See Bynum, *Free State of Jones*, 11–69.

10 Stacy Collins Sr. died within a few years of settling in Texas, leaving Sarah and four sons to go it alone. His untimely death left his son Warren, rather than himself, to be labeled the "Daniel Boone" of East Texas. For a full history of the migrations west of Stacy and Sarah Collins, see Bynum, *Free State of Jones*; and Vinson A. Collins, *Story of My Parents*, 1–7.

11 Vinson A. Collins, "Settling the Old Poplar-Tree Place," 58–68.

12 Buenger, "Riddle of Secession," 1–26. For a full analysis of Texas Unionism and its defeat, see Baum, *Shattering of Texas Unionism*.

13 Hardin County voted 167 for secession, 62 against. See Willis, *Short History of Hardin County*, 23. On Unionism in Texas, see especially Pickering and Falls, *Brush Men and Vigilantes*; Dykes-Hoffman, "Treue der Union"; Baum, *Shattering of Texas Unionism*; McCaslin, *Tainted Breeze*; McCaslin, "Voices of Reason," 180–94; Marten, *Texas Divided*; and Buenger, *Secession and the Union in Texas*. For fresh perspectives on Civil War Texas, see also Howell, *Seventh Star of the Confederacy*.

14 W. D. Douglas, Capt. and Assistant Quartermaster, CSA, Post Quartermaster's Office, Woodville, Tex., 19 Nov. 1863, to E. P. Turner, Assistant Adjutant General, Houston, Tex., Confederate Military Records, Officers for William D. Douglas,

p. 50, ⟨www.footnote.com⟩. My thanks to Vicki Betts of the University of Texas at Tyler Library for supplying me with this letter.

15 Slaves made up 14 percent of Hardin County's and 16.1 percent of Angelina County's total populations in 1860 (McCaslin, "Voices of Reason," 176–94). Historically, more important Unionist rebellions occurred in Texas, among small wheat farmers of North Texas and German Texans of the Hill Country. In these regions, settled communities with strong religious or cultural bonds combined with kin-based, non-slaveholding traditions forged a Unionist solidarity that compared with that of the North Carolina Piedmont.

16 Quoted passage from Wooster and Wooster, "Rarin' for a Fight," 48.

17 Warren and Eboline Valentine Collins were related to a multitude of Knight Company members, including 1st Lt. James Morgan Valentine, 2nd Lt. Simeon Collins, and 1st Sgt. Jasper Collins. Another of Warren's brothers, Riley James Collins, was a private. Privates James Madison, Benjamin Franklin, and Morgan Columbus Collins, all sons of Simeon, were his nephews, as was Private Prentice M. Bynum, son of Warren's sister Margaret. Richard Hampton and John Ira Valentine, brothers of Eboline, were also Knight Company privates, as was Eboline's cousin, William Patrick Valentine. Through her mother, Cynthia Welch Valentine, she was related to four additional Knight Company privates: William M., Timothy L., Harrison R., and R. T. Welch. Kinship links between the Hardin County, Tex., and Jones County, Miss., Collinses were determined by research into Federal Manuscript Censuses and published genealogies. See especially Vinson A. Collins, *Story of My Parents*; and Bynum, *Free State of Jones*, 60–62. Military service, desertion, and membership in the Knight Company were traced from Compiled Service Records, 7th Battalion, Mississippi Infantry, War Department Collection of Confederate Records, NA; and Newton Knight Folder.

18 Knight Company roster, Newton Knight Folder.

19 Baum, *Shattering of Texas Unionism*, 52–56.

20 North Carolina contributed one-fourth of all deserters, although it contributed only one-sixth to one-seventh of the total number of soldiers who served the Confederacy. The state's greatest concentration of deserters was in Randolph County, where Bill Owens lived. See Yearns and Barrett, *North Carolina Civil War Documentary*, xii, 94.

21 Auman and Scarboro, "Heroes of America," 331.

22 Military records show that one William Owens, age thirty-three, from Moore County, N.C., enlisted as a private in the Confederate Army on 28 Apr. 1862 and deserted on 15 June 1862 ("American Civil War Soldiers," Ancestry.com). An unidentified report sent to Piedmont editors E. J. Hale & Sons reported 1,100 deserters in the Randolph, Moore, Chatham Counties border area (Auman, "Neighbor against Neighbor," 77.

23 R. P. Buxton to Gov. Vance, 20 Jan. 1863, Governors' Papers, Vance, NCDAH.

24 The 1863 arrest warrant in the Shamburger case revealed extensive kinship and neighborhood ties among Bill Owens and the fourteen men listed. None of the men owned slaves: Benjamin Northcutt, Elijah Spivey, Mark A. Spivey, Josiah Spivey, Temple Spivey, Asa Owens, William Owens, Emsley Owens, Riley Cagle, Henry

Cagle, James R. Phillips, Kisey Williams, Jesse Jordan, Enoch Jordan, and John Dunlap Jr. The Owens band's abuse of Officer Shamburger and others is described by James S. Dunn in a letter to newspaper editor E. J. Hale, which Hale in turn sent on to Gov. Zebulon Vance (Jas. S. Dunn to E. J. Hale & Sons, 8 Jan. 1863, Governors' Papers, Vance, NCDAH).

25 "Mr. Allen" was likely James G. Allen, who owned six slaves in 1860 and lived in the Montgomery County neighborhood from which the men wrote (U.S. Bureau of the Census, Federal Manuscript Census, Slave Schedules, 1860, Montgomery County, N.C.). The Freemans who petitioned Gov. Vance were brothers, and A. T. Parnell was their brother-in-law. R. W. Freeman, Harrison Freeman, and A. T. Parnell to Gov. Z. B. Vance, 5 July 1863, Governors' Papers, Vance, NCDAH.

26 R. W. Freeman, Harrison Freeman, and A. T. Parnell to Gov. Z. B. Vance, 5 July 1863, Governors' Papers, Vance, NCDAH. In the aftermath of the war, Amos T. Parnell was charged with armed burglary of the home of Lydia Jane Hussey (Criminal Action Papers, fall 1866, Montgomery County, NCDAH).

27 In 1860, Pleasant Simmons, who lived in Montgomery County, near the Randolph County border, owned four slaves (U.S. Bureau of the Census, Federal Manuscript Census, Population and Slave Schedules, 1860, Montgomery County, N.C.). His will, dated 18 March 1863, is posted on "Kay's Family Tree," at ⟨http://www.kaysfamilytree.com/simmons2.html⟩. Information about the Owens band's takeover of Simmons's silversmith shop is from letter of James S. Dunn to E. J. Hale, 8 Jan. 1863. Riley Cagle's status as a member of the Owens band and former employee of Simmons is mentioned in letter of Capt. J. H. Sands to Allen Jordan, 30 Aug. 1864, forwarded on 6 Sept. 1864 to Gov. Vance. Both in Governors' Papers, Vance, NCDAH.

28 Quoted from Auman, "Neighbor against Neighbor" (dissertation), 278–79; this eyewitness account appeared in the *Daily Confederate* on 27 Feb. 1864. William Owens, Murphy Owens, Riley Cagle, and John Latham were charged with the murders of Simmons and Sanders in 1864 and identified as Pleasant Simmons's murderers in 1869, during the settlement of Simmons's estate (*Martha Simmons, Admx, v. J. W. D. Moffitt and James McKenzie*, Minute Dockets of the Superior Court, fall term, 1869, Montgomery County, NCDAH). In the months following the murders, however, Murphy Owens and John Latham identified Riley Cagle as the trigger man. Also, according to Capt. J. H. Sands, Cagle confessed to having shot Pleasant Simmons while being held in the Richmond, Va., military prison on charges of desertion from Co. C, 16th N.C. Regiment (see Allen Jordan to Gov. Vance, 6 Sept. 1864, Governors' Papers, Vance, NCDAH). In 1869, James M. Leach, a pro-Union attorney and politician from Randolph County who represented Murphy Owens, described the fatal confrontation to Gov. Holden. In calling for the acquittal of Murphy Owens, Leach identified John Latham as the man who shot Jacob Sanders (J. M. Leach to Gov. William Holden, 1 Sept. 1869, Governors' Papers, Holden, NCDAH).

29 Peter Shamburger was married to Pleasant Simmons's daughter, Martha. Home Guard Capt. Alexander "Sandy" P. Leach was the son of Archibald Leach, brother to Pleasant Simmons's wife, Christian Leach Simmons (Richter, *Heritage of Montgomery County*, 272–73). Murphy Owens, age forty-two in 1860, apparently was

not a regular member of the Owens band, unlike his sons, Asa and Emsley Owens (see J. M. Leach to Gov. William Holden, 1 Sept. 1869, Governors' Papers, Holden, NCDAH).

30 Sanders's occupation was listed as "carpenter" on the Federal Manuscript Census of 1850; I have not found him on the 1860 Population Schedules, although he clearly still lived in the Randolph County area (see J. M. Leach to Gov. William Holden, 1 Sept. 1869, Governors' Papers, Holden, NCDAH; and U.S. Bureau of the Census, Federal Manuscript Census, Population and Slave Schedules, 1850, Montgomery County, N.C.).

31 For a more comprehensive treatment of women and the inner civil war in the North Carolina Central Piedmont, see chapter 2 in this volume; and Bynum, *Unruly Women*, 130–50.

32 Evidence of deliberate torturing of deserters' wives, most particularly that of Bill Owens, was especially abundant for the North Carolina Piedmont. The story of Mrs. Owens's confrontation with Confederate militia is described by Judge Thomas Settle in two letters to Gov. Zebulon Vance, one dated 21 Sept. 1864 (Governors' Papers, Vance, NCDAH) and the other 4 Oct. 1864 (reprinted from H. L. Carson Papers in Yearns and Barrett, *North Carolina Civil War Documentary*, 103–5). Judge Settle never referred to Mrs. Owens by her given name.

33 Yearns and Barrett, *North Carolina Civil War Documentary*, 104.

34 Ibid.

35 Ibid.; Auman, "Neighbor against Neighbor" (dissertation), 279. On the life and career of Judge Thomas Settle, see Crow, "Thomas Settle Jr.," 689–726.

36 Bynum, *Free State of Jones*, 115–29.

37 For details on the Lowry raid, see also ibid., 124–25. Newton Knight's handwritten roster, submitted to Congress in 1870, lists fifty-five men as having belonged to the Knight Company and delineates which ones were executed, captured, and "cut off," causing them to flee to New Orleans during the war. On 29 Jan. 1895, James Morgan Valentine testified to having been wounded and captured by Col. Lowry's men (Newton Knight Claims). By Newt's own admission, the list does not include every man who ever joined the band, only those who "held true" to its mission. Six of the members joined the Knight Company less than six weeks after Lowry's raid, indicating its continued viability (Newton Knight Folder; Bynum, *Free State of Jones*, 93–113).

38 Riley James Collins and Prentice Bynum enrolled in Co. E of the 1st Regiment, New Orleans Infantry, on 30 Apr. 1864 and 26 May 1864, respectively. Bynum enlisted at Ft. Pike and was mustered in at New Orleans on 28 May 1864. From 30 Oct. 1864 until 20 May 1865, he was hospitalized at University Hospital in New Orleans, at St. Louis General Hospital, and, finally, at McDougall General Hospital in New York harbor. Other Knight Company members listed on Newt Knight's 1870 roster who fled to the same Union regiment in New Orleans included Willis Jones, Elijah Welborn (Laird), Richard Welch, and James Knight. Additional Jones County men who joined the 1st Regiment, New Orleans Infantry, and may at some point have belonged to the Knight Company, include William M. Knight, Tolbert Welborn, Joel Walters, Drury Walters (died of smallpox on 24 Nov. 1864), Marada Walters

(died of chronic diarrhea on 27 Nov. 1864), and Richard Walters. Records of the 1st Regiment, New Orleans Infantry (Union Army), M396, roll 34, NA; Union Pension Files of Riley James Collins and Prentice Bynum, Claims for Pensions, NA.

39 Anonymous officer, Waynesboro, Miss., 3 May 1864, to *Mobile Daily Advertiser and Register*, printed 6 May 1864, clipping from James L. Power Scrapbook, MDAH.

40 Col. William N. Brown to Gov. Charles Clark, 5 May 1864, Governors' Papers, Clark, MDAH.

41 Stacy Collins reportedly died in Texas from erysipelas for lack of a doctor; his wife, Sarah Collins, was still alive in 1860, but apparently she died soon after the census for that year was recorded. Vinson A. Collins, *Story of My Parents*; U.S. Bureau of the Census, Federal Manuscript Census, 1860, Hardin County, Tex.

42 On the intertwined genealogies of the Collins, Valentine, Mathews, and Bynum families, see Bynum, *Free State of Jones*, 20–60, passim.

43 Newton Knight Folder. The report that Lydia Collins implored Col. Lowry to spare the life of her husband, Simeon, is discussed in the testimony of J. M. Valentine (who denied ever hearing it), 29 Jan. 1895, Newton Knight Claims.

44 Compiled Service Records, 7th Battalion, Mississippi Infantry, War Department Collection of Confederate Records, NA; Muster Roll of Capt. Lt. H. M. Hartfield, Co. (F) of the 7th Battalion Regiment of Mississippi Volunteers, Army of the Confederate States, Col. Sam D. Harris from the 31st day of November Oct. 1864 when last mustered, to the 28th day of Feb. 1865, ser. 390, box 273, RG 9, vol. 4, folder "7th Batt. Co. F #13," NA. (As in the case of a number of military records, the muster roll at first erroneously identified the 7th Battalion as a "regiment" but then crossed through that word. "November" was also crossed through and replaced with "Oct.")

45 Narrative of Elder J. K. Womack, quoted from *Confederate Veteran* 6, no. 12 (Dec. 1898), posted on "Treatment of Prisoners at Camp Morton," ⟨http://www.civilwarhistory .com⟩.

46 Information from "Camp Morton, Civil War Camp and Union Prison, Indianapolis, Ind., 1861–1865," ⟨http://freepages.history.rootsweb.com⟩.

47 Pitts, "Civil War and 'Kaiser's Burnout,'" 20–22.

48 For published military records of the Collins brothers, see Peebles, *There Never Were Such Men Before*, 89. On the characteristics of the Texas yeomanry, see Lowe and Campbell, *Planters and Plain Folk*.

49 "S" to Editor, *Houston Tri-Weekly Telegraph*, 21 Dec. 1864. My thanks to Vicki Betts of the University of Texas at Tyler Library for supplying me with this letter.

50 From the account of Lance Rosier, in Loughmiller and Loughmiller, *Big Thicket Legacy*, 71; and Betts, "A Sacred Charge upon Our Hands," 258–59.

51 Tevis, "Battle at Bad Luck Creek," 75–92.

52 Loughmiller and Loughmiller, *Big Thicket Legacy*, 72.

53 On the Collinses as jayhawkers and on the "Kaiser Burnout," see also Wooster and Wooster, "A People at War," 3–16; House, *Big Thicket*, 17–19; and Zuber, "Fire at Union Wells," 28.

54 Willis, *Short History of Hardin County*, 27–29.

55 According to William Auman, extreme secessionist Peter Garner, who combed the

woods in search of deserters, found Bill Owens at his secret camp. Owens was easily captured by the sheriff's posse because of the wound he had received at the Simmons home shoot-out (Auman, "Neighbor against Neighbor" [dissertation], 279, 393).

56 Ibid.

57 Newt Knight's and Warren Collins's postwar activities are analyzed, respectively, in chapters 4 and 5 in this volume.

58 Quoted passage on Warren Collins is from Schaadt, *History of Hardin County*, 20–21; interview with Newt Knight by Meigs Frost, *New Orleans Item*, 20 Mar. 1921.

CHAPTER TWO

1 Franny Jordan's confrontation with Confederate troops is detailed in a letter from Moore County resident Thomas W. Ritter to Gov. Zebulon B. Vance (25 Jan. 1864, Governors' Papers, Vance, NCDAH). Ritter identified Franny only as "Mrs. Jordan" and did not identify her female companions by name. I deduced Franny's first name by using clues in Ritter's letter, such as the surnames of her neighbors and the age of her son, to find the only Jordan family in the U.S. Bureau of the Census, Federal Manuscript Census for Carthage, Moore County, 1860, that matched Ritter's descriptions.

2 Ritter to Vance, 25 Jan. 1864, Governors' Papers, Vance, NCDAH.

3 The fact that Franny Jordan is referred to only as "Mrs. Jordan" by her defender, Thomas Ritter, signifies his equating of her identity with her status as a wife and mother. Likewise, the first name of guerrilla leader Bill Owens's wife, who was tortured by Confederate militia, was not provided by Thomas Settle when he reported the abuse to Gov. Zebulon Vance. On Southern women's behavior on the Civil War home front, see especially Whites, *Gender Matters*; Storey, *Loyalty and Loss*; Bynum, *Free State of Jones*; Williams, Williams, and Carlton, *Plain Folk in a Rich Man's War*; Inscoe and Kenzer, *Enemies of the Country*; and Edwards, *Scarlett Doesn't Live Here Anymore*.

4 Crofts, *Reluctant Confederates*, 133, 147, 154.

5 On slaveholders' opposition to secession in the Upper South, see especially ibid.; on policing of slaves and free blacks in Civil War North Carolina, see Escott, *Many Excellent People*, 41–43.

6 Petition from citizens of Goldsboro (Wayne County) to Gov. Jonathan Worth, Oct. 1867, Governors' Papers, Worth, NCDAH.

7 *State v. Henry Harrison Blalock*, County Court, June 1861, Superior Court, Sept. 1861, Criminal Action Papers, Orange County, NCDAH.

8 Charles Long, Claim #20593, n.d., Orange County, N.C., SCC-NA; Kenzer, *Kinship and Neighborhood*, 8–9, 66–96.

9 Sheffey Lindsey, Claim #6365, 24 Apr. 1874; James Pleasant Mason, Claim #11663; Mager Green quoted in Abner Dixon Claim #12791, Mar. 1877, Orange County, N.C.; all in SCC-NA.

10 Female-headed households made up 16.7 percent of total households in Orange County, compared with 12 percent and 11.5 percent in Granville and Montgomery

Counties, respectively. Their per capita wealth was only 63 percent that of male-headed households, compared to 80 percent and 94 percent in Granville and Montgomery Counties (Bynum, *Unruly Women*, 27–33). On similar conditions in neighboring Alamance County, see Beatty, *Alamance*, 86–88.

11 *State v. Rebecca Davis (or Carson), Nancy Bowers, and Nancy Carroll*, May 1864; *State v. Elizabeth Gilbert and Hawkins Browning*, Jan. 1865; all in Criminal Action Papers, Orange County, NCDAH.

12 Escott, "Poverty and Governmental Aid for the Poor in Confederate North Carolina," 462–80; Bynum, *Unruly Women*, 127–29.

13 U.S. Bureau of the Census, Federal Manuscript Census, 1850, Orange County, N.C.; Minutes of the Wardens of the Poor, Orange County, vol. 1, 1832–56, vol. 2, 1856–79, NCDAH.

14 U.S. Bureau of the Census, Federal Manuscript Census, 1850, Orange County, N.C.; Minutes of the Wardens of the Poor, Orange County, vol. 1, 1832–56, vol. 2, 1856–79, NCDAH; Bastardy Bonds, Orange County, NCDAH; charges of fornication and adultery are from Criminal Action Papers, Orange County, NCDAH.

15 U.S. Bureau of the Census, Federal Manuscript Census, 1850, Orange County, N.C.; Minutes of the Wardens of the Poor, Orange County, vol. 1, 1832–56, vol. 2, 1856–79, NCDAH; charge against Penny Gilbert for operating a disorderly house, Apr. 1862, Criminal Action Papers, Orange County, NCDAH.

16 Martha A. Sheets to Sheriff Aaron H. Sanders, 27 Jan. 1865, Criminal Action Papers, Montgomery County, NCDAH; see also Bynum, *Unruly Women*, 148. Sheriff A. H. Sanders owned twenty-eight slaves in 1860 (U.S. Bureau of the Census, Federal Manuscript Census, Slave Schedules, 1860, Montgomery County, N.C.). Martha Adeline Cranford Sheets was the daughter of Leonard Cranford, a nonslaveholding farmer who claimed property worth $550 in 1850 (U.S. Bureau of the Census, Federal Manuscript Census, Randolph County, N.C.). Martha married Lewis Sheets, a nonslaveholding miller, on 6 Jan. 1859 (Marriage Bonds, North Carolina, 1741–1868, Randolph County, NCDAH). Indicative of the manner in which communities overlapped county borders in the Randolph County area, Sheets threatened the Montgomery County sheriff even though she lived near Lassiter's Mill, on the Randolph County side of her community (U.S. Bureau of the Census, Federal Manuscript Census, 1860, Randolph County, N.C.).

17 I have found no evidence that Aaron H. Sanders obtained exemptions for adult sons Jesse A., Romulus F., or Aaron T. Sanders. In fall 1864, he served as state's witness against widow Sarah Atkins for harboring her son, James Atkins, who failed to report for Confederate duty. His son, Romulus F. Sanders, served as state's witness against James Meachum, James Blake, and John Yarbrough, all charged with harboring Confederate deserters or evaders who shared their surnames (all from Criminal Action Papers, Miscellaneous Records, Desertion, box 2, fall 1864, Montgomery County, NCDAH).

18 B. Craven to Gov. Clark, 13 Mar. 1862, Governors' Papers, Clark, NCDAH. Braxten Craven was the president of Trinity College, located in Randolph County; the school was later moved to Durham, where it became Duke University. Montgomery County was estimated in June 1864 to have about 200 deserters (Lt. T. H. Haughton,

Enrolling Officer of Montgomery County, to Capt. D. C. Pearson, Chief Enrolling Officer, Confederate Conscript Papers, SHC-UNC). Randolph County's desertion figures are from Auman, "Neighbor against Neighbor" (dissertation), 454. Other Central Piedmont Quaker Belt counties with high levels of opposition to the Confederacy were Chatham, Davidson, Forsyth, Guilford, Wilkes, and Yadkin.

19 Escott, *Many Excellent People*, 64–65; Crofts, *Reluctant Confederates*, 133, 154.

20 Kenzer, *Kinship and Neighborhood*, 29–51. On the demise of Quaker antislavery views, see Auman, "Neighbor against Neighbor" (dissertation), 15–16, 64–66. On the Moravians' gradual movement away from a more humane form of slavery that recognized individual rights during the period of the early republic to one more in line with that of traditional Southern slaveholders, see Sensbach, "Interracial Sects," 154–67. In 1852, Wesleyan leader Daniel Wilson reported eleven Wesleyan Methodist churches in four Quaker Belt counties: five in Guilford, one in Chatham, three in Randolph, and two in Montgomery (Auman, "Neighbor against Neighbor" [dissertation], 48–49). Martha Sheets's cousin, Malinda Cranford Beaman, and Malinda's husband, John Beaman, belonged to the same Wesleyan Methodist circle as did Martha Sheets. On Adam Crooks's address before the Lovejoy Church and genealogical links between the Cranford family and the Wesleyan Methodist Beaman, Hulin, Moore, and Hurley families, see Bynum, *Unruly Women*, 135–40; Nicholson, *Wesleyan Methodism in the South*, 53–76, 106–13; and Crooks, *Life of Reverend Adam Crooks*, 28–105.

21 Crofts, *Reluctant Confederates*, 133, 154; David Brown, *Southern Outcast*; David Brown, "Attacking Slavery from Within," 541–76; Helper, *Impending Crisis*, vi.

22 For a reexamination of Helper's racial views and the depth of his antislavery convictions, see David Brown, *Southern Outcast*.

23 For an analysis of the gender divisions among Northern abolitionists and free soil reformers and politicians, see Pierson, *Free Hearts, Free Homes*.

24 Over the course of the war, North Carolina's desertion rate averaged 12.2 percent and Randolph County's averaged 22.8 percent. Reid, "Test Case of the 'Crying Evil,'" 235; Bynum, *Unruly Women*, 130. On the Heroes of America, see Auman and Scarboro, "Heroes of America," 327–44; and Nelson, "Red Strings and Half Brothers," 37–53.

25 Auman, "Neighbor against Neighbor" (dissertation), 142–43; Capt. N. A. Ramsey, Commander of Co. D, 61st Regiment, North Carolina Troops, to Gov. Vance, 1 Feb. 1863, Governors' Papers, Vance, NCDAH.

26 U.S. Bureau of the Census, Federal Manuscript Census, 1860, Randolph County, Moore County, N.C. On Bryan Tyson's career as a Southern Unionist political agitator, see Auman, "Neighbor against Neighbor" (dissertation).

27 Ritter to Vance, 25 Jan. 1864, Governors' Papers, Vance, NCDAH.

28 See Bynum, *Unruly Women*, 132–33, for one example of a woman who delivered a "hearty blow" to an officer who had shot and wounded her son. All of the men quoted above lived near Adams Brewer in 1860. H. K. Trogden to Bryan Tyson, 23 Apr. 1864; Alexander K. Pearce to Bryan Tyson, Oct. 24, 1864; Israel Lowdermilk to Bryan Tyson, Oct. 20, 1864; all in Bryan Tyson Papers, Manuscripts Department, Duke University, Durham, N.C. I have found no record of Brewer in the 1870 cen-

sus, but his indictment for the murder of George Moon (Moore?) in 1866 indicates he survived the war. See Auman, "Neighbor against Neighbor" (dissertation), 277.

29 H. W. Ayer to Gov. Vance, 10 Mar. 1863, Governors' Papers, Vance, NCDAH.

30 H. W. Ayer to Vance, 10 Mar. 1863, ibid.; 1st Lt. Wm. A. Pugh to Maj. Archer Anderson, A. A. General, 21 Mar. 1863, ibid. Henry W. Ayer is identified as state agent for contracts, in Watford, *Piedmont*, 79. I did not find Loton Williams in either the Population or the Slave Schedules for 1860. He is listed as a nonslaveholding farmer in the 1850 U.S. Bureau of the Census, Federal Manuscript Census for Alamance County and as a farmer with combined real and personal property valued at $900 in the 1870 Randolph County Federal Manuscript Census.

31 Ayer to Vance, 10 Mar. 1863, Governors' Papers, Vance, NCDAH.

32 Ibid.; Pugh to Anderson, 21 Mar. 1863, ibid. For a description of Nancy Hoover's losses, estimated at $197.15, and of Pugh's grudging payment to her of $100, see letter from her lawyer, Thomas M. Moore, to Maj. Gen. D. H. Hill, 25 June 1863, ibid.

33 Z. B. Vance to Gen. D. H. Hill, 22 Apr. 1863, ibid.; Pugh to Anderson, 21 Mar. 1863, ibid.

34 Auman and Scarboro, "Heroes of America," 347. D. C. Pearson's remarks came in response to Thomas Morris's petition for exemption (22 Feb. 1864, Office of the Enrolling Officer, Seventh N.C. Congressional District, Confederate Conscript Papers, SHC-UNC).

35 P. H. Williamson to D. C. Pearson, 5 Aug. 1864, Confederate Conscript Papers, SHC-UNC; Auman, "Neighbor against Neighbor" (dissertation), 226, 368.

36 J. M. Worth to Gov. Vance, 9 Aug. 1864 (emphasis mine); Iver D. Patterson to Gov. Vance, 24 Dec. 1864; both in Governors' Papers, Vance, NCDAH. Patterson's personal estate, which included nine slaves in 1860, was valued at $10,000 (U.S. Bureau of the Census, Federal Manuscript Census, 1860, Population and Slave Schedules, Randolph County, N.C.).

37 On the torture of Bill Owens's wife, see chapter 1 in this volume; and Bynum, *Unruly Women*, 143–44. On Confederate policy in regard to millers providing services for deserters' wives, see J. S. Patterson to Gov. Vance, 15 June 1863; and William Thomas to Gov. Vance, 11 Aug. 1864; both in Governors' Papers, Vance, NCDAH.

38 Clarinda Hulin to Gov. Vance, 20 Nov. 1863, Governors' Papers, Vance, NCDAH. Clarinda Crook Hulin and Phebe Crook were the daughters of William and Rachel Crook of Montgomery County (U.S. Bureau of the Census, Federal Manuscript Census, 1850, Montgomery County, N.C.). Clarinda married Nelson Hulin on 15 Jan. 1855 (Marriage Bonds, Montgomery County, NCDAH). Although the couple lived in Montgomery County in 1860, Clarinda's letter was addressed from Randolph County.

39 Phebe Crook to Gov. Vance, 15 Sept. 1864, Governors' Papers, Vance, NCDAH. Crook's letter was addressed from Davidson County, although she advised Gov. Vance to direct his response to Salem Church in Randolph County.

40 Ibid.

41 Hiram Hulin and sons Nelson and Jesse were charged with circulating "seditious publications" in March 1860 (Minute Dockets of the Superior Court, Montgomery County, NCDAH). On the Hulin family's conversion to Wesleyan Methodism,

membership in the Lovejoy Methodist Church, support for Wesleyan antislavery leaders Adam Crooks and Daniel Wilson, and their harassment by neighbors and militia during the war, see Bynum, *Unruly Women*, 24–25, 142–49.

42 The Hulin brothers and Atkins were reportedly killed early on the morning of 28 Jan. after being tied down in a "cold basement," presumably in the jail. It is possible that Sheets's letter was misdated and written in response to the executions (narrative of Thoburn M. Freeman, in Richter, *Heritage of Montgomery County*, 316–17).

43 Hiram Hulin to Col. M. Cogwell, Commanding the Post of Fayetteville, N.C., 28 Sept. 1867, printed in McPherson, "Letters from North Carolina to Andrew Johnson," 118–19. My thanks to William Auman for bringing this letter to my attention. On 9 July 1879, a letter from G. M. Hardy to the *American Wesleyan* recalled the deaths of the Hulin brothers. The writer described the oldest Hulin son as "an exhorter in the Wesleyan Church" and erroneously described the youngest of the executed brothers as "a lad of twelve years."

44 Charges against Sarah Atkins for harboring James Atkins are in Criminal Action Papers, Montgomery County, fall 1864, spring 1865, miscellaneous box #2, NCDAH. As late as 1980, a Hulin descendant recounted that one "Aaron Saunders" was among the "officers in charge" (quoted from narrative of Thoburn M. Freeman, in Richter, *Heritage of Montgomery County*, 316–17). The story of the Hulin brothers' murder was revisited on 22 Oct. 2003 by the *Montgomery Herald* (Troy, N.C.). My thanks to Allen Green of Star, N.C., for providing me with a copy of this article (Bynum files).

45 A. C. McAlister's orders were quoted by Jno. M. Waddill on 6 March 1865, Alexander Carey McAlister Papers, SHC-UNC.

46 For an indication that Confederate soldiers may have aimed guns at women to force compliance or achieve arrest, see an Iredell County letter to Gov. Vance that claimed that military forces had "presented their guns at a lady in Alexander County" (Auman, "Neighbor against Neighbor" [dissertation], 287).

47 Thomas Settle to Gov. Z. B. Vance, 4 Oct. 1864, quoted in Yearns and Barrett, *North Carolina Civil War Documentary*, 104.

48 Maj. J. G. Harris, Commander, 7th NCT, Headquarters, to Lt. Col. McAlister, Asheboro, 27 Mar. 1865, Alexander Carey McAlister Papers, SHC-UNC.

49 Letter of Lt. McAlister, 16 Mar. 1865, contained in Report to Gen. Lee, 30 Mar. 1865, ibid.; Lt. Jno. M. Waddell, to Maj. J. G. Harris, Commander, 7th NCT, 30 Mar. 1865, ibid.

50 U.S. Bureau of the Census, Federal Manuscript Census, 1870, Orange County, N.C.

51 Kenzer, *Kinship and Neighborhood*, 128–47; Escott, *Many Excellent People*. On the gendered nature of Civil War rhetoric and mythmaking, before and after the war, see Whites, *Civil War as a Crisis in Gender*.

52 Ramsey not only ignored Southern unionists but refused even to credit Northern soldiers for the Union's victory, insisting that the Confederacy was "crushed not by the people of the North but by the hundreds of thousands of foreign trash, who fought for money and not for the love of the union." N. A. Ramsey, "61st North Carolina Infantry," Durham, 1901, ⟨http://members.aol.com/jweaver301/nc/61ncinf.htm⟩.

53 Ibid.

PART TWO

1 Testimony of J. M. Valentine, 29 Jan. 1895, Newton Knight Claims.

2 *Journal of the Proceedings and Debates in the Constitutional Convention of the State of Mississippi, August, 1865.* Thomas G. Crawford owned two slaves in 1860. In 1895, he supported remuneration for Newton Knight and his men for having supported the Union during the war and testified on behalf of Knight. In his deposition, he claimed to have joined the Knight band himself, in May 1864, although his name does not appear on Newt Knight's roster (testimony of T. G. Crawford, 8 Mar. 1895, Newton Knight Claims).

CHAPTER THREE

1 Col. Samuel Thomas to [?], Sept. 1865, Records of the Assistant Commissioner for the State of Mississippi, Freedmen's Bureau Papers, M826, reel 1. For a synthesis of the violence and failures of Reconstruction, see especially Fitzgerald, *Splendid Failure*; and Foner, *Reconstruction*.

2 Report of Clinton A. Cilley, Brevet Col. A.A.G., superintendent of the West District, Salisbury, N.C., to Col. E. Whittlesey, 30 Dec. 1865, Raleigh, N.C., ser. 2837, Letters Received, Freedmen's Bureau Papers.

3 Ibid.

4 On Reconstruction North Carolina, see especially Edwards, *Gendered Strife and Confusion*, 24–65; Zipf, "Whites Shall Rule the Land or Die," 499–534; and Escott, *Many Excellent People*, 85–135.

5 Kenzer, *Kinship and Neighborhood*, 66–70; Crofts, *Reluctant Confederates*, 334–47; Auman, "Neighbor against Neighbor" (dissertation), 494–500. Lloyd, Bowers, and Ivey were described as Unionists by witness William Lloyd Sr., in Joseph Ivey Claim #37087, 24 Mar. 1875, Orange County, N.C., SCC-NA.

6 William W. Guess described his own Unionist views while a witness for John Cole Claim #12789 and Samuel Cole Claim #12790, Mar. 1877, Orange County, SCC-NA.

7 Nancy Brewer purchased her husband, Green Brewer, a slave, sometime before 1858, when she bought a home and lot in the town of Chapel Hill. Brewer and Nelly Stroud quoted in Nancy Brewer Claim #11545, Orange County, SCC-NA.

8 Escott, *Many Excellent People*, 150–52. On mountain Republicans, see McKinney, *Southern Mountain Republicans*.

9 Zipf, "Whites Shall Rule the Land or Die," 503–4; Crow, "Thomas Settle Jr.," 701–6.

10 Zipf, "Whites Shall Rule the Land or Die," 524–25, 534; Escott, *Many Excellent People*, 152–67. For a profile of North Carolina's black legislators during Reconstruction, see Balanoff, "Negro Legislators in the North Carolina General Assembly," 22–55.

11 Escott, *Many Excellent People*, 158, 160; Beatty, *Alamance*, 110–17. For an account of Orange County Reconstruction written from the perspective of a local multiracial family, see Murray, *Proud Shoes*, 166–228.

12 *The State*, Mar. 1961.

13 David Schenck Diary, Dec. 1868, David Schenck Books, SHC-UNC; Reminiscences of Jacob Alson Long, SHC-UNC. Long so believed that Klan violence was justified by events that in 1915 he freely admitted to many Klan acts of terrorism.

14 David Schenck Diary, Dec. 1868, David Schenck Books, SHC-UNC; Petition to Gov. Worth from Citizens of Chapel Hill, 18 Nov. 1867, Governors' Papers, Worth, NCDAH.

15 Petition on behalf of Green Durham, 18 Nov. 1867, Orange County, Governors' Papers, Worth, NCDAH.

16 Crow, "Thomas Settle Jr.," 705–16.

17 Testimony of Squire Alston, Criminal Action Papers, 1868–69, Orange County, NCDAH. Alston identified the three men as John Alvis Thompson, Calvin Gibson, and James Gibson.

18 S. B. Williams to Gov. Holden, 16 Sept. 1869, Governors' Papers, Holden, NCDAH.

19 James B. Mason to Gov. Holden, 22 Sept. 1869, Governors' Papers, Holden, NCDAH. Wright Malone was reported hanged by "persons unknown"; witness Squire Malone described his captors to the coroner. I was unable to identify Wright Malone, but Squire, more than likely kin to him, was described as a fifty-one-year-old black laborer in 1870. Coroner's Report, Sept. 1869, Orange County, N.C., NCDAH; U.S. Bureau of the Census, Federal Manuscript Census, 1870, Wake County, N.C.

20 Beatty, *Alamance*, 110–11.

21 Gov. Holden to Chief Justice Richmond Pearson, 19 July 1870, no. 386, Governors' Letter Books, Holden, NCDAH; Escott, *Many Excellent People*, 162–63.

22 One month later, E. McCroray of Hillsboro informed Gov. Holden that the sheriff of that town had been forced to release two black prisoners to Klansmen. One was shot to death; the other escaped, only to be captured later along with his father and hanged (E. McCroray to Gov. Holden, 13 Feb. 1871, William Woods Holden Collection, Manuscripts Department, Duke University, Durham, N.C.). Other blacks listed by Mason and the others as beaten by Klan members included Giss Loyd (described as almost hanged), Champion Mason, and Dapper Davis. In addition to Nathaniel King, several white Orange County Republicans were also listed as beaten: Eaton Walker, David Reeves, William Husky, Sidney Dollar, and Henry Snipes (Report of KKK Outrages in Orange County by James B. Mason, Andrew J. King, and Turner King to Gov. Holden, 10 Jan. 1871, ibid.).

23 For reasons unspecified, the wife and son of Jerry Mason, a black man, were also reported beaten by the Klan; ibid. For charges of fornication against Sampson and Mary Atwater, see *State v. Mary Atwater and Sampson Atwater*, Superior Court, fall 1869, Criminal Action Papers, Orange County, NCDAH. On freedwomen during Reconstruction, see O'Donovan, *Becoming Free*; Bercaw, *Gendered Freedoms*; Schwalm, *A Hard Fight for We*; Hunter, *To 'Joy My Freedom*, 21–43; Edwards, *Gendered Strife and Confusion*; Clinton, "Reconstructing Freedwomen," 306–19; and Jacqueline Jones, *Labor of Love*, 44–78.

24 Kenzer, *Kinship and Neighborhood*, 133–41.

25 Tinnin, born around 1800, owned fourteen slaves in 1860. The men attending the corn shucking may all have been his former slaves (U.S. Bureau of the Census, Federal Manuscript Census, Population and Slave Schedules, 1850, 1860, 1870, Orange

County, N.C.). Details of the case are from *State v. Catlett C. Tinnin*, Superior Court, spring 1867, Criminal Action Papers, 1866–67, Orange County, NCDAH.

26 *State v. Catlett C. Tinnin.*

27 Ibid.

28 On race mixing and social control in the Old South, see especially Forret, *Race Relations at the Margins*, 184–222; Edwards, "Law, Domestic Violence," 733–70; and Bynum, *Unruly Women*, 88–110.

29 Bynum, *Unruly Women*, 88–110.

30 Bastardy Bonds, 1866, Orange County, NCDAH.

31 Graham's use of plural nouns indicated that he did not intend that the favor be extended to only his "young friend." John W. Graham, Hillsboro, N.C., to Col. H. B. Guthrie, Chapel Hill, N.C., 19 Aug. 1866. I found Graham's letter lying loose among the Bastardy Bonds, Orange County, NCDAH.

32 19 Aug. 1866, 21 Aug. 1866, Bastardy Bonds, Orange County, NCDAH.

33 Zipf, *Labor of Innocents*, 8–39.

34 Bynum, *Unruly Women*, 99–103; Franklin, *Free Negro in North Carolina*, 122–30.

35 Litwack, *Been in the Storm So Long*, 191, 237–38, 365–66. On Reconstruction policies concerning apprenticeship of former slaves, see Indentures of Apprenticeship, Sept. 1865–Dec. 1866, ser. 2489, and Register of Indentured Apprentices, Nov. 1865–June 1866, ser. 2488, Freedmen's Bureau Papers.

36 Petition of Lila McDonald, Civil Action Papers, 12 Apr. 1869, Montgomery County, NCDAH.

37 Zipf, *Labor of Innocents*, 129–52.

38 Petition of Alex Corbin, Probate Court, 13 May 1871, Civil Action Papers, Orange County, NCDAH.

39 Ibid.

40 Appeal in the matter of the Petition of Alex Corbin from Probate Court, Superior Court, 7th Judicial District, Albion W. Tourgee, Judge, ibid. On the political affiliation of Isaac Strayhorn, see Kenzer, *Kinship and Neighborhood*, 138. On Albion Tourgee's career as a Klan-fighting Republican judge in Reconstruction North Carolina, see Olsen, *Carpetbagger's Crusade*.

41 Ben Harris to Mr. W. L. Miller, agent, 15 Jan. 1867, and Wm. Andrews to Col. Jno R. Edie, Superintendent, 15 Feb. 1867, both in Letters Received, Freedmen's Bureau Papers; Zipf, *Labor of Innocents*, 49.

42 D. C. Parrish to Lt. Isaac Porter, Assistant Superintendent, Sub-district of Orange and Alamance Counties, 14 Sept. 1867, Letters Received, May 1866–Dec. 1868, ser. 2686, Freedmen's Bureau Papers.

43 Some former slaveholders wanted nothing to do with freedpeople at all; see Escott, *Many Excellent People*, 120–21; E. A. Harris, Lt. and Assistant Superintendent, 25 Dec. 1865, to Col. C. A. Cilley, Letters Received, ser. 2837, Freedmen's Bureau Papers; and Zipf, *Labor of Innocents*, 47.

44 G. R. Marcom to Benjamin Markham, 11 June 1866, Benjamin Markham Papers, Manuscripts Department, Duke University, Durham, N.C. On black men and issues of masculinity in the nineteenth century, see Black, *Dismantling Black Manhood*; Hine, *19th Century*; and hooks, "Plantation Patriarchy," in hooks, *We Real Cool*, 1–14.

45 Quoted in Kenzer, *Kinship and Neighborhood*, 136–37. On black women's assertive-
ness during Reconstruction, see especially Schwalm, "Sweet Dreams of Freedom,"
11–40; Edwards, *Scarlett Doesn't Live Here Anymore*, 125–48; Edwards, *Gendered Strife
and Confusion*, 145–56; Mann, "Slavery, Sharecropping, and Sexual Inequality"; and
Jacqueline Jones, *Labor of Love*, 52–72.

46 John W. Graham was the son of antebellum North Carolina senator and governor
William A. Graham. He served as Conservative Party delegate to the 1868 state convention. While running as the Democratic candidate for state treasurer, the younger
Graham supported amnesty for members of the Klan. For a contemporary attack on
his role in "redeeming" North Carolina from Republican rule during Reconstruction, see Republican campaign essay "Read and Circulate! The Elections in August
Impose upon the People of North Carolina One of the Most Solemn and Important
Duties That Citizens Were Ever Called Upon to Perform" [1872?], 2002, *Documenting the American South*, SHC-UNC. On Graham's political history, see Zipf, "Whites
Shall Rule the Land or Die," 509–15; and Kenzer, *Kinship and Neighborhood*, 129–30,
139–40.

47 Henderson warned Yarbro that he and Harriet had signed a contract with the Freed-
men's Bureau twelve months before and that it was "against civil law" to evict her.
Chas. Yarbro, to Mr. Henderson, 8 Feb. 1867, and W. J. Henderson to J. R. Edie, 7
Feb. 1867, Letters Received, ser. 2837, Freedmen's Bureau Papers.

48 J. Cowles to Capt. Wm. Jones, subdivision of Statesville, 23 July 1867, and W. H.
Worden to Col. Edie, 27 Aug. 1866, ibid.

49 Alfred Gray to Gen. Sickels, Commander, Military District #2, 12 Apr. 1867, and
A. Dilworth, Agent, to Col. Edie, 15 May 1867, ibid.

50 McFeely, *Yankee Stepfather*, 317; *State v. Scinthia Mary McQuin* [Linda Mary McQueen],
woman of color, for concealing the birth of a child, 28 Aug. 1867, Minute Dockets
of the Superior Court, Montgomery County, NCDAH.

51 Ten of Butler's seventeen witnesses at the new trial were African American; all nine
state's witnesses, except for Linda McQueen, were white. *State (Linder McQueen) v.
Harry Butler*, Mar. 1867, Criminal Action Papers, Montgomery County, NCDAH;
Scinday Mary McQuin [Linda Mary McQueen] *v. Harry Butler*, 28 Aug. 1867, Minute
Dockets of the Superior Court, Montgomery County, NCDAH.

52 *Scinday Mary McQuin* [Linda Mary McQueen] *v. Harry Butler*, 11 Sept. 1867, Criminal
Action Papers, Montgomery County, NCDAH; Attorney B. F. Simmons to Brevet
Maj. Gen. Nelson A. Miles, Commissioner, Freedmen's Bureau for N.C., and Wm.
McFarland, Agent, Freedmen's Bureau, to Col. M. Cogswell, Sub Assistant Com-
missioner, 10 Oct. 1867, Letters Received, Freedmen's Bureau Papers. This case is also
discussed in Bynum, "On the Lowest Rung," 40–44.

53 On wartime and postwar attacks on previously tolerated interracial marriages, see
Bynum, *Unruly Women*, 124–25. On postwar changes in the law in Southern states
in regard to race relations, see especially Bardaglio, *Reconstructing the Household*,
115–213.

54 Deed of Diza Ann Williams, sworn before I. M. Deaton, Registrar of Deeds, 6 Feb.
1884, Miscellaneous Books, #3, folder #25, Montgomery County, NCDAH.

55 Evidence that Wilson and Dicey Williams's marriage was treated as legal may be

found in Wilson's application for an exemption from military service during the Civil War. See letter of enrolling officer Lt. T. H. Haughton recommending Williams be exempted even "though his wife [is] a white woman"; Letter Book of Chief Enrolling Office, Seventh Congressional District, Lexington, N.C., 1864, Confederate Conscript Papers, SHC-UNC; Federal Manuscript Census, Population Schedule, 1860, Montgomery County, NCDAH. (In the same census for 1880, Wilson Williams was noted as divorced.) For a theoretical overview of the political construction of racial identification, see Powell, "*Passing" for Who You Really Are.*

56 *John Hopkins, Alexander Hopkins, Sally Hopkins (by Alexander Hopkins), Robert Daniel and wife Emma Daniel, Thomas Adcock and wife Larcena, Jordan Nance and wife Sally v. Ann (Bowers) Boothe and daughters Eliza and Nannie (Bowers) Boothe*, Superior Court, 1888–92, Estate Records, Orange County, NCDAH. At the time she was sued, Ann was living in a separate house on John Johnston's land. Johnston, his brother, and his mother, Polly Johnston, had all been harassed by the Klan in 1869, as had another black neighbor, Madison Nunn (Report of KKK Outrages in Orange County by James B. Mason et al., William Woods Holden Collection, Manuscripts Department, Duke University, Durham, N.C.). Ann was also linked to Unionism through Cannon Bowers, a prosperous Durham farmer (Federal Manuscript Census, Population Schedules, 1860, 1870, Orange County, NCDAH).

57 Mary Jane Boothe charged her husband, Nash, with marrying her and then abandoning her and their child in 1873 and with committing adultery with Easter Carroll in 1874. Charges of adultery also included the name of Ann Bowers, which was later crossed out. In 1870, Lydia Bowers, age thirty-eight, was listed as head of a household in Durham Township that included George Bowers, age twenty-one, Ann Eliza Bowers, age sixteen, Nash Boothe, age thirty-eight, and Annie Dollar, age thirty. I have found no marriage record for Nash Boothe and Ann Bowers, although Ann claimed they were married in Wake County on 30 May 1876. The ages listed for Ann and Nash in the 1870 census conflict with her statement that she was twenty-four and he thirty-eight years old when they married, which shortened the gap in their ages from twenty-two to fourteen years. Lydia Bowers disappears from the records after 1872 and probably died around that time. *Mary Jane Boothe v. Nash Boothe*, Superior Court, fall 1875, Divorce Records, Orange County; U.S. Bureau of the Census, Federal Manuscript Census, Population Schedule, 1870, Orange County, N.C.; *State v. Lydia Bowers and Nash Boothe*, fornication, Superior Court, 1872, Criminal Action Papers, Orange County, all in NCDAH.

58 *State v. Dr. Bartlett L Durham*, A&B [assault and battery] on Nash Boothe, and *State v. Nash Boothe*, A&B on Bartlett Durham, both in May 1854; *State v. Nash Boothe*, A&B on George Trice, fall 1866; Peace Warrant against Nash Boothe by Cate and Victoria Dezerne and Tapley Patterson, Aug. 1871; all in Criminal Action Papers, Orange County, NCDAH. Petition of Nash Boothe and seventeen signatories to Gov. Holden, 17 June 1870, Governors' Papers, Holden, NCDAH; Deposition of Katy Carroll, *Hopkins et al. v. Bowers et al.*, NCDAH.

59 Deposition of Katy Carroll, *Hopkins et al. v. Bowers et al.*, NCDAH.

60 *Hopkins et al. v. Bowers et al.*, NCDAH.

61 Ibid. Quote from Lewis Pratt's half-brother, Louis Jenkins. Lydia Bower's friend,

Katy Carroll (aka Katy Gilbert), insisted that Alexander Copley was Ann's father and that Lydia had sworn to that in a court of law.

62 Ibid.

63 Ibid.

64 In 1870, forty-year-old Katy Carroll, aka Katy Gilbert, was living in a household headed by eighty-seven-year-old Archy Carroll, likely her father. The household also included Betsy Rue, age thirty-seven, and Easter Carroll (named in Mary Ann Boothe's 1872 divorce petition as having committed adultery with her husband, Nash Boothe), age twenty-two. In 1850, 1860, and 1870, Archy Carroll was listed as a farmer, but no value was assigned him in real estate. In 1860, his personal estate was valued at $300. U.S. Bureau of the Census, Federal Manuscript Census, Population Schedules, 1850, 1860, 1870, Orange County, N.C.

65 *Hopkins et al. v. Bowers et al.*, NCDAH.

66 Ibid.

67 Ibid.

68 Ann Boothe appears to have continued to be identified as "black" after this trial. The 1900 Federal Manuscript Census for Orange County listed an "Annie Boothe," age forty (according to the 1870 census, Ann would have been forty-six in 1900) and "black," living in Chapel Hill. This Boothe was listed as having given birth seven times, twice since the trial, which is consistent with Ann's statement that she and Nash Boothe had five children together. In the household is a daughter named Nannie, also consistent with court records. *Hopkins et al. v. Bowers et al.*, NCDAH; quoted passage from Col. Samuel Thomas, Sept. 1865, Letters Received, Freedmen's Bureau Papers. On the historical progression of the "one drop rule," see Sweet, *Legal History of the Color Line.*

CHAPTER FOUR

1 J. F. H. Claiborne to Attorney General of United States, 10 Aug. 1873, in Records of the Commissioner of Claims, 1871–80 (microfilm no. 18333, reel 3), NA. Claiborne, who lived in New Orleans in 1873, served in the Mississippi House of Representatives from 1830 to 1834 and in the U.S. House of Representatives from 1835 to 1837. He was a Unionist during the Civil War. His famous essay, "A Trip through the Piney Woods," was published in the *Natchez Free Trader and Gazette*, 1841–42, and reprinted in *Publications of the Mississippi Historical Society* 9 (1906): 487–538. For a discussion of that article, see Bynum, *Free State of Jones*, 68–72.

2 The Southern Claims Commission (SCC) began accepting petitions in March 1871, after Newt Knight had filed under previous claims rules. When Congress closed the SCC in 1880, only one-third of claim applications had been allowed. More research is needed on the history of the SCC and on the reluctance of Congress to approve its claims. The most complete work, Klingberg, *Southern Claims Commission*, is now fifty-five years old. A promising recent work on African Americans' appeals to the SCC during their transition to freedom is Penningroth, *Claims of Kinfolk.*

3 *New South*, 15 June 1895, in B. T. Collins Jr. research files. For excellent analyses of the rewriting of Civil War history according to nostalgic memories and a desire for

national reconciliation, see Brundage, *Southern Past*; Fahs and Waugh, *Memory of the Civil War*; and Blight, *Race and Reunion*.

4 The voluminous documentation for Newt's three claims was filed away, the pre-1873 claim in one place and the post-1887 claims in another. The National Archives and Records Commission, created in Washington, D.C., in 1946, thus holds two separate sets of Newton Knight Claims. The first set, pertaining to the years 1870–73, is filed as Newton Knight Folder, box 15, Records of the U.S. House of Representatives, RG 233, NA (here cited as Newton Knight Folder), and is discussed in Bynum, *Free State of Jones*, 141–42. The second set, pertaining to the years 1887–1907, is filed as Claims of Newton Knight and Others, #8013 and #8464, Committee on War Claims, Records of the U.S. Court of Claims, 1835–1966, RG 123 (here cited as Newton Knight Claims). The latter claims are cited and quoted in Jenkins and Stauffer, *State of Jones*, as proof of Newt Knight's Unionism, but the authors offer no analysis of the claims process itself. Independent researcher Kenneth Welch obtained copies of the second set of Newton Knight's claim files in 1981. I am grateful to him for sharing these files with me in 2001.

5 Affidavit of Newton Knight, certified by T. J. Collins, Acting Justice of the Peace, Jones County, Miss., 15 Oct. 1870, Newton Knight Folder. In letters concerning Newt's claim, Benagah Mathews sometimes signed himself as "B. A. Mathews, Probate Judge," but usually used no official title. Mathews was kin to Lazarus Mathews, a member of the Knight band. His daughter, Caroline, married band member James Madison (Matt) Collins.

6 Staples to be handed over to Newton Knight included 2,400 lbs of bacon, 2,000 lbs of flour, 1,250 lbs of bread, 82 lbs of soap, 82 lbs of salt, and a large quantity of molasses. Requisition, O. S. Coffin, 16 July 1865, Newton Knight Folder.

7 The above-cited letters are in Newton Knight Folder. For more details on the military orders obeyed by Newt Knight in July and August 1865 and on his conflicted relationship with Amos Deason, see Bynum, *Free State of Jones*, 133–35.

8 The original roster is in the possession of Florence Knight Blaylock, of Soso, Miss., great-granddaughter of Newt Knight and Rachel Knight; Copy of Roster, Newton Knight Folder.

9 Certified letter of John Mathews, Allen Valentine, H. L. Sumrall, James Hinton, and Madison Herrington, 15 Oct. 1870, Newton Knight Folder. The statement that these men had "no interest" in the outcome of the suit ignored kinship ties: John Mathews was the son of Benagah Mathews; Allen Valentine was the father of several men who belonged to the band; James Hinton was the uncle of band member Richard (Dick) Hinton; H. L. Sumrall was the brother of William W. Sumrall; and Madison Herrington's daughter, Annabelle, was married to Benagah Mathews's son, Joel.

10 Ibid.

11 Ibid. Prentice M. Bynum was a former member of the band. T. J. Collins is not listed on the roster as a member, but his father and three brothers are. The printed bill for relief of Newton Knight et al. spelled out the amount of financial compensation sought and identified each Knight Company man's "rank": Capt. Newton Knight, $2,000; 1st Lt. James Morgan Valentine, $1,800; 2nd Lt. Simeon Collins, $1,600; 1st Sgt. J. J. Collins, $350; 2nd Sgt. W. P. Turnbow, $350; 1st Corp. Alpheus Knight, $325;

2nd Corp. Samuel G. Owens, $325. Forty-eight privates, or their survivors, were to receive $300 each. The total requested was $21,150.

12 B. A. Mathews to Honorable L. W. Price [Perce] & G. C. McKee, 8 Dec. 1870, Newton Knight Folder.

13 Wm. M. Hancock's letter is dated 10 Dec. 1870; Richard Simmons's is dated 6 Dec. 1870. Both are in Newton Knight Folder.

14 H.R. 2775, 16 Jan. 1871, *Journal of the House of Representatives, 3rd Sess., 41st Cong.*, 158; L. W. Perce to B. A. Mathews, 14 Jan. 1871, 16 Jan. 1871, 20 Jan. 1871, 3 July 1871, in Ames Family Papers, Sophia Smith Collection, Smith College, Northampton, Mass. In his 16 Jan. letter to Mathews, Perce explained that he arrived too late to introduce the bill and that he arranged for Rep. George Whitmore of Texas to do so in his stead.

15 L. W. Perce to B. A. Mathews, 16 Apr. 1872, Ames Family Papers, Smith College, Northampton, Mass. For Rep. Perce's presentation of the bill, see H.R. 1814, 4 Mar. 1872, *Journal of the House of Representatives, 2nd Sess., 42nd Cong.*, 446.

16 G. C. McKee to B. A. Mathews, 20 June 1872, Ames Family Papers, Sophia Smith Collection, Smith College, Northampton, Mass.; Simmons to McKee, 6 Dec. 1870, Newton Knight Folder. For more on McKee's politics, see Bond, *Political Culture*, 275; and Wharton, *Negro in Mississippi*, 158, 181.

17 B. A. Mathews to Hon. A. Ames, 21 Nov. 1873, 28 Nov. 1873, Ames Family Papers, Sophia Smith Collection, Smith College, Northampton, Mass. Mathews included in his "package" a new copy of the Knight Company roster that appears from the handwriting to have been written by Mathews himself.

18 Note from A. Ames directing secretary to answer to B. A. Mathews, 4 Dec. 1873, Ames Family Papers, Sophia Smith Collection, Smith College, Northampton, Mass. For Sen. Ames's presentation of the bill, see S. 219, 18 Dec. 1873, *Journal of the Senate, 1st Sess., 43rd Cong.*, 85; For Rep. Howe's presentation of the bill, see H.R. 822, 18 Dec. 1873, *Journal of the House of Representatives, 1st Sess., 43rd Cong.*, 160.

19 Albert Richards Howe, a Panola County Republican born in Massachusetts, represented Mississippi in the 43rd Congress from Mar. 1873 to Mar. 1875.

20 I have found no reference to the Knight Company as the "Jones County Scouts," either before or after the period of these latter claims. Following the narrative of Newt's petition was a list of the same fifty-five men identified on the roster that Newt had prepared for the original bills submitted between 1870 and 1873. This list, however, was not written in Newt's hand and contained none of the details of enlistment, execution, or "reenlistment" at New Orleans contained on the first roster. It was titled, simply, "Roll of Jones County Scouts, Jones Co., Miss." Petition of Newton Knight, a citizen of the State of Mississippi, to the Senate and House of Representatives of the United States of America, in Congress assembled, 22 Nov. 1887, Newton Knight Claims.

21 Ibid.

22 John Bynum's name appears alongside his father's and brother's names on a petition to Gov. William Sharkey protesting the appointments of Newt Knight's allies to office. He also signed a petition calling on the state legislature to change the name of Jones County to Davis County on account of the notoriety and shame brought

to the county by the Knight Company. Petition to Gov. William Sharkey, 29 July 1865, Governors' Papers, Sharkey, MDAH; Petition to Mississippi Senate and House of Representatives, 16 Oct. 1865, Senate Journal, MDAH.

23 Brig. Gen., Chief of Ordnance, and Acting Secretary of War S. V. Benet to Hon. J. R. Hawley, Chairman, Committee on Military Affairs, U.S. Senate; Report to accompany S. 1443, "For the Relief of Newton Knight and Others, Citizens of Mississippi," *Journal of the Senate of the United States, 1st Sess., 50th Cong.*, 26 Mar. 1888.

24 Written statement by Newton Knight, 3 Aug. 1889, Jones County Court, Miss., Newton Knight Claims. The census enumerator of 1880 listed Gilbert Moyers's occupation as Claim Agent. In 1880, Moyers was renting a room in Washington, D.C.; in 1890 he was renting a residence; by 1900, he had moved his family there from Memphis. Federal Manuscript Censuses for Memphis, Shelby County, Tenn., 1880, and Washington, D.C., 1900; City Directories for Memphis, Tenn., 1890–91, and Washington, D.C., 1890. Civil War information on Moyers is from "3rd Michigan Cavalry," Vicksburg National Military Park website, ⟨http://www.nps.gov/vick/historyculture/3rd-michigan-cavalry.htm⟩. Although many men of the 7th Battalion, Mississippi Infantry, served at Vicksburg, evidence does not support the contention of Jenkins and Stauffer that Newt Knight served there, too (*State of Jones*, 99, 114).

25 "Case of Jones County Scouts, United States Army, War of 1861," to the Senate and House of Representatives of the United States of America, In Congress Assembled, 3 Aug. 1889, Newton Knight Claims. Six men, M. M. Coats, R. H. Hinton, M. W. Kurven, Montgomery Blackwell, G. M. Hathorn, and R. H. Valentine, signed a statement at the bottom of the petition proclaiming all statements to be "true in every particular."

26 The Committee on War Claims was formed in 1873 to replace the Committee on Revolutionary Claims. The citizens' petition on behalf of Newt Knight, 10 Feb. 1890, was signed by Hiram Anderson, James Knight, A. M. Drennan, A. T. Wilborn, Berry Sims, W. P. Ainsworth, J. R. Stringer, G. W. Kennedy, R. M. Blackwell, and George M. Brumfield. Just five days earlier, on 5 Feb. 1890, several of these same citizens signed affidavits on behalf of former members of the band, including Joseph Yaughn, J. M. Valentine, Ausberry McDaniel, J. J. Collins, William Wesley Sumrall, and W. M. Welch, verifying the men's support of the Union through membership in the Jones County Scouts and indicating they would provide statements for the defense. All in Newton Knight Claims.

27 Depositions for Client [Newton Knight], *Newton Knight v. United States*, filed 29 Nov. 1890, case #8013; Motion to Secretary of War from Gilbert Moyers, filed 13 Mar. 1891; Reports of War Department, filed 24 Mar. 1891; Motion to consolidate congressional claims #8013 and #8464 by Attorney Gilbert Moyers, approved 24 Apr. 1891; Notice to Hon. J. E. Dodge, from Gilbert Moyers, Attorney for Claimant, case #8013 & 8464, of intent to take testimony of "Lieut. John Valentine, J. W. Blackwell, A. McDaniel, Capt. Knight, James Knight, and others," before J. R. Owen, Commissioner of the Court of Claims, at his office in Hillsboro, Miss., beginning on 10 Aug. 1894, filed 16 July 1894; all in Newton Knight Claims. Because of the two phases of interviews, several men were interviewed twice. On 25 Nov. 1890,

Moyers took depositions from Newton Knight, James Morgan Valentine, Richard Hinton, and Harmon Levi Sumrall. In March of the following year, he applied to the War Department for any records regarding service to the Union by the Jones County Scouts. After receiving notice that no such records were found, the two claims were merged. New depositions were then initiated, and typed copies of the depositions were added to the file. Unfortunately, some were edited, presumably to eliminate what was considered extraneous material. I have thus based my analysis on the original handwritten depositions.

28 Testimony of Newton Knight, 29 Jan. 1895, Newton Knight Claims. Dougherty, who replaced Luke Lee as government defense attorney, also badgered Newt about why he had cited fifty-five members of the band when the petition listed fifty-six.

29 Motion for call on Clerk, House of Representatives, for original papers in case of Newton Knight, *"Jones County Scouts," Scott Co., Miss., v. The United States*; and Motion for Call on Hon. Secretary of War for original papers in case of the "Jones County Scouts," *Capt. Newton Knight v. The United States*, both filed 13 Mar. 1891 by Gilbert Moyers, Attorney for Claimant, in Newton Knight Claims. The House of Representatives replied on 3 June 1891 that said papers were "not returned to files of the House by the Committee on War Claims." The War Department likewise (and predictably) found no records of Union service for Capt. Newton Knight and the Jones County Scouts (Endorsements to Court of Claims from War Department, filed 24 Mar. 1891, Newton Knight Claims).

30 *Official Records*, ser. I, vol. 24, pt. 2, 513–16. The Rocky Creek Bridge Battle is recounted by Kohl, "On Grant's Front Line," 41–56; and Bearss, *Decision in Mississippi*, 398–401.

31 Capt. W. Wirt Thomson to James A. Seddon, 29 Mar. 1864, Daniel Logan to Maj. J. C. Denis, 7 Apr. 1864, *Official Records*, ser. I, vol. 32, pt. 3, 711–12, 755; Brig. Gen. W. L. Brandon to Maj. Gen. D. H. Maury, 14 Aug. 1864, *Official Records*, ser. I, vol. 39, pt. 3, 777.

32 Testimony of Newton Knight, Newton Knight Claims. When the Rocky Creek Bridge skirmish was first included in Newt's petition, in 1887, the penned-in replacement of "Leaf River Bridge" with "Rocky Creek Bridge" suggests the careless haste with which the story was added as an example of Gen. Grant's efforts to muster the Knight Company into service.

33 Testimonies of Joel E. Welborn, 6 Mar. 1895, C. M. Edmonson, 6 Mar. 1895, E. M. Devall, 30 Jan. 1895, and J. M. Valentine, 29 Jan. 1895, Newton Knight Claims. Joel E. Welborn was captain of Co. E., 7th Battalion, Mississippi Infantry. Newt's 1st Lt., James Morgan Valentine, echoed Newt's claims about Rocky Creek Bridge. Although Newt's account of the Rocky Creek Bridge skirmish was discredited by defense witnesses, he never backed down from it, and neither, apparently, did Jasper Collins. Around 1946, Jasper's son Loren claimed to have heard his father tell the story over the years. Certain details differed, however. Loren claimed that Gen. Benjamin Butler, rather than Gen. Grant, sent the detachment of men from New Orleans in 1864 to muster the Knight band into the Union. He then made the improbable assertion that it was Col. Robert Lowry's forces that had captured Capt. Mann's forces at Rocky Creek. Gen. Butler's failed attempt to aid the Knight

Company, he concluded, was what prompted so many Jones County men to flee to Union forces in New Orleans in the immediate aftermath of Lowry's raid (Loren Collins, "The Free State of Jones, or, Two Ways to Tell a Story," unpublished manuscript, B. T. Collins Jr. research files). Depositions for Newt's claim were taken at the courthouse in Ellisville, Miss.

34 Testimony of J. J. Collins, 6 Mar. 1895, Newton Knight Claims.

35 Maj. Gen. W. T. Sherman to Maj. Gen. Halleck, 29 Feb. 1864, *Official Records*, ser. I, vol. 32, pt. 2, 498–99; Testimony of J. J. Collins, 7 Mar. 1895, Newton Knight Claims.

36 Testimony of Newton Knight, 29 Jan. 1895, and Testimony of J. J. Collins, 7 Mar. 1895, Newton Knight Claims. Jasper also claimed to have visited Randolph, Tenn., just outside Memphis.

37 Testimony of J. J. Collins, 7 Mar. 1895, Newton Knight Claims. Because of his travels, Jasper escaped both Col. Maury's and Col. Lowry's raids on Jones County.

38 Testimony of J. J. Collins, 7 Mar. 1895, Newton Knight Claims. Jasper also testified that T. J Collins was a member of the Knight band, even though his name does not appear on Newt's roster.

39 Petition of Newton Knight, filed 3 Aug. 1889, and Exhibit A, Muster Roll of the Jones County Scouts, filed 4 Feb. 1895, Newton Knight Claims.

40 Testimony of Newton Knight, 29 Jan. 1895, Newton Knight Claims.

41 Ibid.

42 Testimonies of Harmon Levi Sumrall (emphasis mine), 29 Jan. 1895, and W. M. Welch, 6 Mar. 1895, Newton Knight Claims.

43 Testimonies of J. M. Valentine, 29 Jan. 1895, and R. M. Blackwell, 7 Mar. 1895, Newton Knight Claims.

44 Testimony of J. J. Collins (emphasis mine), 7 Mar. 1895, Newton Knight Claims.

45 Ibid.

46 Ibid. B. A. Mathews is identified as probate judge in 1869, in Jones County Chancery Court, Final Records, First District, 1857–90, 301, MDAH.

47 Among witnesses who identified themselves as members of the Knight Company, only T. J. Huff and T. G. Crawford did not remember taking an oath with the band, probably the reason they were called as witnesses by the defense. As Newt's lawyers pointed out, these men joined the band after the date the oath was allegedly taken. Neither one is listed on Newt's copy of his wartime roster. Testimonies of T. J. Huff and T. G. Crawford, 8 Mar. 1895, Newton Knight Claims.

48 In 1860, E. M. Devall, age thirty, was living with his seventeen-year-old wife, Mary Jane, in the household of her father, Joel E. Welborn. Devall claimed real estate valued at $2,500 and personal property at $3,550. His father-in-law claimed $36,000 in real estate and $13,000 (including six slaves) in personal property. In 1860, C. M. Edmonson, a twenty-eight-year-old Williamsburg merchant, claimed $800 in real estate and $5,000 in personal property. He was appointed clerk of the Covington County Court on 19 July 1865 (U.S. Bureau of the Census, Federal Manuscript Census, Population and Slave Schedules, 1860, Covington County, Jones County, Miss.; Bonds, Oaths of Office, 1863–65, RG 28, MDAH). A. (Ausberry) B. Jordan and his wife, Retinsey Mary Ann, daughter of Amos and Eleanor Deason, appear in the

1870 but not in the 1860 Population Schedule for Jones County (U.S. Bureau of the Census, Federal Manuscript Census, 1870, 1860, Jones County, Miss.). Jordan was administrator for Amos Deason's estate upon Deason's death in 1874. His sureties included E. M. Devall and John M. Baylis, Jones County's unsuccessful prosecession candidate as delegate to Mississippi's 1861 state convention (Jones County Chancery Court, Final Records, First District, 1857–90, MDAH).

49 Testimony of E. M. Devall, 30 Jan. 1895, Newton Knight Claims.

50 E. M. Devall to Gov. Charles Clark, 21 Mar. 1864, Governors' Papers, Clark, MDAH.

51 Testimony of A. B. Jordan, 6 Mar. 1895, Newton Knight Claims. According to family histories, Jordan married Retinsy Mary Ann Deason on 12 June 1856. Mrs. Jordan died in 1879.

52 Testimony of A. B. Jordan, 6 Mar. 1895, Newton Knight Claims. On the election of cooperationist candidate John H. Powell over secessionist candidate John M. Baylis, see Bynum, *Free State of Jones*, 98.

53 Testimony of O. C. Martin, 6 Mar. 1895, Newton Knight Claims.

54 On kin relations between pro- and anti-Confederate Jones County families and on economic and political differences among the Welborns of Jones County during the Civil War era, see Bynum, *Free State of Jones*, 47–69, passim.

55 Younger and William Turner Welborn, brothers, J. C. C. Welborn, and Aaron Terrell Welborn were cousins to Joel E. Welborn. All came from nonslaveholding families except for J. C. C., who owned one slave in 1860. All four men deserted the Confederate Army. Younger and William Turner joined the Knight band. J. C. C. was paroled to camp and subsequently died at Vicksburg. From Compiled Service Records, Co. F, 7th Battalion, Mississippi Infantry, War Department Collection of Confederate Records, NA; and U.S. Bureau of the Census, Federal Manuscript Census, Population and Slave, 1860, Jones County, Miss. Though not a member of the band, Aaron T. Welborn signed an 1890 petition in support of the Knight Company (see Newton Knight Claims).

56 Testimony of J. E. Welborn, 7 Mar. 1895, Newton Knight Claims. According to family accounts, Welborn died on 28 Nov. 1895.

57 Findings of Fact; Defendant's Brief on Merits, filed 3 Aug. 1899, 3–4, 7–12; Defendant's Supplemental Brief on Merits, filed 31 Aug. 1899, 4; all in Newton Knight Claims.

58 Claimant's Reply, Brief on Merits, filed 16 Aug. 1899; 2nd Claimant's Reply, Brief on Merits, undated, 2–3; both in Newton Knight Claims.

59 Defendant's Supplemental Brief on Merits, 31 Aug. 1899, 5, Newton Knight Claims. Assistant attorney Collins's remark that Newt Knight's lawyers offered "not a particle of disinterested evidence . . . and this will apply also to orders which it claimed were issued to Newton Knight and his men by General [Capt. H. T.] Elliott stationed at Meridian [Raleigh, Miss.], Mississippi," indicates that he had not seen Newt's 1870 evidence (Defendant's Brief on Merits, 3 Aug. 1899, 11, Newton Knight Claims).

60 Defendant's Supplemental Brief on Merits, 31 Aug. 1899, 3, 5, Newton Knight Claims. General Grant died in 1885, Sherman in 1891, and Butler in 1893. The court stated only that it "assumed" that "McMillen" was Brevet Gen. William Linn McMillen,

even though B. A. Mathews had carefully provided his full name and address in 1870. Further indicative of the Court of Claims' failure to view the claim's original evidence was its comment that the Knight claimants specified no financial amount, when in fact they had done so several times. Although the War Department found no records confirming contact between the Union Army and the "Jones County Scouts," in 1897 it verified that both McMillen and Elliott had been stationed in Mississippi during the relevant period, May–August 1865, as cited in Newt Knight's testimony (Record and Pension Office, War Department, 11 Jan. 1897, Newton Knight Claims).

61 For the final report on the claim of "Newton Knight and Others," see Letter from the Assistant Clerk of the Court of Claims Transmitting a Copy of the Finding Filed by the Court in the Case of Newton Knight and Others against the United States, 4 Feb. 1907, 59th Cong., 2nd Sess., House of Representatives, Doc. #672.

62 See especially Brundage, *Southern Past*; and Blight, *Race and Reunion*.

63 Kennedy, "History of Jasper County." J. M. Kennedy gave no date for his visit with Newt Knight but specified that it was sometime after Newt testified at the 1891 murder trial of Walter Simpson (box ID 6063, series 6 [Supreme Court], Case 7048, 1892, MDAH). My thanks to independent historians Ralph Poore of Boise, Idaho, who provided copies of Kennedy's two-part article, and Ed Payne of Jackson, Miss., who supplied the date for the murder trial of Walter Simpson.

CHAPTER FIVE

1 The "Free State of Jones" refers to a region that encompassed parts of four counties: Jones, Covington, Jasper, and Smith (see Bynum, *Free State of Jones*). On Populists Gore, Burkitt, and Hathorn, see especially Cresswell, *Multiparty Politics*, 114–15, 147–48; and McCain, "Populist Party in Mississippi," 32–35.

2 U.S. Bureau of the Census, Federal Manuscript Census, Population Schedule, 1860, Covington County, Miss. Prentice M. Bynum was identified as a member of the Knight Company on Newt Knight's 1870 handwritten roster of men (Newton Knight Folder). *Pearl River News*, 2 Aug. 1895, identified Nevin C. Hathorn as chairman and Prentice M. Bynum as secretary of the Marion County People's Party.

3 In 1910, W. J. Collins ran for the U.S. Congress from the Second Congressional District on the Socialist ticket against Democrat Martin Dies. Collins received 129 votes to Dies's 849 (Election Returns, 1910, Hardin County, Records of the Secretary of State, Election Division, 1846–1984, TSLAAC). Martin Dies of Beaumont, Tex., served as representative from the Second Congressional District from 1909 until 1919 and was the father of Congressman Martin Dies Jr. See James R. Green, *Grass-Roots Socialism*, 8, 25–26.

4 On Jackie Knight's opposition to secession and the genealogical connections between the Hathorns and the Knights of Covington County, Miss., see Bynum, *Free State of Jones*, 85, 192.

5 History of Early Settlers, Marion County, unpublished papers, WPA-MDAH.

6 On sectional loyalties as a barrier to Populist unity, see especially Goodwyn, *Democratic Promise*, 4–10.

7 Goodwyn, *Democratic Promise*, 26–31; Cresswell, *Multiparty Politics*, 3–5, 8; Weeks, "South in National Politics," 221–40; Moneyhon, *Texas after the Civil War*, 152, 162–65.

8 Goodwyn, *Democratic Promise*, 25–31; Cresswell, *Multiparty Politics*, 9–10.

9 Goodwyn, *Democratic Promise*, 31–33; Moneyhon, *Texas after the Civil War*, 163–64.

10 In 1860, Simeon Collins owned land valued at $6,000 and personal goods, most of it livestock, none of it slaves, at $2,000. By 1870, forty-eight-year-old Lydia was living on a farm located near the county seat of Paulding, Jasper County, with her four youngest children. The farm's value, $490, and her personal property, assessed at $600, document a steep ten-year decline in wealth. To make ends meet, she and her kinfolk pooled resources and shared labor. Surrounding her household were those of son Matt, twenty-five, who lived with his wife and four children on a farm valued at $100; son Harrison, twenty-one (married to Emeline Welch); and daughter Frances Loftin, eighteen (married to Leonard Lee Loftin). The farms of these families were assigned no value by the census enumerator. Other nearby kinfolk included Jonathan Anderson, fifty-four, cousin of Lydia's late husband, who lived with his married daughter on a farm valued at $250. Next door was Jonathan's son, Asa Anderson, and his family. U.S. Bureau of the Census, Federal Manuscript Census, Population, Agricultural, and Slave Schedules, 1860, Jasper County, Miss.

11 In Hardin County, Lydia's son Benjamin Franklin "Frank" Collins was soon elected justice of the peace (Records of the Secretary of State, TSLAAC). A comparison of the 1870 Jones County and Jasper County, Miss., and 1880 Hardin County, Tex., Federal Manuscript Censuses reveals many of the families who moved west. According to Donald Howard Loftin (*Loftin Chronicles*, provided to author by Catherine McKnight), Giles Loftin, member of the Knight Company, also moved his family to Texas after the war. He later moved back to Mississippi, where he died around 1880. Bill and Sarah Holifield moved first to Simpson County, Miss., then on to Hardin County, Tex. Bill had hung out with the Knight band during the war, but he joined the Union Army in New Orleans with Riley Collins after Col. Lowry's raid. His wife, Sarah, was the sister of Lydia Bynum Collins (see Bynum, *Free State of Jones*, 197). Like many of his kin, Holifield joined the Union Army in New Orleans after Col. Lowry's raid. Like several Jones County men who died of dysentery while serving the Union Army in that city, Bill immediately got sick. Permanently impaired by the effects of smallpox and rheumatism, he tried after the war to make a fresh start in Texas. Application of William Holifield, 16 Feb. 1894, Pension Application Files Based on Service in the Civil War and Spanish-American War ("Civil War and Later"), Records of the Department of Veterans' Affairs, NA.

12 James R. Green, *Grass-Roots Socialism*, 1.

13 Sitton and Conrad, *Nameless Towns*, 34–78; Moneyhon, *Texas after the Civil War*, 190–91. After 1890, numerous Polk County Collinses appear on delinquent land tax lists (Registers of Lands and Town Lots Sold by Tax Collector, Polk Co., Tex., List of Delinquent or Insolvent Tax Payers, 1891, 1892, 1894, 1897, 1902, Sam Houston Library and Archives, Liberty, Tex.).

14 Frank Knight's full name was George Franklin Knight and his wife was Emma Jane Turnbow. After the war, the Knights and Turnbows lived in Rusk, Tex. In an appar-

ent attempt to erase his Civil War connections to the Knight Company and to his brother Newt, Frank Knight told many of his descendants that he was born in Grayson, Tex. (Eldon Knight to author, e-mail, 10 Feb. 2005, 21 Mar. 2005, Bynum files). According to Turnbow genealogist Martha Miller, both of Jane Turnbow's brothers accompanied the Knights on their move to Texas and also became Mormons after Latter Day Saints Elders visited the family in Texas (Martha Miller to author, e-mail, 22 May 2006, Bynum files).

15 Stein, *Communities of Dissent.* Violence against religious dissenters in the Deep South, including what some Southern leaders deemed the "Mormon Monster," included lynching, murder, rape, tar and feathering, and destruction of property. See Mason, "Sinners in the Hands of an Angry Mob." Shortly before her death, in 1889, Rachel Knight, Newt Knight's wartime collaborator and postwar lover, joined the Mormon Church, as did her daughter, Fannie (Bivins, "Rachel Knight").

16 Danny Coats to author, e-mail, 29 Nov. 2003, 30 Nov. 2003, 10 Aug. 2005, 28 Nov. 2006, 29 Nov. 2006; Dwayne Coats to author, e-mail, 1 Dec. 2003, 21 June 2004, 16 Aug. 2005; all in Bynum files.

17 On political offices held by former members of the Knight Company during Reconstruction, see also Bynum, *Free State of Jones*, 132–41. On Democratic politics during this era, see Bond, *Political Culture in the Nineteenth-Century South*, 156–81; Wharton, *Negro in Mississippi*, 131–215; and Cresswell, *Multiparty Politics*, 13–18.

18 My thanks to Ralph Poore, independent scholar, for sharing evidence with me that former Confederate whites from the Mississippi Piney Woods were involved as early as 1868 in the Ku Klux Klan or forerunner groups to punish blacks who crossed them (Ralph Poore to author, e-mail, 14 June 2006, Bynum files). On whitecapping, see Holmes, "Whitecapping," 165–85; Bond, *Political Culture in the Nineteenth-Century South*; Wharton, *Negro in Mississippi*; and Cresswell, *Multiparty Politics*, 177.

19 Tom Watson's efforts to build a biracial movement ended after the 1896 presidential election, when he ran on the Democratic fusion ticket as William Jennings Bryan's Populist running mate. He is today remembered as much for his reactionary racism and anti-Semitism as his earlier, more hopeful, brand of Populism. Woodward, *Tom Watson*, 220–21.

20 *Pearl River News*, 7 July, 18 June 1894.

21 Cantrell and Barton, "Texas Populists," 659–92; Goodwyn, "Populist Dreams and Negro Rights," 1435–56. For a profile of Andrew Jackson Spradley, see *New Handbook of Texas*, Online.

22 The story of Newt and Rachel Knight and the multiracial community they founded is told in Bynum, *Free State of Jones*, 132–90.

23 On Newt Knight's ongoing efforts to win compensation from the U.S. government for having supported the Union during the Civil War, see chapter 4 in this volume; and Bynum, *Free State of Jones*, 141.

24 On the political careers of Stockdale, McKee, and Hathorn, see Cresswell, *Multiparty Politics*, 76, 132–34, 141–48, 173–74.

25 Ibid., 146–47.

26 Burruss, "History of Universalism in Mississippi," ML-USM. According to Burruss, Orange Herrington requested that he write the history. The Universalist message

resonated among a widening circle of Jones County folks over the years. In 1902, Burruss (sometimes spelled Burris) Universalist Church was organized by Rev. A. G. Strain of Ariton, Ala., "under a bush arbor in the Union Community." Among its founding members were Jasper Collins and several members of the Herrington, Tucker, Kirkland, and Sholar families. Jasper's neighbor, Martin Van Buren Tucker, an early Universalist convert, was also from a Unionist family. Tucker's daughter, Samantha Ardella ("Della"), married Elijah T. Kirkland, grandson of Universalist convert Sherod Sholar. In 1905, Della and Elijah Kirkland's daughter, Hilda, married Buford T. Collins Sr., grandson of Jasper Collins. All belonged to the Burruss Universalist Church. Interview with J. Brackin Kirkland, Mississippi Oral History Program, USM; U.S. Bureau of the Census, Federal Manuscript Census, Population Schedule, 1870, Jones County, Miss.; B. T. Collins Jr. to Ed Payne, e-mail, 23 Oct. 2006, Ed Payne research files.

27 McCarty, "History of the Universalist Church," 5–11, 122–26.

28 Bynum, *Free State of Jones*, 29–46; McCarty, "History of the Universalist Church," 93.

29 Our Home Universalist Church had its own building by 1907. Located a few miles west of Laurel, on land donated by Orange Herrington (one of seven founding members), it is still active as the Our Home Universalist-Unitarian Church, recently celebrating its 100th anniversary. See McCarty, "History of the Universalist Church," 88–93; Burruss, "History of Universalism in Mississippi," ML-USM; and Addie West, 7 Dec. 1937, unpublished papers, WPA-MDAH.

30 *Clarion-Ledger*, 8 Aug. 1895.

31 *New South*, 4 May 1894, 15 June 1895 (B. T. Collins Jr. research files). No extant issues of the *Ellisville Patriot* have been located, but the appearance of its first issue was announced in *Ellisville (Miss.) News*, 2 May 1895, as well by the *New South*. J. F. Parker's editorials identify Jasper Collins and his son Loren as the newspaper's cofounders. Loren seems to have been editor of the *Patriot*, but Jasper contributed the articles to which Parker responded in the pages of the *New South*.

32 Cresswell, *Multiparty Politics*, 145; McCain, "Populist Party in Mississippi," 32–35, 73; *Clarion-Ledger*, 20 June, 8 Aug., 12 Sept., 28 Sept., 10 Oct. 1895.

33 Quoted phrases from "The Populist Convention" and "Populite Convention," both in *Clarion-Ledger*, 8 Aug. 1895.

34 *Clarion-Ledger*, 27 Feb. 1896. N. C. "Scott" Hathorn served as the delegate from Marion County in 1896; Jasper Collins was one of two alternates elected from the Sixth Congressional District; Loren was appointed assistant secretary of the convention.

35 *Clarion-Ledger*, 27 Feb. 1896; McCain, "Populist Party in Mississippi," 73–74; Cresswell, *Multiparty Politics*, 108–9, 142–43, 153–54, 186–89.

36 Cantrell and Barton, "Texas Populists," 660, 684, 687.

37 Vinson A. Collins, *Story of My Parents*, 11–14. For more on Vinson Collins's portrayal of his father, see epilogue in this volume.

38 Vinson A. Collins, *Story of My Parents*, 12–13.

39 Ibid., 20–24. According to Vinson, during this time Warren ran a small blacksmith shop and then tried contracting himself and his sons out to clear farmland for others.

40 Ibid., 18–20.

41 Ibid., 11, 12, 21–22.

42 James R. Green, *Grass-Roots Socialism*, 4–5, 8–11, 24–29. See also Alter, "E. O. Meitzen."

43 Woodward, *Tom Watson*, 406.

44 Foley, *White Scourge*, 92–117; Zamora, *World of the Mexican Worker*, 133–61.

45 Quoted material on W. J. Collins from the *Rebel*, 14 Dec. 1912. Collins's run for Congress is recorded in Election Returns, 1910, Hardin County, Election Division, Records of the Secretary of State, TSLAAC. For his identification as the Socialist candidate, see "The Collins Are Coming," in *Rebel*, 19 Aug. 1911. Martin Dies of Beaumont, Tex., served as House representative from the Second Congressional District from 1909 until 1919. Collins's run for county judge with a Socialist slate of candidates from Hardin County was announced by L. F. Rigby, Hardin County secretary for the Socialist Party, in *Rebel*, 23 Mar. 1912.

46 *Rebel*, 23 Mar., 14 Dec. 1912.

47 Ibid.

48 Both Nathan C. Hathorn Jr. and Prentice Bynum became Democrats after the decline of Populism. In 1895, Orange Herrington was Jones County's candidate for treasurer on the People's Party ticket. In 1899, he served as delegate to the party's state convention. In 1900, he was the party's presidential elector candidate from the Sixth Congressional District. In April 1905, Herrington's "Farmers' Page" was renamed "Farmer Folks"; by the end of 1905, it was called "Farmers' Department." The information on election of Southern Cotton Growers Association officers is from the *Laurel (Miss.) Ledger*, 16 Dec. 1905.

49 *Laurel (Miss.) Ledger*, 2 Dec. 1909. Men who attended the original meeting and signed the resolution included Walter Boler, H. C. Collins, B. T. Collins (Socialist), Hubert Herrington, J. S. Sumrall, J. B. Praytor (Socialist), W. E. Grantham, W. W. Hopkin, U. S. Collins, E. C. Tisdale, W. P. Moss, Rev. R. J. Loper, P. C. Jourdan, J. L. Shows, J. J. Collins (Populist), E. E. Kirkland, A. T. Long, C. S. Jourdan, T. D. Williams, G. B. Boler, Jerry Moss, R. L. Barfield, and A. J. Runnels.

50 Farmers' Union president G. R. Hightower placed an announcement in the *Laurel (Miss.) Ledger*, 13 May 1909, stating that the Union had taken on "new life" in the state and urged members who were in arrears to take advantage of a "special dispensation" of past dues by rejoining within thirty days. Orange Herrington signed the letter as well.

51 Buford T. Collins Sr.'s candidacy was announced in the *Jones County News*, 11 Sept. 1913. Political affiliations of Mississippi's "oppositional" candidates for office were compiled by Stephen Cresswell, "Who Was Who in Mississippi's Opposition Political Parties, 1878–1963," MDAH. Timothy Wyatt Collins was the son of Riley James Collins, a member of the Knight Company during the war who joined the Union Army in New Orleans and died of disease while serving.

52 The Socialist candidates were Lazarous Marvin Bynum (county sheriff), William H. F. Mauldin (circuit clerk), Thomas J. Lyon (railroad commissioner), and W. Thomas Loftin (county assessor). Lazarous Marvin Bynum was the nephew of Unionist/Populist Prentice M. Bynum. William H. F. Mauldin was the son of W. H. Mauldin, a member of the Knight Company who joined the Union Army at New

Orleans in 1864 and soon died of disease. His mother, Dicey Bynum, was the sister of Prentice M. Bynum. Both Bynum's and Mauldin's grandparents were Benjamin Bynum and Margaret "Peggy" Collins Bynum, a sister of Jasper Collins. W. Thomas Loftin's father, Giles Loftin, was a member of the Knight Company. T. J. Lyon's father, William A. Lyon, deserted but later rejoined the Confederacy, was captured by Yankees, and died at Fort Douglas Prison Camp. T. J.'s father-in-law was Jasper Collins, whom he cited as his greatest political influence. A lifelong Socialist after his conversion around 1915, Lyon also ran for the Sixth Congressional District seat in 1920 (Donnis Lyon research files). See also the epilogue in this volume.

53 "Ye Oldest Native: Interesting Interview with Mr. J. J. Collins," *Jones County News*, 10 Apr. 1913.

54 Ibid. Jasper's political activism of earlier years indicated he admired the courageous, articulate Tom Watson of 1895 rather than the bitter, demoralized one of 1913. On the rise and fall of Tom Watson, see Woodward, *Tom Watson*.

55 *Laurel (Miss.) Ledger*, 4 Feb. 1905; obituary of Jasper Collins, *Jones County News*, 12 Aug. 1913.

56 *Beaumont Enterprise*, 31 Jan. 1928, reprinted in Vinson A. Collins, *Story of My Parents*.

CHAPTER SIX

1 Painter, *Southern History across the Color Line*; Hunter, *To 'Joy My Freedom*; Leslie, *Woman of Color*; Bullard, *Robert Stafford*; Alexander, *Ambiguous Lives*.

2 Gilmore, *Gender and Jim Crow*; Higginbotham, *Righteous Discontent*.

3 Eva B. Dykes to Anna Knight, scrapbook, 10 Mar. 1964, Anna Knight Papers, Oakwood Archives and Museum, Oakwood College, Huntsville, Ala.; Erle Johnston Jr. to Honorable Jack Tubb and Honorable F. Gordon Lewis, 12 Dec. 1963, Mississippi Sovereignty Commission Papers, USM.

4 *State of Mississippi v. Davis Knight*, Clerk's Office, Mississippi Supreme Court, MDAH; Bynum, "White Negroes," 247–76. The verdict was reported in many newspapers, including the *New York Times*, 19 Dec. 1948.

5 U.S. Bureau of the Census, Federal Manuscript Census, 1900, Jasper County, Miss.; *St. Louis Post-Dispatch*, 18 Dec. 1948, 19 Dec. 1948, 20 Dec. 1948, 9 Jan. 1949, 10 Jan. 1949, 14 Nov. 1949.

6 Bivins, "Martha Ann Ainsworth Notes." See also Pieratt, *Ainsworth-Collins Clan*, 110–11.

7 Pieratt, *Ainsworth-Collins Clan*, 110–11; Bivins, "Martha Ann Ainsworth Notes"; Bivins, "Lucy Ann 'Jane' Ainsworth." Martha Ann's children's names and approximate years of birth are Charity, 1846; Louis, 1850; Pernicia, 1853; Susanna, 1856; and Lucy Ann, 1857. U.S. Bureau of the Census, Federal Manuscript Census, 1850, 1860, 1870, Smith County, Miss.

8 Bivins, "Open Secret"; Bynum, "White Negroes," 247–76.

9 Ethel Knight, *Echo of the Black Horn*, 250, 265, 283–87, 302–9. On white Southern women who challenged the South's segregated social order during this period, see Lumpkin, *Making of a Southerner*; Smith, *Killers of the Dream*; and Hall, "You Must Remember This," 439–65.

10 Bynum, *Free State of Jones*, 144–45.

11 After Mollie's death in 1917, Serena lived with her son Tom. U.S. Bureau of the Census, Federal Manuscript Census, 1900, 1910, 1920, Jasper County, Miss.

12 Bivins, "Open Secret." On increased legal and extralegal persecution of interracial marriages, see Hodes, *White Women, Black Men*, 176–97; and Gilmore, *Gender and Jim Crow*, 71.

13 Frances Jackson to author, e-mail, 30 Apr. 2000, Bynum files.

14 Frances Jackson to author, e-mail, 30 Apr. 2000, and Dianne Walkup to author, e-mail, 31 May 2005, Bynum files; Knight, *Mississippi Girl*, 16, 23.

15 *Martha Ann Musgrove et al. v. J. R. McPherson et al.*, 27 Jan. 1914, Jones County Chancery Court, Laurel, Miss., Kenneth Welch research files.

16 Ibid.

17 Ibid.

18 Ibid.

19 Rhonda Benoit to author, e-mail, 14 Jan. 2000, Bynum files.

20 Addie Knight was first cousin, one generation removed, to her husband, Otho, who was the son of Mollie and Jeffrey Knight (Bynum, "White Negroes," 251–58).

21 *Musgrove et al. v. McPherson et al.*, 27 Jan. 1914, Kenneth Welch research files.

22 Nancy Knight quoted in F. A. Behymer, "The Remote No-Man's Land of Soso," *St. Louis Post-Dispatch*, 10 Jan. 1949; Florence Knight Blaylock and Annette Knight, interview by author, Soso, Miss., 22 July 1996, ML-USM; Report, West Jasper County School Board, Bay Springs, Miss., 18 Aug. 1960, Mississippi Sovereignty Commission File, Leesha Faulkner Civil Rights Collection, ML-USM.

23 Lessie Robertson, death certificate, 21 Feb. 1944, Texas Department of Health, Bureau of Vital Statistics, Obituaries, TSLAAC; Obituaries, *Beaumont Enterprise*, 21 Feb. 1944.

24 Anna Knight, *Mississippi Girl*, 20–24; Graves, "Historical View," 2–3.

25 Anna Knight, *Mississippi Girl*, 29–32, 39–47, 52–57.

26 Medallion of Merit Award for Anna Knight, brochure, 17 Nov. 1971, Anna Knight Papers, Oakwood Archives and Museum, Oakwood College, Huntsville, Ala.

27 Johnston to Tubb and Lewis, 12 Dec. 1963, Mississippi Sovereignty Commission File, Leesha Faulkner Civil Rights Collection, ML-USM; Anna Knight to Rachel Green, 18 June 1963, 24 Aug. 1967, 23 Sept. 1971, Wynona G. Frost research files.

28 Anna Knight, *Mississippi Girl*, 11.

29 Hine, "Rape and the Inner Lives of Southern Black Women," 177–89.

30 Anna Knight, "The Great Contest," undated, unpublished essay, Anna Knight Papers, Oakwood Archives and Museum, Oakwood College, Huntsville, Ala.

31 Graves, "Historical View," 1; Rosetta Baldwin and Natelkka E. Burrell, letters, 4 Mar. 1964, Scrapbook, Anna Knight Collection.

32 On Anna's family's resistance to Adventism, see Anna Knight, *Mississippi Girl*, 33–37; Graves, "Historical View," 2–4; and Knight, "The Great Contest," Anna Knight Collection.

33 Anna Knight, *Mississippi Girl*, 147–48, 153.

34 Ibid.

35 Ibid., 18.

36 Ibid., 31.

37 Ibid., 32, 43.

38 Ibid., 40, 42, 46.

39 Ibid., 75–76.

40 Ibid., 82–87.

41 Ibid., 88–91, 108–9; "Miss Anna Knight," 3, Anna Knight Papers, Oakwood Archives and Museum, Oakwood College, Huntsville, Ala.

42 Anna Knight, *Mississippi Girl*, 90, 108–9, 159, 163.

43 Miscellaneous records, Anna Knight Collection.

44 Ibid.

45 Anna Knight, *Mississippi Girl*, 168, 171, 176–80. Quoted passages from Van Buren Watts to Anna Knight, 2 Mar. 1964, scrapbook, Anna Knight Collection; and *North American Regional Voice* (Apr. 1988), 15, Anna Knight Papers, Oakwood Archives and Museum, Oakwood College, Huntsville, Ala.

46 T. B. Corley to George and Sylvia [Corley], 29 June 1948, Ardella Knight Barrett Papers.

47 Grace Knight to Della Knight Bramwell [Barrett], 21 May 1948; T. B. Corley to Mrs. Ardella Bramwell [Barrett], 15 July 1948; copy of Oil, Gas, and Mineral Lease agreement between T. B. Corley and Della Bramwell, 29 June 1948; all in Ardella Knight Barrett Papers. Davis Knight was charged with miscegenation the same year that the Knights sought to sell mineral rights from land inherited from Newt Knight. It may be that interested parties sought to make race an issue of inheritance, as was successfully done in 1914.

48 Anna Knight, *Mississippi Girl*, preface.

EPILOGUE

1 Ethel Knight, *Echo of the Black Horn*.

2 Thomas J. Knight, *Life and Activities*; Street, *Tap Roots*. Universal Studio produced the movie, *Tap Roots*, in 1948.

3 *New South*, 1 June 1895 (B. T. Collins research files). For more on the feud between Jasper Collins and J. Frank Parker, see chapter 5 in this volume.

4 Loren Collins was particularly irritated by the unsubstantiated remarks that abound in interviews conducted by the Works Progress Administration during the 1930s (Loren Collins, "Two Ways to Tell a Story"). Jenkins and Stauffer, *State of Jones*, inexplicably subtitle their book "The Small Southern County That Seceded from the Confederacy." They offer no evidence within that such an event occurred.

5 Bynum, *Free State of Jones*, 98, 107. For a recent history of Jasper's sister, Sarah (Sally) Collins, that sheds new light on the Free State of Jones, see Payne, "Kinship, Slavery, and Gender."

6 Loren R. Collins, born 1871, and his cousin Timothy W. Collins served as delegates to the 1895 Mississippi Populist Convention; Jasper Collins was delegate to the 1896 Populist Convention. See McCain, "Populist Party in Mississippi," 16–17; *Clarion-Ledger*, 20 June, 8 Aug., 12 Sept., 28 Sept., 10 Oct. 1895, 27 Feb. 1896; and Bynum, *Free State of Jones*, 146–48.

7 The candidacy of B. T. Collins Sr., son of Henry Clay Collins and Vina Herrington, was not supported by the area's overwhelmingly Democratic newspapers, and he lost the election to J. T. Herrington. *Jones County News*, 11 Sept., 18 Sept. 1913 (my thanks to Ed Payne for providing these citations). Charles C. Evans, the minister who presided at Lyon's funeral, was the Socialist candidate for the Mississippi legislature from the Fifth District in 1920, the same year Lyon ran from the Sixth District. Stephen Cresswell, "Who Was Who in Mississippi's Oppositional Parties," MDAH; Obituary of T. J. Lyon, *Laurel (Miss.) Leader Call*, 5 Dec. 1938, Donnis Lyon research files; Keith Lyon to author, telephone conversation, 25 June 2006, and Donnis Lyon to author, telephone conversation, 7 July 2006, Bynum files.

8 Elizabeth "Betty" Lyon Myrick Burrow, born in 1885, was the daughter of T. J. Lyon and Theodocia "Docia" Collins. In her preamble, Burrow, who was still "Myrick" at that time (her first husband, John Myrick, died in 1948), thanked Tom Knight for sharing materials from "Captain Knight's trunk" with her. Typed on its front page are the words "written in 1934." If that date is accurate, Burrow did indeed produce the earliest version. In January 1962, the *Ellisville (Miss.) Progress-Item* began publishing Burrow's version in serial form (Research Files, Dorothy Lyon Thomas).

9 Thomas J. Knight, *Life and Activities*, 20–24; Loren Collins, "Two Ways to Tell a Story," 1–2.

10 Lyon, "Function and Survival of Legend." On concepts of Southern honor, both primal and genteel, see Wyatt-Brown, *Southern Honor*; and Greenberg, *Honor and Slavery*.

11 Henry Clay Collins, born in 1856, was considerably younger than twelve during the war. Loren Collins, "Two Ways to Tell a Story," 3.

12 On the political career of Vinson Allen Collins, see Norman D. Brown, *Hood, Bonnet, and Little Brown Jug*, 211–12, 388, 390–91; Tyler, *New Handbook of Texas*, 2:218; Wharton, *Texas under Many Flags*, 112; and *Dallas News*, 14 July 1953.

13 *Rebel*, 19 Aug. 1911. Vinson Allen Collins, born in 1867, served twice in the Texas State Senate, 1910–14 and 1916–17. On this era of Texas politics, see Gould, *Progressives and Prohibitionists*; and George Norris Green, *Establishment in Texas Politics*.

14 Vinson Collins, *Story of My Parents*.

15 Warren J. Collins quoted by T. A. Hickey in the *Rebel*, 19 Aug. 1911. In a retrospective article about Vinson Collins published on 30 Nov. 1970, the *Dallas Morning News* claimed that Collins had turned against the Klan by 1924 and opposed the Klan-backed candidate, Felix D. Robertson of Dallas. Historical records tell a different story. The Klan suspended Collins's membership in the organization after he entered the governor's race without first consulting the Dallas Klan leadership. On issues of race, gender, and religion, Vinson typified conservative Southern progressivism. Like many proponents of woman suffrage, he also supported protective legislation for women workers based on their feminine frailty. In 1928, he joined the "Constitutional Democrats," who bolted the national party rather support the Catholic candidate, Alfred E. Smith. See Tyler, *New Handbook of Texas*, 2:218; Wharton, *Texas under Many Flags*, 112; and Norman D. Brown, *Hood, Bonnet, and Little Brown Jug*, 211–12.

16 Morgan C. Collins, a son of Simeon Collins, who was a member of the Knight

band, was granted a pension based on the testimony of two relatives who, like him, were from Mississippi. T. J. Loftin, his uncle, testified that Morgan had served in Co. F of the 7th Battalion, Mississippi Infantry. Sarah P. Collins, Morgan's sister-in-law, likewise testified that she remembered when Morgan "left home and went to war." In his letter of 22 Sept. 1926, Hickman specifically identified Warren Collins's brother Newton Carroll as having deserted "my company, Co. F 22nd Texas Infantry." The other brother who joined Warren's jayhawkers was Stacy Collins Jr. Hickman's second letter was dated 4 Oct. 1926. See pension application and records of Morgan C. Collins, #41265, Records of the War Department, Adjutant General's Office, TSLAAC. On the migration of Simeon Collins's widow and children from Mississippi to Texas around 1872, see chapter 5 in this volume. My thanks to James McNabb, Alicia McNabb, and Lois McNabb, descendants of Morgan C. Collins, for their support and help in tracing this branch of the Collins family.

17 Military records, 7th Battalion, Mississippi Infantry. U.S. Bureau of the Census, Federal Manuscript Census, 1870, Hardin County, Tex.; pension records of James Madison Collins (application of widow Mary Collins), #46415, Records of the War Department, Adjutant General's Office, TSLAAC. For evidence that Morgan C. Collins joined the Knight band during the war, see Newton Knight Claim.

18 Tevis, "Battle at Bad Luck Creek"; V. A. Collins, "A Little Sketch of the Descendants of Stacey Collins."

19 Both Vinson A. Collins and his grandson, Carr P. Collins Jr., documented the family's kinship links between Hardin County, Tex., and Jones County, Miss., but failed to mention either branch's Civil War Unionism or membership in the Jones County Knight Company or the Big Thicket jayhawkers. See Vinson Collins, *Story of My Parents*; and Carr P. Collins Jr., *Royal Ancestors*.

20 Carr P. Collins Jr., *Royal Ancestors*, 279.

21 Vinson Collins, *Story of My Parents* 11–12.

22 Carr P. Collins Jr., *Royal Ancestors*, 294–95. The Collinses' tilt toward the Republican Party began when Vinson Collins bolted the Democratic Party in 1928 and continued in 1952 when they supported Dwight Eisenhower for president. On the career of Vinson's son, Carr P. Collins, see Tyler, *New Handbook of Texas*, 2:217. On the politics of Carr P. Collins Jr. and James P. Collins, grandchildren of Vinson Collins, see Davidson, *Race and Class in Texas Politics*, 76, 201, 213, 217–18, 234, 250; and George Norris Green, *Establishment in Texas Politics*, 25, 37–38, 55, 92.

23 Quoted passage from Neville, *Carr P. Collins*, 45.

24 Quoted passage from Vinson Collins, *Story of My Parents*, 14. Revealing studies on the increasing prominence of "poor white trash" stereotypes in the twentieth century include Wray, *Not Quite White*; Harkins, *Hillbilly*; and Rafter, *White Trash*.

25 Entertaining accounts of Warren J. Collins as a Civil War jayhawker and backwoods brawler appear in various essays in Abernethy, *Tales from the Big Thicket*. For an example of how stereotypes of stubborn backwoodsmen have shaped images of East Texas Unionists, see *Tempo Magazine*, 17 May 1970. More politically astute studies include Pitts, "Civil War and 'Kaiser's Burnout,'" 20–22; Wooster and Wooster, "A People at War," 3–16; House, *Big Thicket*, 17–19; and Zuber, "Fire at Union Wells."

26 Quoted in Loughmiller and Loughmiller, *Big Thicket Legacy*, 70–71.

27 Quoted in *Tempo Magazine*, 17 May 1970. An important exception to historians' neglect of Big Thicket dissent is Wooster and Wooster, "A People at War."

28 In 1921, reporter Meigs O. Frost reported both Jasper Collins's and Newt Knight's statements that Lowry never dared enter Jones County after the war (*New Orleans Item*, 20 Mar. 1921). Loren R. Collins reiterated this in "Two Ways to Tell a Story." The image of Jones County deserters as violent, poor, white backwoodsmen who attempted "secession within secession" was first popularized by Galloway, in "Confederacy within a Confederacy," 387–90.

29 A clipping of this article, which lacks the title of the publication that printed it, is contained in the Ardella Knight Barrett Papers.

30 To create the impression that this article was an update of Meigs O. Frost's original interview (*New Orleans Item*, 20 Mar. 1921), it was signed with the initials "M.O.F."

31 My thanks to Ed Payne (e-mail to author, 28 Jan. 2008, Bynum files) for his thoughts on the differences between Vinson Collins of Texas and Loren Collins of Mississippi.

32 B. T. Collins, "Are There Moral Issues That We Need to Recognize."

33 Ibid.

Bibliography

PRIMARY SOURCES

Manuscripts

Austin, Tex.
   Center for the Study of American History, University of Texas
      Special Collections
   Texas State Libraries and Archives and Archives Commission
      Genealogy Collections
         Index, Texas Department of Health, Bureau of Vital Statistics, Obituaries
      Governors' Papers, 1865–74
         Edmund Jackson Davis
         Elijah M. Pease
      Records of the Secretary of State, Election Division, 1846–1984, RG 307, series 84
         Election Returns, 1910, Hardin County, Tex.
      Records of the War Department, Adjutant General's Office
         Confederate Pension Records
Chapel Hill, N.C.
   Southern Historical Collection, University of North Carolina
      Confederate Conscript Papers
      Confederate Papers
      Documenting the American South, Electronic Edition, ⟨http://docsouth.unc.edu/⟩
         Diary of Samuel A. Agnew
         "Read and Circulate! The Elections in August Impose Upon the People of
            North Carolina One of the Most Solemn and Important Duties That
            Citizens Were Ever Called Upon to Perform" [1872?]
      Reminiscences of Jacob Alson Long
      Alexander Carey McAlister Papers

Richmond Pearson Papers
David Schenck Books
Charlottesville, Va.
Valley of the Shadow Project, Electronic Text Center, ⟨http://valley.vcdh.virginia.edu/⟩
Augusta County Letters and Diaries, Civil War Letters
Rachel Cormany Diary
Durham, N.C.
Manuscripts Department, Duke University
William Woods Holden Collection
Ku Klux Klan Collection
Benjamin Markham Papers
Bryan Tyson Papers
Hattiesburg, Miss.
University of Southern Mississippi, McCain Library and Archives
Author's Letters and Conversation Notes (deposited copies)
Florence Knight Blaylock
Annette Knight
Earle Knight
Ethel Knight
Dorothy Knight Marsh
Olga Watts Nelson
John C. Burruss, "History of Universalism in Mississippi," n.p., file box M245
L. Clinton Kirkland Papers, 1894–1979, Papers, 1886–1983, boxes 1 and 2
Mississippi Oral History Program
Interview with J. Brackin Kirkland by Dr. C. Paul Massey, 1 Oct. 1973,
vol. 41 (1974)
Mississippi Sovereignty Commission File, Leesha Faulkner Civil Rights
Collection
Huntsville, Ala.
Oakwood Archives and Museum, Oakwood College
Anna Knight Papers
North American Regional Voice (Apr. 1988)
Jackson, Miss.
Mississippi Department of Archives and History
Bonds, Oaths of Office, 1863–65, RG 28
Confederate Records, RG 9
County Records (microfilm)
Jones County Chancery Court, Final Records, First District, 1857–90
Governors' Papers, RG 27
James L. Alcorn
Adelbert Ames
Charles Clark
Robert Lowry
John J. Pettus
William L. Sharkey

Legislative Records, RG 47
Petitions and Memorials, 1817–39
Senate Journal, vol. 88
James L. Power Scrapbook
Walter Simpson Trial, box ID 6063, series 6 (Supreme Court), Case no. 7048, 1892
Unpublished Manuscripts
Stephen Cresswell, "Who Was Who in Mississippi's Oppositional Political Parties, 1878–1963"
Thomas J. Knight, "Intimate Sketch of Activities of Newton Knight and 'Free State of Jones County'" (1935)
Works Projects Administration, RG 60, unpublished files, Jones, Covington, Jasper, and Marion Counties
Mississippi Supreme Court, Clerk's Office
State of Mississippi v. Davis Knight, 13 Dec. 1948, Case no. 646, court record and transcript of the Circuit Court, Jones County, Miss.
Laurel, Miss.
Lauren Rogers Museum of Art Library Collection
Newspaper Clipping file
Northampton, Mass.
Sophia Smith Collection, Smith College
[Adelbert] Ames Family Papers
Raleigh, N.C.
North Carolina Department of Archives and History
General Assembly Session Records
Petitions to Assembly
Governors' Letter Books
William W. Holden
Governors' Papers, 1861–70
William W. Holden
Zebulon Vance
Jonathan Worth

Official Records

Washington, D.C.
National Archives
Records of the Adjutant General's Office, 1780s–1917, RG 94
Compiled Service Records of Volunteer Union Soldiers Who Served in Organizations from the State of Louisiana, M396, 50 rolls
Records of the Bureau of Refugees, Freedmen, and Abandoned Lands, RG 105 (microfilm)
Indentures of Apprenticeship, Sept. 1865–Dec. 1866, series 2489
Letters Received, May 1866–Dec. 1868, Hillsboro, N.C., series 2686
Letters Received, Dec. 1865–Dec. 1868, Salisbury, N.C., series 2837

Records of the Assistant Commissioner for the State of Mississippi,
Bureau of Refugees, Freedmen, and Abandoned Lands, 1865–69,
M826, 50 rolls

Records Relating to Cases Tried and Destitute Freedmen, 1868, Hillsboro,
N.C., series 2690

Register of Indentured Apprentices, Nov. 1865–June 1866, series 2488

Records of the Commissioner of Claims (Southern Claims Commission), 1871–80,
M87, 14.00 rolls

Records of the Department of Justice, RG 60
Letters Received by the Department of Justice from Mississippi, 1871–84,
M970

Records of the Department of Veterans' Affairs, 1773–1985, RG 15
Pension Application Files Based on Service in the Civil War and Spanish-
American War ("Civil War and Later")

Records of the General Accounting Office, Third Auditor's Office, Southern
Claims Commission, RG 217

Records of the U.S. Court of Claims, 1835–1966, RG 123
Committee on War Claims
Claims of Newton Knight and Others, #8013 and #8464

Records of the U.S. House of Representatives, RG 233
Barred and Disallowed Case Files of the Claims Commission, 1871–80,
M1407, 4,829 cards (microfiche)
Newton Knight Folder, box 15

War Department Collection of Confederate Records, RG 109
Compiled Service Records of Confederate Soldiers Who Served in
Organizations from the States of Mississippi (M269), North Carolina
(M270), and Texas (M323)

Local Court Records

Ellisville, Miss.
Office of the Circuit Clerk, Jones County
Circuit Court Minutes, First District, Books 3, 5, 7
Folder, Trial Papers of Davis Knight, 1948, case #646
Justice's Docket, 1887–95
Liberty, Tex.
Sam Houston Library and Research Center
Delinquent or Insolvent Tax Payers, Polk County, 1891, 1892, 1897, 1902, 1911
Election Return Record, Hardin County
Laborer's Lien Record, Polk County, 1885–1929
List of Delinquent Tax Payers, Polk County, 1892–1913
Minutes of Election Precincts, Hardin County
Record of Election Judges, Hardin County, 1904–20
Record of Lands and Town Lots Sold by Tax Collector, Polk County, 1877–86,
1888, 1889, 1897, 1899, 1900, 1903, 1909, 1910

Raleigh, N.C.
North Carolina Department of Archives and History
Apprentice Bonds, Orange and Montgomery Counties
Bastardy Bonds, Orange and Montgomery Counties
Civil Action Papers, Montgomery County
Coroner's Reports, Orange County
County Court Minutes, Orange and Montgomery Counties
Criminal Action Papers, Orange and Montgomery Counties
Divorce Records, Orange and Montgomery Counties
Estate Records, Orange and Montgomery Counties
Land Entry Book, Orange County
Marriage Bonds, North Carolina
Minute Dockets of the County Court, Orange and Montgomery Counties
Minute Dockets of the Superior Court, Orange and Montgomery Counties
Minutes of the Wardens of the Poor, Orange and Montgomery Counties
Miscellaneous Records, Orange and Montgomery Counties
Official Bonds and Records, 1837–1918, Montgomery County
Wills, Orange and Montgomery Counties

Private Collections

Ardella Knight Barrett Papers, in possession of Florence Knight Blaylock, Soso, Miss.
Anna Knight Collection, in possession of Dorothy Knight Marsh, Washington, D.C.
Shirley Insall Pieratt Collection, Ainsworth-Collins Papers, in possession of Victoria
   Bynum
Research Files
Sondra Yvonne Bivins, Rochester, N.Y.
Florence Knight Blaylock, Soso, Miss.
Victoria Bynum, San Marcos, Tex.
B. T. Collins Jr., Laurel, Miss.
Wynona G. Frost, Detroit, Mich.
Donnis Lyon, Laurel, Miss.
Keith Lyon, Laurel, Miss.
Ed Payne, Jackson, Miss.
Ralph Poore, Boise, Idaho
Dorothy Lyon Thomas, Hattiesburg, Miss.
Dianne Walkup, Tacoma, Wash.
Kenneth Welch, Soso, Miss.

U.S. Censuses and Census Reports

U.S. Bureau of the Census, Federal Manuscript Agricultural and Manufacturing
   Schedule, 1850, 1860, 1870, 1880. National Archives, microfilm.
———. Federal Manuscript Census, Population Schedules, 1820, 1830, 1840, 1850, 1860,
   1870, 1880, 1900, 1910, 1920, 1930. National Archives, microfilm.

————. Federal Manuscript Census, Slave Schedules, 1850, 1860, Mississippi, North Carolina. National Archives, microfilm.

Published Proceedings of the U.S. Congress

Journal of the House of Representatives of the United States. 3rd Sess., 41st Cong. 5 Dec. 1870. Washington, D.C.: Government Printing Office, 1871.
————. *2nd Sess., 42nd Cong.* 4 Dec. 1871. Washington, D.C.: Government Printing Office, 1872.
————. *1st Sess., 43rd Cong.* 1 Dec. 1873. Washington, D.C.: Government Printing Office, 1873.
Journal of the Senate of the United States. 1st Sess., 43rd Cong. 18 Dec. 1873. Washington, D.C.: Government Printing Office, 1874.
————. *1st Sess., 50th Cong.* 26 March 1888. Washington, D.C.: Government Printing Office, 1888.

Published Proceedings of State Supreme Courts and Legislatures

Journal of the Proceedings and Debates in the Constitutional Convention of the State of Mississippi, August, 1865 (Mississippi Constitutional Convention, 1865), 122, Making of America Books Collection, ⟨http://quod.lib.umdl.umich.edu⟩.
Journal of the Proceedings in the Constitutional Convention of the State of Mississippi, 1868. Jackson: E. Stafford, Printer, 1871.

Published Documents and Compilations of Records

Ancestry.com, ⟨www.Ancestry.com⟩. American Civil War Soldiers
————. City Directory, Memphis, Tenn., 1890–81
————. City Directory, Washington, D.C., 1890
Bettersworth, John K., ed. *Mississippi in the Confederacy: As They Saw It.* 1962. New York: Kraus Reprint Co., 1970.
Civil War History, ⟨www.civilwarhistory.com⟩. "Treatment of Prisoners at Camp Morton"
Edwards, Patricia N., and Jean Strickland. *Who Married Whom, Jones County, Mississippi.* Moss Point, Miss.: N.p., 1986.
Jaquette, Henrietta S., ed. *Letters of Cornelia Hancock from the Army of the Potomac.* Lincoln: University of Nebraska Press, 1998 (E-Book edition).
Joslyn, Mauriel Phillips, ed. *Charlotte's Boys: Civil War Letters of the Branch Family of Savannah.* Berryville, Va.: Rockbridge, 1996.
"Kay's Family Tree," ⟨http://www.kaysfamilytree.com/simmons2.html⟩
Lackey, Richard S., ed. "Minutes of Zion Baptist Church of Buckatunna, Wayne County, Mississippi" (original manuscript at Mississippi Baptist Historical Commission Library, Mississippi College, Clinton, Miss.). *Mississippi Genealogical Exchange* 19 (Spring 1973): 13–21, 59–65, 85–93, 123–25.

McPherson, Elizabeth Gregory, ed. "Letters from North Carolina to Andrew Johnson."
  North Carolina Historical Review 39 (Jan. 1952): 118–19.
Peebles, Ruth, ed. *There Never Were Such Men Before: The Civil War Soldiers and
  Veterans of Polk County, Texas, 1861–1865*. Livingston, Tex.: Polk County Historical
  Commission, n.d.
Pryor, Sara Rice. *Reminiscences of Peace and War*. New York: Macmillan, 1904.
Rawick, George P., ed. *The American Slave: A Composite Autobiography*. Supplement,
  ser. 1, vols. 8–10, Mississippi Narratives, pts. 3–5. Westport, Conn.: Greenwood
  Press, 1972.
Rootsweb.com, ⟨www.rootsweb.com⟩. "Camp Morton, Civil War Camp and Union
  Prison, Indianapolis, Ind., 1861–1865." "The Owens Family," files of Jen Taylor.
Smith, Janet, Jean Strickland, and Patricia N. Edwards. *Who Married Whom, Covington
  County, Mississippi*. Moss Point, Miss.: N.p., 1991.
Strickland, Ben, and Jean Strickland. *Records of Jones County, Mississippi: Deed Book
  A & B, 1827–1856*. Moss Point, Miss.: N.p., 1981.
Strickland, Jean, and Patricia N. Edwards. *Confederate Records: Covington, Wayne and
  Jones County*. Moss Point, Miss.: N.p., 1987.
———. *Miscellaneous Records of Jones County, MS*. Moss Point, Miss.: N.p., 1992.
———. *Records of Jones County, Mississippi*. Moss Point, Miss.: N.p., n.d.
U.S. War Department. *War of the Rebellion: A Compilation of the Official Records of the Union
  and Confederate Armies*. Washington, D.C.: Government Printing Office, 1880–1901.
———. *Supplement to the Official Records of the Union and Confederate Armies*, edited by
  Janet B. Hewett. Wilmington, N.C.: Broadfoot, 1996.
Vicksburg National Military Park, ⟨http://www.nps.gov/vick/historyculture/
  3rd-michigan-cavalry.htm⟩. 3rd Michigan Cavalry.
Watford, Christopher M. *The Piedmont*. Vol. 1 of *The Civil War in North Carolina:
  Soldiers' and Civilians' Letters and Diaries, 1861–1865*. Jefferson, N.C.: McFarland, 2003.
Yearns, W. Buck, and John G. Barrett, eds. *North Carolina Civil War Documentary*.
  Chapel Hill: University of North Carolina Press, 1980.

Newspapers and Magazines

Adams Sentinel (Gettysburg, Pa.)
American Wesleyan (New York, N.Y.)
Beaumont Enterprise (Beaumont, Tex.)
Clarion-Ledger (Jackson, Miss.)
Confederate Veteran, ⟨http://www
  .civilwarhistory.com⟩ (Nashville, Tenn.)
Ellisville (Miss.) News
Ellisville (Miss.) Progress-Item
Ellisville (Miss.) Progressive
Jasper County News (Bay Springs, Miss.)
Jones County News (Laurel, Miss.)
Laurel (Miss.) Daily Leader
Laurel (Miss.) Leader Call

Laurel (Miss.) Ledger
Natchez (Miss.) Courier
New Orleans Item
New South (Ellisville, Miss.)
New York Times
Pearl River News (Columbia, Miss.)
The Rebel (Hallettsville, Tex.)
The State: Down Home in North Carolina
  (Raleigh, N.C.)
St. Louis Post-Dispatch
Tempo Magazine (*Houston Post*)
  (Houston, Tex.)
True Wesleyan (New York, N.Y.)

Books

Crooks, Mrs. E. W. *Life of Reverend Adam Crooks, A.M.* Syracuse, N.Y.: Wesleyan Methodist Publishing Company, 1871.

Helper, Hinton Rowan. *The Impending Crisis of the South and How to Meet It.* New York: Burdick Brothers, 1857.

Surby, R. W. *Grierson's Raids, and Hatch's Sixty-Four Days' March, with Biographical Sketches and the Life and Adventures of Chickasaw, the Scout.* Chicago: Rounds and James, 1865.

Weeks, Steven B. *Southern Quakers and Slavery: A Study in Institutional History.* New York: Bergman, 1896.

Articles

Claiborne, J. F. H. "A Trip through the Piney Woods" (1841–42), reprinted in *Publications of the Mississippi Historical Society* 9 (1906): 487–538.

Ramsey, N. A. "61st North Carolina Infantry." Durham, N.C.: N.p., 1901. ⟨http://members.aol.com/jweaver301/nc/61ncinf.htm⟩ (Sept. 2006).

SECONDARY SOURCES

Family Genealogies and Biographical Dictionaries

Collins, Carr P., Jr. *Royal Ancestors of Magna Charta Barons.* Dallas: N.p., 1959.

Collins, Vinson Allen. *A Story of My Parents: Warren Jacob Collins and Tolitha Eboline Valentine Collins.* Livingston, Tex.: N.p., 1962.

Leverett, Rudy. "Ole Rosinheels: A Genealogical Sketch of the Family of Major Amos McLemore, 27th Mississippi Infantry Regiment, C.S.A. Unpublished manuscript, 1988.

Loftin, Donald Howard. "Loftin Chronicles." N.p.: N.p., n.d., author's possession.

Pieratt, Shirley Insall. *The Ainsworth-Collins Clan in Texas, 1838.* Boerne, Tex.: N.p. 2004.

Richter, Winnie, ed. *The Heritage of Montgomery County, North Carolina.* Troy, N.C.: Montgomery County Historical Society, n.d.

Sumrall, Jan, and Kenneth Welch. *The Knights and Related Families.* Denham Springs, La.: N.p., 1985.

Thomas, Winnie Knight, Earle W. Knight, Lavada Knight Dykes, and Martha Kaye Dykes Lowery. *The Family of John "Jackie" Knight and Keziah Davis Knight, 1773–1985.* Magee, Miss.: Robert and Delores Knight Vinson, 1985.

Tyler, Ron, ed. *New Handbook of Texas.* 6 vols. Austin: Texas State Historical Association, 1996.

Wharton, Clarence Ray. *Texas under Many Flags.* Chicago: American Historical Society, 1930.

Books

Abernethy, Francis E. ed. *Tales from the Big Thicket.* Denton: University of North Texas Press, 1967.

Alexander, Adele Logan. *Ambiguous Lives: Free Women of Color in Rural Georgia, 1789–1879*. Fayetteville: University of Arkansas Press, 1991.

Alexander, Roberta Sue. *North Carolina Faces the Freedmen: Race Relations during Presidential Reconstruction, 1865–67*. Durham, N.C.: Duke University Press, 1985.

Ames, Blanche Ames. *Adelbert Ames, 1835–1933*. New York: Argosy-Antiquarian, 1964.

Ash, Stephen V. *When the Yankees Came: Chaos and Conflict in the Occupied South, 1861–1865*. Chapel Hill: University of North Carolina Press, 1995.

Ayers, Edward L. *Vengeance and Justice: Crime and Punishment in the Nineteenth-Century South*. New York: Oxford University Press, 1984.

Bardaglio, Peter. *Reconstructing the Household: Families, Sex & the Law in the Nineteenth-Century South*. Chapel Hill: University of North Carolina Press, 1995.

Baum, Dale. *The Shattering of Texas Unionism: Politics in the Lone Star State in the Civil War Era*. Baton Rouge: Louisiana State University Press, 1998.

Beals, Carleton. *War within a War: The Confederacy against Itself*. Philadelphia: Chilton Press, 1965.

Bearss, Edwin C. *Decision in Mississippi: Mississippi's Important Role in the War between the States*. Jackson: Mississippi Commission on the War between the States, 1962.

Beatty, Bess. *Alamance: The Holt Family and Industrialization in a North Carolina County, 1837–1900*. Baton Rouge: Louisiana State University Press, 1999.

Bercaw, Nancy. *Gendered Freedoms: Race, Rights, and the Politics of Household in the Delta, 1861–1875*. Gainesville: University Press of Florida, 2003.

Betts, Vicki. "'A Sacred Charge upon Our Hands.'" In *The Seventh Star of the Confederacy: Texas during the Civil War*, edited by Kenneth W. Howell, 244–65. Denton: University of North Texas Press, 2009.

Billingsley, Carolyn Earle. *Communities of Kinship: Antebellum Families and the Settlement of the Cotton Frontier*. Athens: University of Georgia Press, 2004.

Black, Daniel P. *Dismantling Black Manhood: An Historical and Literary Analysis of the Legacy of Slavery*. London: Routledge, 1997.

Blair, William. *Virginia's Private War: Feeding Body and Soul in the Confederacy, 1861–1865*. New York: Oxford University Press, 1998.

Blight, David W. *Race and Reunion: The Civil War in American Memory*. Cambridge, Mass.: Harvard University Press, 2001.

Bolton, Charles C. *Poor Whites of the Antebellum South: Tenants and Laborers in Central North Carolina and Northeast Mississippi*. Durham, N.C.: Duke University Press, 1994.

Bolton, Charles C., and Scott Culclasure, eds. *The Confessions of Edward Isham: A Poor White Life of the Old South*. Athens: University of Georgia Press, 1998.

Bond, Bradley G. "Herders, Farmers, and Markets on the Inner Frontier: The Mississippi Piney Woods, 1850–1860." In *Plain Folk of the South Revisited*, edited by Samuel C. Hyde Jr., 73–99. Baton Rouge: Louisiana State University Press, 1997.

———. *Political Culture in the Nineteenth-Century South: Mississippi, 1830–1900*. Baton Rouge: Louisiana State University Press, 1995.

Brown, David. *Southern Outcast: Hinton Rowan Helper and the Impending Crisis*. Baton Rouge: Louisiana State University Press, 2006.

Brown, Norman D. *Hood, Bonnet, and Little Brown Jug: Texas Politics, 1921–1928*. College Station: Texas A&M University Press, 1984.

Brundage, W. Fitzhugh. *Lynching in the New South: Georgia and Virginia, 1880–1930.* Urbana: University of Illinois Press, 1993.

———. *The Southern Past: A Clash of Race and Memory.* Cambridge, Mass.: Belknap Press, 2005.

Buenger, Walter L. "The Riddle of Secession." In *Lone Star Blue & Gray: Essays on Texas in the Civil War,* edited by Ralph A. Wooster, 1–26. Austin: Texas State Historical Association, 1995.

———. *Secession and the Union in Texas.* Austin: University of Texas Press, 1984.

Bullard, Mary R. *Robert Stafford of Cumberland Island: Growth of a Planter.* Athens: University of Georgia Press, 1995.

Burton, Orville Vernon. *The Age of Lincoln.* New York: Hill and Wang, 2007.

Bynum, Victoria E. *The Free State of Jones: Mississippi's Longest Civil War.* Chapel Hill: University of North Carolina Press, 2001.

———. "Refashioning the Bonds of Womanhood: Divorce in Reconstruction North Carolina." In *Divided Houses: Gender and the Civil War,* edited by Catherine Clinton and Nina Silber, 320–33. New York: Oxford University Press, 1992.

———. *Unruly Women: The Politics of Social and Sexual Control in the Old South.* Chapel Hill: University of North Carolina Press, 1992.

Cantrell, Gregg. *The People's Revolt: Populism in Texas.* Work-in-progress under contract with Yale University Press.

Clinton, Catherine. "Reconstructing Freedwomen." In *Divided Houses: Gender and the Civil War,* edited by Catherine Clinton and Nina Silber, 306–19. New York: Oxford University Press, 1992.

Clinton, Catherine, and Michele Gillespie, eds. *The Devil's Lane: Sex and Race in the Early South.* New York: Oxford University Press, 1997.

Clinton, Catherine, and Nina Silber, eds. *Divided Houses: Gender and the Civil War.* New York: Oxford University Press, 1992.

Collins, Vinson Allen. "Settling the Old Poplar-Tree Place." In *Tales from the Big Thicket,* edited by Francis E. Abernethy, 58–68. Denton: University of North Texas Press, 2002.

Cresswell, Stephen. *Multiparty Politics in Mississippi, 1877–1902.* Jackson: University Press of Mississippi, 1995.

———. *Rednecks, Redeemers and Race: Mississippi after Reconstruction: 1877–1917.* Jackson: University Press of Mississippi/Mississippi Historical Society, 2006.

Crofts, Daniel W. *Reluctant Confederates: Upper South Unionists in the Secession Crisis.* Chapel Hill: University of North Carolina Press, 1989.

Dailey, Jane, Glenda Gilmore, and Bryant Simon, eds. *Jumpin' Jim Crow: Southern Politics from Civil War to Civil Rights.* Princeton, N.J.: Princeton University Press, 2000.

Davidson, Chandler. *Race and Class in Texas Politics.* Princeton, N.J.: Princeton University Press, 1990.

Degler, Carl N. *The Other South: Southern Dissenters in the Nineteenth Century.* New York: Harper and Row, 1974.

Dominquez, Virginia R. *White by Definition: Social Classification in Creole Louisiana.* New Brunswick, N.J.: Rutgers University Press, 1968.

Durrill, Wayne. *War of Another Kind: A Southern Community in the Great Rebellion.* New York: Oxford University Press, 1990.

Edwards, Laura. *Gendered Strife and Confusion: The Political Culture of Reconstruction.* Urbana: University of Illinois Press, 1997.

———. *Scarlett Doesn't Live Here Anymore: Southern Women in the Civil War Era.* Urbana: University of Illinois Press, 2000.

Elder, Pat Spurlock. *Melungeons: Examining an Appalachian Legend.* Blountville, Tenn.: Continuity Press, 1999.

Escott, Paul D. *Many Excellent People: Power and Privilege in North Carolina, 1850–1890.* Chapel Hill: University of North Carolina Press, 1985.

Eubanks, W. Ralph. *The House at the End of the Road: The Story of Three Generations of an Interracial Family in the American South.* New York: Harper, 2009.

Fahs, Alice, and Joan Waugh, eds. *The Memory of the Civil War in American Culture.* Chapel Hill: University of North Carolina Press, 2004.

Faust, Drew Gilpin. *Mothers of Invention: Women of the Slaveholding South in the American Civil War.* Chapel Hill: University of North Carolina Press, 1996.

Fellman, Michael. *Inside War: The Guerrilla Conflict in Missouri during the American Civil War.* New York: Oxford University Press, 1989.

Fitzgerald, Michael W. *A Splendid Failure: Postwar Reconstruction in the South.* Chicago: Ivan R. Dee, 2007.

Foley, Neil. *The White Scourge: Mexicans, Blacks, and Poor Whites in Texas Cotton Culture.* Berkeley: University of California Press, 1997.

Foner, Eric. *Reconstruction: America's Unfinished Revolution, 1863–1877.* Baton Rouge: Louisiana State University Press, 1988.

Forret, Jeff. *Race Relations at the Margins: Slaves and Poor Whites in the Antebellum Countryside.* Baton Rouge: Louisiana State University Press, 2006.

Franklin, John Hope. *The Free Negro in North Carolina, 1790–1860.* Chapel Hill: University of North Carolina Press, 1943.

Gallagher, Gary. *The Confederate War.* Cambridge, Mass.: Harvard University Press, 1999.

Gilmore, Glenda Elizabeth. *Gender and Jim Crow: Women and the Politics of White Supremacy in North Carolina, 1896–1920.* Chapel Hill: University of North Carolina Press, 1996.

Goodwyn, Lawrence. *Democratic Promise: The Populist Moment in America.* New York: Oxford University Press, 1976.

Gould, Lewis L., ed. *Progressives and Prohibitionists: Texas Democrats in the Wilson Era.* Austin: Texas State Historical Association, 1992.

Green, George Norris. *The Establishment in Texas Politics: The Primitive Years, 1938–1957.* Norman: University of Oklahoma Press, 1979.

Green, James R. *Grass-Roots Socialism: Radical Movements in the Southwest, 1895–1943.* Baton Rouge: Louisiana State University Press, 1978.

Gunter, Pete A. Y. *The Big Thicket: An Ecological Reevaluation.* Denton: University of North Texas Press, 1993.

Hahn, Steven. *The Roots of Southern Populism: Yeoman Farmers and the Transformation of the Georgia Upcountry, 1850–1890.* New York: Oxford University Press, 1983.

Hale, Grace Elizabeth. *Making Whiteness: The Culture of Segregation in the South, 1890–1940*. New York: Pantheon, 1998.

Hall, Jacquelyn Dowd. "'The Mind That Burns in Each Body': Women, Rape, and Racial Violence." In *Powers of Desire: The Politics of Sexuality*, edited by Ann Snitow, Christine Stansell, and Sharon Thompson, 328–49. New York: Monthly Review Press, 1983.

———. *Revolt against Chivalry: Jessie Daniel Ames and the Women's Campaign against Lynching*. 2nd ed. New York: Columbia University Press, 1988.

Harkins, Anthony. *Hillbilly: A Cultural History of an American Icon*. New York: Oxford University Press, 2004.

Harris, J. William. *The New South: New Histories*. New York: Routledge, 2008.

Harris, William C. *The Day of the Carpetbagger: Republican Reconstruction in Mississippi*. Baton Rouge: Louisiana State University Press, 1979.

———. *Presidential Reconstruction in Mississippi*. Baton Rouge: Louisiana State University Press, 1967.

Higginbotham, Evelyn Brooks. *Righteous Discontent: The Women's Movement in the Black Baptist Church, 1880–1920*. Cambridge, Mass.: Harvard University Press, 1993.

Hilliard, Sam Bowers. *Hog Meat and Hoe Cake: Food Supply in the Old South, 1840–1860*. Carbondale: Southern Illinois University Press, 1972.

Hine, Darlene Clark. "Rape and the Inner Lives of Southern Black Women: Thoughts on the Culture of Dissemblence." In *Southern Women: Histories and Identities*, edited by Virginia Bernhard, Betty Brandon, Elizabeth Fox-Genovese, and Theda Purdue, 177–89. Columbia: University of Missouri Press, 1992.

———, ed. *The 19th Century: From Emancipation to Jim Crow*. Vol. 2 of *A Question of Manhood: A Reader in U.S. Black Men's History and Masculinity*. Bloomington: Indiana University Press, 2001.

Hirschman, Elizabeth Caldwell. *Melungeons: The Last Lost Tribe in America*. Macon, Ga.: Mercer University Press, 2005.

Hodes, Martha, ed. *Sex, Love, Race: Crossing Boundaries in North American History*. New York: New York University Press, 1999.

———. *White Women, Black Men: Illicit Sex in the 19th-Century South*. New Haven, Conn.: Yale University Press, 1997.

hooks, bell. *We Real Cool: Black Men and Masculinity*. London: Routledge, 2003.

House, Aline. *Big Thicket: Its Heritage*. San Antonio, Tex.: Naylor, 1967.

Howell, Kenneth W., ed. *The Seventh Star of the Confederacy: Texas during the Civil War*. Denton: University of North Texas Press, 2009.

Hunter, Tera W. *To 'Joy My Freedom: Southern Black Women's Lives and Labors after the Civil War*. Cambridge, Mass.: Harvard University Press, 1997.

Hyde, Samuel C., Jr., ed. "Backcountry Justice in the Piney-Woods South." In *Plain Folk of the South Revisited*, edited by Samuel C. Hyde Jr., 228–49. Baton Rouge: Louisiana State University Press, 1997.

Inscoe, John, and Robert Kenzer. *Enemies of the Country: New Perspectives on Unionists in the Civil War South*. Athens: University of Georgia Press, 2001.

Jenkins, Sally, and John Stauffer. *State of Jones: The Small Southern County That Seceded from the Confederacy*. New York: Doubleday, 2009.

Johnson, Guion Griffis. *Antebellum North Carolina: A Social History*. Chapel Hill: University of North Carolina Press, 1937.

Jones, Jacqueline. *Labor of Love, Labor of Sorrow: Black Women, Work, and the Family from Slavery to the Present*. New York: Vintage, 1985.

Jones, Katherine M. *Heroines of Dixie: Confederate Women Tell Their Side of the War*. New York: Bobbs-Merrill, 1955.

Kennedy, N. Brent, with Robyn Vaughan Kennedy. *The Melungeons: The Resurrection of a Proud People, an Untold Story of Ethnic Cleansing in America*. Macon, Ga.: Mercer University Press, 1994.

Kenzer, Robert C. *Kinship and Neighborhood in a Southern Community: Orange County, North Carolina, 1849–1881*. Knoxville: University of Tennessee Press, 1987.

Kirwan, Albert D. *Revolt of the Rednecks: Mississippi Politics, 1876–1925*. 1951. Gloucester, Mass.: Peter Smith, 1964.

Klingberg, Frank. *The Southern Claims Commission*. 1955. New York: Octagon Books, 1978.

Knight, Anna. *Mississippi Girl: An Autobiography*. Nashville, Tenn.: Southern Publishing Association, 1952.

Knight, Ethel. *The Echo of the Black Horn: An Authentic Tale of "The Governor" of "The Free State of Jones"*. N.p.: n.p., 1951.

Knight, Thomas Jefferson. *The Life and Activities of Captain Newton Knight and His Company and the "Free State of Jones County."* 1935. Rev. ed., Laurel, Miss.: N.p., 1946.

Kruman, Marc W. *Parties and Politics in North Carolina, 1834–1865*. Baton Rouge: Louisiana State University Press, 1983.

Leslie, Kent Anderson. *Woman of Color, Daughter of Privilege: Amanda America Dickson, 1849–1893*. Athens: University of Georgia Press, 1995.

Leverett, Rudy. *Legend of the Free State of Jones*. Jackson: University Press of Mississippi, 1984.

Litwack, Leon F. *Been in the Storm So Long: The Aftermath of Slavery*. New York: Alfred A. Knopf, 1979.

———. *Trouble in Mind: Black Southerners in the Age of Jim Crow*. New York: Alfred A. Knopf, 1998.

Lonn, Ella. *Desertion during the Civil War*. 1928. Lincoln: University of Nebraska Press, 1998.

Loughmiller, Campbell, and Lynn Loughmiller, comp. and eds. *Big Thicket Legacy*. Austin: University of Texas Press, 1977.

Lowe, Richard G., and Randolph B. Campbell. *Planters and Plain Folk: Agriculture in Antebellum Texas*. Dallas: Southern Methodist University Press, 1987.

Lumpkin, Katharine Du Pre. *The Making of a Southerner*. 1947. Athens: University of Georgia Press, 1991.

MacLean, Nancy. *Behind the Mask of Chivalry: The Making of the Second Ku Klux Klan*. New York: Oxford University Press, 1994.

Marten, James. *Texas Divided: Loyalty and Dissent in the Lone Star State, 1856–1874*. Lexington: University Press of Kentucky, 1990.

McCaslin, Richard. *Tainted Breeze: The Great Hanging at Gainesville, Texas, 1862*. Baton Rouge: Louisiana State University Press, 1994.

McFeely, William S. *Yankee Stepfather: General O. O. Howard and the Freedman.* New York: W. W. Norton, 1994.

McKinney, Gordon. *Southern Mountain Republicans, 1865–1900: Politics and the Southern Appalachian Community.* 1978. Nashville: University of Tennessee Press, 1998.

McMillen, Neil R. *Dark Journey: Black Mississippians in the Age of Jim Crow.* Urbana: University of Illinois Press, 1989.

Mills, Gary B. *The Forgotten People: Cane River's Creoles of Color.* Baton Rouge: Louisiana State University Press, 1977.

Moneyhon, Carl. *Texas after the Civil War: The Struggle of Reconstruction.* College Station: Texas A&M University Press, 2004.

Montgomery, Rebecca S. *The Politics of Education in the New South: Women and Reform in Georgia, 1890–1930.* Baton Rouge: Louisiana State University Press, 2006.

Murray, Pauli. *Proud Shoes: The Story of an American Family.* 1956. New York: Harper and Row, 1978.

Nelson, Scott Reynolds. "Red Strings and Half Brothers: Civil Wars in Alamance County, North Carolina, 1861–1871." In *Enemies of the Country: New Perspectives on Unionists in the Civil War South,* edited by John C. Inscoe and Robert C. Kenzer, 37–53. Athens: University of Georgia Press, 2001.

Neville, Dorothy. *Carr P. Collins: Man on the Move.* Dallas: Park Press, 1963.

Nicholson, Ray S. *Wesleyan Methodism in the South.* Syracuse, N.Y.: Wesleyan Methodist Publishing House, 1933.

Noe, Kenneth W., and Shannon H. Wilson. *The Civil War in Appalachia: Collected Essays.* Knoxville: University of Tennessee Press, 1997.

O'Donovan, Susan Eva. *Becoming Free in the Cotton South.* Cambridge, Mass.: Harvard University Press, 2007.

Olsen, Otto. *Carpetbagger's Crusade: The Life of Albion Winegar Tourgee.* Baltimore: Johns Hopkins University Press, 1965.

Painter, Nell Irvin. *Southern History across the Color Line.* Chapel Hill: University of North Carolina Press, 2002.

Paludan, Phillip Shaw. *Victims: A True Story of the Civil War.* Knoxville: University of Tennessee Press, 1981.

Pascoe, Peggy. *What Comes Naturally: Miscegenation Law and the Making of Race in America.* New York: Oxford University Press, 2009.

Penningroth, Dylan C. *The Claims of Kinfolk: African American Property and Community in the Nineteenth-Century South.* Chapel Hill: University of North Carolina Press, 2002.

Pickering, David, and Judy Falls. *Brush Men and Vigilantes: Civil War Dissent in Texas.* College Station: Texas A&M University Press, 2000.

Pierson, Michael D. *Free Hearts, Free Homes: Gender and American Antislavery Politics.* Chapel Hill: University of North Carolina Press, 2003.

———. *Mutiny at Fort Jackson: The Untold Story of the Fall of New Orleans.* Chapel Hill: University of North Carolina Press, 2008.

Pitts, Edna. "The Civil War and 'Kaiser's Burnout.'" In *History of Hardin County,* edited by Robert L. Schaadt, 20–22. Kountze, Tex.: Hardin County Historical Commission, n.d.

Polk, Noel, ed. *Mississippi's Piney Woods: A Human Perspective.* Jackson: University Press of Mississippi, 1986.

Powell, A. D. *"Passing" for Who You Really Are: Essays in Support of Multiracial Whiteness.* Palm Coast, Fla.: Backintyme Publishing, 2005.

Rable, George C. *But There Was No Peace: The Role of Violence in the Politics of Reconstruction.* Athens: University of Georgia Press, 1984.

————. *Civil Wars: Women and the Crisis of Southern Nationalism.* Urbana: University of Illinois Press, 1989.

Rafter, Nicole Hahn, ed. *White Trash: The Eugenic Family Studies, 1877–1919.* Boston: Northeastern University Press, 1988.

Rienstra, Ellen Walker. "A Family Full of Legends." In *Tales from the Big Thicket,* edited by Francis E. Abernethy, 181–98. 1967. Denton: University of North Texas Press, 2002.

Sandweiss, Martha. *Passing Strange: A Gilded Age Tale of Love and Deception across the Color Line.* New York: Penguin, 2009.

Schaadt, Robert L., ed. *History of Hardin County.* Kountze, Tex.: Hardin County Historical Commission, n.d.

Schwalm, Leslie. *A Hard Fight for We: Women's Transition from Slavery to Freedom in South Carolina.* Urbana: University of Illinois Press, 1997.

————. "'Sweet Dreams of Freedom': Freedwomen's Reconstruction of Life and Labor in Lowcountry South Carolina." In *The Black Worker: A Reader,* edited by Eric Arnesen, 11–40. Urbana: University of Illinois Press, 2004.

Sensbach, Jon F. "Interracial Sects: Religion, Race, and Gender among Early North Carolina Moravians." In *The Devil's Lane: Sex and Race in the Early South,* edited by Catherine Clinton and Michele Gillespie, 154–67. New York: Oxford University Press, 1997.

Silber, Nina. *The Romance of Reunion: Northerners and the South, 1865–1900.* Chapel Hill: University of North Carolina Press, 1993.

Sitton, Thad, and James H. Conrad. *Nameless Towns: Texas Sawmill Communities, 1880–1942.* Austin: University of Texas Press, 1998.

Smith, Lillian. *Killers of the Dream.* New York: W. W. Norton, 1949.

Stein, Stephen J. *Communities of Dissent: A History of Alternative Religions in America.* New York: Oxford University Press, 2003.

Storey, Margaret. *Loyalty and Loss: Alabama's Unionists in the Civil War and Reconstruction.* Baton Rouge: Louisiana State University Press, 2004.

Street, James. *Look Away! A Dixie Notebook.* New York: Viking Press, 1936.

————. *Tap Roots.* Garden City, N.Y.: Sun Dial Press, 1943.

Sutherland, Daniel E. *A Savage Conflict: The Decisive Role of Guerrillas in the American Civil War.* Chapel Hill: University of North Carolina Press, 2009.

————, ed. *Guerrillas, Unionists, and Violence on the Confederate Home Front.* Fayetteville: University of Arkansas Press, 1999.

Sweet, Frank W. *Legal History of the Color Line: The Rise and Triumph of the One-Drop Rule.* Palm Coast, Fla.: Backintyme Press, 2005.

Tatum, Georgia Lee. *Disloyalty in the Confederacy.* 1934. Lincoln: University of Nebraska Press, 2000.

Tevis, Dean. "The Battle at Bad Luck Creek." In *Tales from the Big Thicket*, edited by Francis E. Abernethy, 75–92. 1967. Denton: University of North Texas Press, 2002.

Trelease, Allen. *White Terror: The Ku Klux Klan Conspiracy and Southern Reconstruction.* New York: Harper and Row, 1971.

Weitz, Mark. *More Damning Than Slaughter: Desertion in the Confederate Army.* Lincoln: University of Nebraska Press, 2005.

Wetherington, Mark V. *Plain Folk's Fight: The Civil War and Reconstruction in Piney Woods, Georgia.* Chapel Hill: University of North Carolina Press, 2009.

Wharton, Vernon. *The Negro in Mississippi, 1865–1890.* 1947. New York: Harper and Row, 1965.

Whites, LeeAnn. *The Civil War as a Crisis in Gender: Augusta, Georgia, 1860–1890.* Athens: University of Georgia Press, 1995.

————. *Gender Matters: Civil War, Reconstruction, and the Making of the New South.* New York: Palgrave MacMillan, 2005.

Williams, David. *Bitterly Divided: The South's Inner Civil War.* New York: New Press, 2008.

————. *A People's History of the Civil War: Struggles for the Meaning of Freedom.* New York: New Press, 2005.

Williams, David, Teresa Crisp Williams, and David Carlton. *Plain Folk in a Rich Man's War: Class and Dissent in Confederate Georgia.* Gainesville: University Press of Florida, 2002.

Williamson, Joel. *Crucible of Race: Black-White Relations in the American South since Emancipation.* New York: Oxford University Press, 1984.

————. *New People: Miscegenation and Mulattoes in the United States.* New York: Free Press, 1980.

Willis, Harold W. *A Short History of Hardin County.* Kountze, Tex.: Hardin County Historical Commission, 1998.

Winkler, Wayne. *Walking toward the Sunset: The Melungeons of Appalachia.* Macon, Ga.: Mercer University Press, 2004.

Woodward, C. Vann. *Tom Watson, Agrarian Rebel.* New York: Macmillan, 1938.

Wooster, Ralph A., and Robert Wooster. "'Rarin' for a Fight': Texans in the Confederate Army." In *Lone Star Blue & Gray: Essays on Texas in the Civil War*, edited by Ralph A. Wooster, 47–78. Austin: Texas State Historical Association, 1995.

Wooster, Ralph A. ed. *Lone Star Blue & Gray: Essays on Texas in the Civil War.* Austin: Texas State Historical Association, 1995.

Wray, Matt. *Not Quite White: White Trash and the Boundaries of Whiteness.* Durham, N.C.: Duke University Press, 2006.

Zamora, Emilio. *The World of the Mexican Worker in Texas.* College Station: Texas A&M University Press, 1993.

Zipf, Karin. *Labor of Innocents: Forced Apprenticeship in North Carolina, 1715–1919.* Baton Rouge: Louisiana State University Press, 2005.

Articles, Essays, Dissertations, and Theses

Alter, Thomas. "E. O. Meitzen: Agrarian Radical in Texas, 1855–1906." Master's thesis, Texas State University, San Marcos, 2008.

Auman, William T. "Neighbor against Neighbor: The Inner Civil War in the Central Counties of Confederate North Carolina." Ph.D. diss., University of North Carolina at Chapel Hill, 1988.

————. "Neighbor against Neighbor: The Inner Civil War in the Randolph County Area of Confederate North Carolina." *North Carolina Historical Review* 61 (Jan. 1984): 60–90.

Auman, William T., and David D. Scarboro. "The Heroes of America in Civil War North Carolina." *North Carolina Historical Review* 58 (Oct. 1981): 327–44.

Balanoff, Elizabeth. "Negro Legislators in the North Carolina General Assembly, July 1868–February 1872." *North Carolina Historical Review* 49 (Jan. 1972): 22–55.

Behymer, F. A. "The Tragic Story of Davis Knight." *St. Louis Post-Dispatch*, 8 Jan. 1949.

Bivins, Sondra Yvonne. "Lucy Ann 'Jane' Ainsworth." Unpublished essay, Sondra Yvonne Bivins research files.

————. "Martha Ann Ainsworth Notes." Unpublished essay, Sondra Yvonne Bivins research files.

————. "Open Secret." Unpublished essay, Sondra Yvonne Bivins research files.

————. "Rachel Knight." Unpublished essay, Sondra Yvonne Bivins research files.

Bondurant, Alexander L. "Did Jones County Secede?" *Publications of the Mississippi Historical Society* 1 (1898): 103–6.

Brown, David. "Attacking Slavery from Within: The Making of *The Impending Crisis of the South*." *Journal of Southern History* 40 (Aug. 2004): 541–76.

Burrow, Betty. "Memories of the Free State of Jones" (ca. 1934?). Unpublished essay, Dorothy Lyon Thomas research files.

Bynum, Victoria. "On the Lowest Rung: Court Control over Poor White and Free Black Women." *Southern Exposure* 12 (Nov./Dec. 1984): 40–44.

————. "'White Negroes' in Segregated Mississippi: Miscegenation, Racial Identity, and the Law." *Journal of Southern History* 84, no. 2 (May 1998): 247–76.

Cantrell, Gregg, and D. Scott Barton. "Texas Populists and the Failure of Biracial Politics." *Journal of Southern History* 55, no. 4 (Nov. 1989): 659–92.

Collins, B. T., Jr. "Are There Moral Issues That We Need to Recognize?" Unpublished essay, B. T. Collins Jr. research files.

Collins, Loren. "The Free State of Jones, or, Two Ways to Tell a Story." Unpublished essay, ca. 1942, B. T. Collins Jr. research files.

Collins, V. A. "A Little Sketch of the Descendants of Stacey Collins." Unpublished essay, 1949, Lauren Rogers Museum of Art Library Collection, Laurel, Miss.

Crow, Jeffrey. "Thomas Settle Jr. and the Memory of the Civil War." *Journal of Southern History* 62, no. 4 (Nov. 1996): 701–6.

Duval, Mary V. "The Making of a State." *Publications of the Mississippi Historical Society* 3 (1900): 155–65.

Dykes-Hoffman, Judith. "'Treue der Union': German Texas Women on the Civil War Homefront." Master's thesis, Southwest Texas State University, 1996.

Edwards, Laura F. "Law, Domestic Violence, and the Limits of Patriarchal Authority in the Antebellum South." *Journal of Southern History* 65, no. 4 (Nov. 1999): 733–70.

Escott, Paul D. "Poverty and Governmental Aid for the Poor in Confederate North Carolina." *North Carolina Historical Review* 61 (Oct. 1984): 462–80.

Galloway, G. Norton. "A Confederacy within a Confederacy." *Magazine of American History* (Oct. 1886): 387–90.

Genovese, Eugene. "Yeoman Farmers in a Slaveholders' Democracy." *Agricultural History* 49 (Apr. 1975): 331–42.

Goins, Craddock. "The Secession of Jones County." *American Mercury* (Jan. 1941): 33–35.

Goodwyn, Lawrence C. "Populist Dreams and Negro Rights: East Texas as a Case Study." *American Historical Review* 76, no. 5 (Dec. 1971): 1435–56.

Graves, Tiah. "A Historical View of the Life of Anna Knight." ⟨www.oakwood.edu/history/Faculty/knight⟩.

Hall, Jacquelyn Dowd. "'You Must Remember This': Autobiography as Social Critique." *Journal of American History* 85 (Sept. 1998): 439–65.

Holmes, William F. "Whitecapping: Agrarian Violence in Mississippi, 1902–1906." *Journal of Southern History* 35 (1969): 165–85.

Kennedy, J. M. "History of Jasper County." *Jasper County News*, 16 May 1957, 13 June 1957.

Kohl, Rhonda M. "On Grant's Front Line: The Fifth Illinois Cavalry in Mississippi." *Illinois Historical Journal* 91 (Spring 1998): 41–56.

Lang, Herbert H. "J. F. H. Claiborne at 'Laurel Wood' Plantation, 1853–1870." *Journal of Mississippi History* 32 (Feb. 1970): 3–42.

Lyon, Keith. "Function and Survival of Legend: The Case of the Free State of Jones." Unpublished essay, ca. 1991, Keith Lyon research files.

Mann, Susan A. "Slavery, Sharecropping, and Sexual Inequality." *Signs: A Journal of Women in Culture and Society* 14, no. 4 (Summer 1989): 776–98.

Mason, Patrick Q. "Sinners in the Hands of an Angry Mob: Violence against Religious Outsiders in the U.S. South, 1865–1910." Ph.D. diss., Notre Dame, 2005.

McCain, William David. "The Populist Party in Mississippi." Master's thesis, University of Mississippi, 1931.

McCarty, G. Wayman. "A History of the Universalist Church in the Mid-South." Master's thesis, Mississippi State College, Columbus, 1964.

McCaslin, Richard B. "Voices of Reason: Opposition to Secession in Angelina County, Texas." *Locus: An Historical Journal of Regional Perspectives on National Topics* 3, no. 2 (Spring 1991): 177–94.

McNeilly, J. S. "The Enforcement Act of 1871 and the Ku Klux Klan in Mississippi." *Publications of the Mississippi Historical Society* 9 (1906): 109–71.

Miller, Worth Robert. "Building a Progressive Coalition in Texas: The Populist-Reform Democratic Rapprochement, 1900–1907." *Journal of Southern History* 52 (May 1986): 163–82.

Montgomery, Goode. "Alleged Secession of Jones County." *Publications of the Mississippi Historical Society* 8 (1904): 13–22.

Payne, Ed. "Kinship, Slavery, and Gender in the Free State of Jones: The Life of Sarah Collins." *Journal of Mississippi History* 71, no. 1 (Spring 2009): 55–84.

Reid, Richard. "A Test Case of the 'Crying Evil': Desertion among North Carolina Troops during the Civil War." *North Carolina Historical Review* 58 (Summer 1981): 234–62.

Vogt, Daniel C. "A Note on Mississippi Republicans in 1912." *Journal of Mississippi History* 49, no. 1 (Feb. 1987): 49–55.

Weeks, O. Douglas. "The South in National Politics." *Journal of Politics* 26, no. 1 (Feb. 1964): 221–40.

Wooster, Ralph A., and Robert Wooster. "A People at War: East Texas during the Civil War." *East Texas Historical Journal* 28, no. 1 (1990): 3–16.

Zipf, Karin L. "'The Whites Shall Rule the Land or Die': Gender, Race, and Class in North Carolina Reconstruction Politics." *Journal of Southern History* 65, no. 3 (Aug. 1999): 499–534.

Zuber, Macklyn. "Fire at Union Wells." *Frontier Times* (Oct.–Nov. 1963): 28–29, 62.

Acknowledgments

I can never adequately acknowledge all those who have assisted or encouraged me in the writing of this book, particularly since some of its research was conducted twenty-five years ago. More than I ever imagined it would, *The Long Shadow of the Civil War* has evolved into a sampler of the major historical events and issues that have fascinated me since I first discovered the joys of archival research as a college undergraduate. Along the way, I have met and exchanged ideas with an amazing number of people.

The first person to thank is Gregg Andrews, my husband and colleague, who has shared my journeys into the past like no one else. Gregg's own fascination with Newt Knight and the Free State of Jones inspired him to write and perform (as Dr. G and the Mudcats) "Jones County Jubilee," the signature song for my website, Renegade South. Our partnership is truly the best part of being a historian!

Several independent writers have shared ideas and resources with me, none more so than historian Ed Payne of Jackson, Mississippi, and I thank him for his generosity, friendship, and moral support over the years. Likewise, novelist Jonathan Odell of Minneapolis, Minnesota, has inspired me with essays and drafts of his own works-in-progress, while supporting my own efforts to understand Mississippi's turbulent past.

Many individuals, including Sondra Yvonne Bivins, Florence Knight Blaylock, B. T. Collins Jr., Donnis and Keith Lyon, Wynona Green Frost, Dorothy Lyon Thomas, Dianne Walkup, and Kenneth Welch, shared their research files with me, providing materials as crucial to this volume as any held in archives and libraries. Photographs, documents, family stories, and simple encouragement were likewise provided by Rhonda Benoit, Vicki Betts, Danny Coats, Dwayne Coats, Allen Green, Frances Jackson, Ralph Kirkland, Eldon Knight, Dorothy Ladoceour, James McNabb, Martha Miller, Catherine and Harlen McKnight, Ralph Poore, Elaine Reynolds, Betty Zimmerman, and many more. The enthusiasm and helpfulness of my internet correspondents added enormously to the pleasure of writing this book.

My ability to communicate far and wide on the blogosphere was facilitated by Robin Keen of Desert Star Media, who designed and created my website, Renegade South. Likewise, Brigitte London of Outlaw Magazine. com nudged me into the world of blogging. Besides introducing me to the thoughtful comments of folks who revere the craft of history, various internet blogsites have brought cyberspace debates about race, the Civil War, and the Myth of the Lost Cause right to my desktop. Wading into discussions on Frank Sweet and A. G. Powell's "Study of Racialism" or Kevin M. Levin's "Civil War Memory" is not for the faint of heart but always stimulating! My thanks to Robert Moore of "Cenantua" for inviting me to post on his special blogsite "Southern Unionist Chronicles." Serious bloggers, I have learned, are among the hardest-working and most intellectually astute members of the history profession.

Other of my history colleagues supported the development of this book by including me on conference panels or inviting me to contribute essays to anthologies. LeeAnn Whites has done both, and I especially value her support, encouragement, and friendship. Thanks also to Charles Bolton, Brad Bond, Ann Elwood, John Inscoe, Marjoleine Kars, Daniel Letwin, Alecia Long, Elizabeth Payne, Brooks Simpson, Aaron Sheehan-Dean, Jonathan Sarris, Marjorie Spruill, Martha Swain, Sarah Wilkerson-Freeman, David Williams, David Woodbury, Gerald Prokopowicz, and Karen Zipf for the interest they have shown in my scholarship over the years.

I am grateful to the Texas State Historical Association for awarding me the Lawrence T. Jones III Research Fellowship in 2003, which enabled me to conduct statewide research in Texas records. I appreciate as well those Texas State University administrators, notably Dean Ann Marie Ellis and Associate Provost Gene Bourgeois, who have made the research needs of faculty a high priority. I would be remiss not to mention that dean assistant Pam Lemoine has also made life at the university infinitely more fun.

My history department colleagues recognize all too well the difficulty of producing scholarship while meeting a demanding teaching schedule. Department chair Frank de la Teja came to my technological rescue many times, unlocking the mysteries of the latest computer program or cheerfully correcting my word processing mistakes. Mary Brennan, Denny Dunn, Paul Hart, Bill Liddle, Ken Margerison, Liz Makowski, Rebecca Montgomery, Angie Murphy, Ana Romo, Dwight Watson, and Tug Wilson good-naturedly listened to my complaints about plodding academic bureaucracies and committees more than once. I appreciate their friendship and collegiality.

It is a pleasure to produce a third book with the University of North Carolina Press. My gratitude to Kate Torrey is deep and ongoing; and with each passing year I appreciate Vicky Wells's good sense and sense of humor that much more. For the third time, Paula Wald has worked to improve the final product of my efforts. Excellent copyediting was provided by Dorothea Anderson. The process of producing this latest work was enhanced by the manuscript's two superb readers—J. William Harris and Fitzhugh Brundage—whose insightful comments and advice immeasurably improved the final product.

Index

sentiment, 16, 30; effects on secessionist vote, 25; effects on Civil War crimes, 40; in antebellum South, 91; during Civil War, 102–3; in New South, 106, 107. *See also* Quaker Belt

Coffin, O. S., 79

Cogwell, Col. M., 48

Cold War, 114, 145

Collins, B. T., Jr., 148

Collins, Benjamin Franklin "Frank," 104

Collins, Buford T., Jr. *See* Collins, B. T., Jr.

Collins, Buford T., Sr., 113, 139

Collins, Caroline Mathews, 32

Collins, Carr P., Jr., 142, 144, 145

Collins, Carr P., Sr., 142, 144, 145

Collins, Edwin, 8, 24

Collins, Francis, 104

Collins, Franklin W., 94, 95

Collins, Henry Clay, 140

Collins, James Madison "Matt," 32, 104, 143

Collins, Jasper J., 8, 14, 31, 116; political and religious views of, 12, 98, 101, 107–9, 114, 138; 1st sergeant of Knight Company, 26, 88, 101, 138, 155 (n. 17); deposed for Newt Knight claim, 87–91; death of, 114

Collins, Laurence Yeager, 104

Collins, Loren, 14, 147; as Populist, 108, 138–39; son of Jasper Collins, 138; author of essay about father, 138, 140; childhood of, 139; as Republican, 139, 147

Collins, Lydia Bynum, 32, 104

Collins, Margaret. *See* Bynum, Margaret "Peggy" Collins

Collins, Morgan Columbus, 104, 143,

Collins, Nancy. *See* Riley, Nancy Collins

Collins, Newton, 24, 33

Collins, Patience, 104

Collins, Riley James, 8, 24; death of, 31; as member of Knight Company, 155 (n. 17)

Collins, Sarah. *See* Parker, Sarah Collins Walters

Collins, Sarah Anderson Gibson, 24

Collins, Simeon, 8, 24, 31, 32; death of, 104; 2nd lieutenant of Knight Company, 155 (n. 17)

Collins, Stacy, Jr., 24, 33

Collins, Stacy, Sr., 8, 32; frontier migrations of, 24; republican ideals of, 108

Collins, T. J. (Thomas Jefferson), 78, 88, 89, 90–93, 104

Collins, Theodocia. *See* Lyon, Theodocia Collins

Collins, Thomas Jefferson. *See* Collins, T. J.

Collins, Timothy Wyatt, 108, 113

Collins, Tolitha Eboline Valentine, 24, 110; domestic duties of, 111, 145

Collins, Vinson Allen (Miss.), 8, 89, 90–91

Collins, Vinson Allen (Tex.): author of family history, 14, 110, 142, 144; political differences with father, 110, 111, 142, 143, 145, 148; education of, 111; as progressive Democrat, 112, 142; son of Warren J. Collins, 142; increasing conservatism of, 142, 144, 145

Collins, Warren Jacob: as leader of jayhawkers, 8, 14, 16, 19, 21–26, 33–35, 116, 143; literary caricatures of, 21, 145, 146, 148; kinship networks of, 24, 25, 104; life in Big Thicket, 24, 111; as Socialist, 98, 110, 112, 142. *See also* Guerrilla bands; Socialist Party

Collins family: as members of Knight Company, 24; as Unionists in Mississippi and Texas, 26, 139, 144; postwar migration to Big Thicket, 104; as Universalists, 108; political convictions of, 144

Colorado: Mormon communities in, 56

Communities: anti-Confederate sentiment in, 16, 23, 39, 46; non–plantation belt locations, 23; importance of kinship ties to, 23, 40, 46, 93–94; inner civil wars in, 41, 55. *See also* Guerrilla bands; Quaker Belt; Unionists

Compton, Allen, 68

Compton, Green, 68

Confederacy: policies of, 2, 3, 15, 41, 42, 49–50; Southern opposition to, 5, 15, 28, 30, 38, 102; attempts to quell desertion and disaffection, 16, 28–34, 38, 43–45, 47–49; Northern defeat of, 35, 55; abuse of civilians, 44, 45, 50, 140. *See also* Quaker Belt; Twenty-Negro law; Unionists

Confederate Conscript Bureau (N.C.), 43

Conservative Party (N.C.), 61–65

Conservative Union Party (N.C.), 9

Corbin, Alexander, 68, 73, 74

Corinth, battle of, 93

Corley, T. B., 133–34

Cotton, Dick, 64

Courtney, Alzada, 141

Cowles, Rep. Andrew C., 46

Cowles, Agent J., 70

Crane, Martin M., 13

Craven, Braxton, 41

Crawford, Thomas G., 9, 56; deposed for Newt Knight claim, 94

Crook, Clarinda. *See* Hulin, Clarinda Crook

Crook, Phebe, 47, 48

Crook family, 49

Crooks, Rev. Adam, 42

Crop lien system, 12, 103

Davie County, N.C., 21

Davis, Rebecca, 40

Davis County, Miss., 10. *See also* Jones County, Miss.

Deason, Amos, 92, 140

Debs, Eugene, 112

Democratic Party: Southern wing of, 12, 13, 57, 92, 97–99, 105–10, 147; agrarian reform wing of, 107; effects of Populism on, 109, 110; political tactics of, 110, 116. *See also* New South

Desertion: of Confederate Army, 5, 15; in North Carolina Piedmont, 28, 38. *See also* Big Thicket of East Texas; Jones County, Miss.; Quaker Belt; Unionists

Devall, Edmond M., 91, 93; deposed for Newt Knight claim, 87, 92, 94

Dies, Martin, 112

Dillie (freedwoman), 70

Disorderly house. *See* Prostitution

Dissent: religious, 9, 16, 21, 30, 36, 38, 50, 98, 105; political, 21, 30, 36, 38, 50, 114, 115, 139, 148. *See also* Class relations; Kinship

Dougherty, John C., 85, 89, 90, 91

Dunkers, German (N.C.), 108

Durham, Dr. Bartlett, 72

Durham, Green, 62

Durham, N.C., 40, 72

Edie, Col. John R., 68

Edmonson, C. M., 91; deposed for Newt Knight claim, 87

Elliott, 2nd Lt. H. T., 78, 86, 95

Ellisville, Miss., 77, 108

Ellisville (Miss.) Patriot, 108, 138

Embree, Edith, 126

Fairbanks, Capt. J., 78

Farmer's Alliance, 106. *See also* Populist movement

Farmer's Union: affiliate of American Federation of Labor (AFL), 113

Faucet, Bill, 65

Fayetteville, N.C., 48

Ferguson, Gov. Miriam "Ma", 142

First Regiment of New Orleans Infantry, 31

Food riots, 4, 5

Forcible trespass, 40

Fornication, 40

Forsyth County, N.C., 21

Fourteenth Amendment to Constitution, 67

Foust, Esquire, 45, 46

Martin, Oquin C.; deposed for Newt Knight claim, 92
Mason, James B., 63–64
Mason, James Pleasant, 39
Mathews, Benagah, 32, 78, 81–82, 85, 90, 95
Mathews, Caroline. *See* Collins, Caroline Mathews
Mathews, John, 78
Mauldin, W. H., 180 (n. 52)
Mauldin, William H. F., 180 (n. 52)
Maury, Gen. D. H., 87
Maury, Col. Henry, 86
McAlister, Lt. Col. Alexander Carey, 49
McCauley, William, 40
McCown, William, 40
McDonald, Lila, 67, 69
McDonald, Neill, 44, 45
McKee, George, 81
McKinley, William, 110
McKnight, George Monroe, 124
McLemore, Maj. Amos: murder of, 21, 92, 140
McMillen, Brig. Gen. William Linn, 80, 95
McQueen, Linda, 71
McQueen, Mary Ann, 72
Memphis, Tenn., 31, 88
Meridian, Miss., 78, 87
Minerva (slave), 68
Mississippi: New South politics in, 1, 11, 12, 13; dissent in Piney Woods of, 5, 15; 1865 Constitutional Convention of, 9, 10; supreme court, 119; antimiscegenation laws of, 119, 123–25. *See also* Jones County, Miss.
Mississippi Territory, 24
Mobile and Ohio Railroad Bridge, 86
Montgomery, Goode, 124
Montgomery County, N.C., 15, 29, 41, 47, 49, 50, 61, 67, 70. *See also* Quaker Belt
Moore, George, 44
Moore County, N.C., 21, 23, 28, 43, 46, 47, 52, 61. *See also* Quaker Belt
Moravians, 16, 42
Mormons, 56, 105

Morris, Thomas, 46
Moselle, Miss., 107
Moyers, Gilbert, 83, 84, 89, 94
Mulattoes. *See* Multiracial people
Multiracial people, 1, 10, 13, 122; effects of Civil War and Reconstruction on, 2; postwar communities of, 97, 107. *See also* Knight community, multiracial; Women

Nacogdoches, Tex., 107. *See also* Populist movement
Native Americans, 117, 123, 124
New Orleans, Jackson, and Great Northern Railroad, 86
New South: politics of, 52, 57, 95–97, 103, 116; economic conditions in, 110. *See also* Populist movement; Socialist Party; White supremacy
New South, The (Jones County, Miss.), 78, 108
Nonslaveholders: ideology and, 16. *See also* Jones County, Miss.; Quaker Belt
North Carolina, 5, 10, 21, 43–44, 63. *See also* Interracial relations; Orange County, N.C.; Quaker Belt; Randolph County, N.C.; Unionists; Women
Nunn, Madison, 64

Oakwood College (Huntsville, Ala.), 129, 133
Official Records (Confederate Army), 34
Oklahoma, 124
"One drop" rule, 117, 123
Orange County, N.C., 8, 11, 17, 56, 61, 64, 67; prosecession politicians in, 39; poverty in, 40, 41, 50; pro-Unionist sentiment in, 40, 60; civil disorder in, 50, 52; biracial political coalition in, 55, 56. *See also* Interracial relations; Ku Klux Klan; Reconstruction
Our Home Universalist Church (Ellisville, Miss.), 108
Outlaw bands. *See* Guerrilla bands
Overstreet, Bud, 146